MASHARIPOVA Gularam Kamilovna

THE ROLE OF THE DEVELOPMENT OF CIVILIZATION OF NATURAL SCIENTIFIC, SOCIO-PHILOSOPHICAL AND SPIRITUAL INFORMATION OF SCIENTISTS OF THE KHOREZM MAMUN ACADEMY

MONOGRAPHY

© Masharipova Gularam Kamilovna
The role of the development of civilization of natural scientific, socio-philosophical and spiritual information of scientists of the Khorezm Mamun Academy
By: Masharipova Gularam Kamilovna
Edition: May '2024
Publisher:
Taemeer Publications LLC (Michigan, USA / Hyderabad, India)

© Masharipova Gularam Kamilovna

Book	:	The role of the development of civilization of natural scientific, socio-philosophical and spiritual information of scientists of the Khorezm Mamun Academy
Author	:	Masharipova Gularam Kamilovna
Publisher	:	Taemeer Publications
Year	:	'2024
Pages	:	242
Title Design	:	*Taemeer Web Design*

The monograph scientifically analyzes the place of the natural science heritage of scientists from the Khorezm Mamun Academy in the development of civilizations.

It is well known that «humanity» is a comprehensive concept encompassing all people on Earth, regardless of nationality, religion, language, customs, traditions, and values.

However, despite their uniqueness, individuals, nations, and peoples differ not only in characteristics but also in appearance. These differences, in turn, lead to diverse interests.

This situation is particularly evident at the national level. Because a nation expresses its identity through language, customs, traditions, values, and mentality, it strives to preserve and further develop this identity, especially when necessary.

One of the most pressing problems is analyzing the great heritage and works of world significance created by the scientists of the Khorezm Mamun Academy.

Responsible editor: Doctor of Philosophy, Professor **S.Otamuratov**

Reviewers:

Doctor of Philosophy, Professor **G.M.Ruzmatova**
Doctor of Philosophy **Sh.S.Akhzamxodjayeva**

The monograph was recommended for publication on the basis of the № 8 meeting of the Academic Council of the Tashkent Institute of Textile and Light Industry, held on March 29, 2024.

TABLE OF CONTENTS:

INTRODUCTION..5

CHAPTER I. THEORETICAL AND METHODOLOGICAL BASIS FOR STUDYING THE TOPIC "ROLE IN THE DEVELOPMENT OF CIVILIZATIONS OF THE NATURAL SCIENTIFIC, SOCIO-PHILOSOPHICAL AND SPIRITUAL HERITAGE OF SCIENTISTS OF THE KHOREZM MAMUN ACADEMY..26-95

1.1. Integral connection of natural science and historical-philosophical heritage in the views of scientists of the Khorezm Mamun Academy..................................26

1.2. The main directions of research into the sources of the scientists of the Khorezm Academy of Mamun and their natural science and historical and philosophical analysis..60

1.3. Classification of the natural science and historical-philosophical heritage of scientists of the Khorezm Mamun Academy..75

Chapter summaries..93

CHAPTER II. DEVELOPMENT OF SOCIAL AND PHILOSOPHICAL THINKING IN NATURAL SCIENTIFIC APPROACHES OF SCIENTISTS OF THE KHOREZM MAMUN ACADEMY..97-139

2.1. Creation of the Khorezm Mamun Academy, transformation into a natural-scientific and socio-philosophical center..97

2.2. Development of natural science and historical-philosophical thought in the heritage of the Khorezm Academy of Mamun...111

2.3. Social and philosophical views in the natural science thinking of scientists of the Khorezm Academy of Mamun..123

Chapter summaries..137

CHAPTER III. SOCIAL RELATIONS AND PUBLIC LIFE IN THE HISTORICAL AND PHILOSOPHICAL HERITAGE OF SCIENTISTS OF THE KHOREZM MAMUN ACADEMY..141-201

3.1. Views on social relations, science, education, lifestyle and social life in the historical and philosophical heritage of scientists of the Khorezm Mamun Academy..142

3.2. Dialectics of the natural science paradigm and ontological views of Abu Nasr ibn Iraq and Abu Rayhon Beruni...158

3.3. Neoplatonic elements in the ontological teaching of Abu Ali ibn Sina, classification of sciences, humanistic essence of moral views and their influence on the development of historical and philosophical thinking..........................176

Chapter summaries..189

CONCLUSION..192

LIST OF REFERENCES..198

INTRODUCTION

Under the influence of modern socio-political processes, the issue of stabilizing the changes occurring in the human worldview and way of thinking in modern society becomes increasingly relevant. Especially important is adhering to the principle of historicity when standardizing cultural transformation processes. This involves enriching the value set with universal ideas and upholding the ideals and norms of knowledge in the information society.

From this perspective, ensuring the inheritance of knowledge, the intellectual development of young people with a new worldview, and the utilization of cultural exchange, forms, and mechanisms of cultural memory becomes crucial in the spiritual and moral formation of great thinkers. To achieve this, harmonizing views on the development of natural science and socio-philosophical thought with the innovations of the modern era is necessary.

In the development of the world's scientific and philosophical heritage, fundamental research is carried out within the frameworks of educational, philosophical, and natural science teachings of encyclopedists[1]. In particular, their views on the knowledge of the world, nature, the Universe, and social essence are of great interest. Notably, the creation of the world narrative in the scientific heritage of thinkers who have significantly contributed to world civilization is acquiring renewed significance today. This includes exploring the scientific aspects of the doctrines of the creator, humanity, the Universe, nature, and social life, revealing the essence of the relationship between humans and nature, and substantiating the place of natural scientific views in the development of socio-philosophical thought.

In Uzbekistan, special attention is paid to studying views on the universe, humanity, nature, social life, personal spirituality, education, and upbringing in the heritage of ancestors. The focus is on using their ideas, adapted to the modern era, to educate the younger generation as worthy successors.

---

[1] The historical heritage of Eastern scientists and thinkers, its place and significance in modern civilization. - Materials of the international conference. - Samarkand-Tashkent: Uzbekistan, 2014. - 47 p.

"Since we have set ourselves the great goal of creating the foundations of the Third Renaissance in our country, we must create an environment and conditions that will cultivate new Khorezmians, Berunis, Ibn Sinas, Ulugbeks, Navois, and Baburs. At the same time, the main pillars of our national identity should be, first and foremost, the development of education and training, the formation of a healthy lifestyle, and the promotion of science and innovation"[2].

From this perspective, there is a need for a comprehensive scientific and theoretical study of the philosophical and natural scientific views of the scientists of the Khorezm Academy of Mamun. This study should be based on universal human values and existential ideas that have constructive significance for human betterment.

If we look at the history of Khorezm, in 998 the ruler, Ali ibn Mamun, needed wise and intelligent advisors in a difficult political situation. Fortunately for him, his uncle, Abu Nasr ibn Iraq, was a highly knowledgeable scholar of his time. During his lifetime, he earned the nickname "Ptolemy of his time". Additionally, Ibn Iraq raised Abu Rayhan Biruni in his house. Thanks to these two figures, favorable conditions were created in the Iraqi palace for scholars. These two scholars maintained personal correspondence with many scholars in the Near and Middle East.

At the end of the 10th century, the Samanid dynasty ceased to exist. At the suggestion of Ibn Iraq and Abu Rayhan Biruni, from 1004 onwards, scientists from Nishapur, Balkh, Bukhara, and even Iraq began coming to Gurganj. Thus, a scientific institution called the "Bayt al-Hikmah wa Ma'arif" (House of Wisdom) was fully formed. It conducted studies and research in all fields of science, similar to the Bayt al-Hikmah in Baghdad. According to encyclopedic sources, translations from Syriac and Greek were also made at this institution.

After the death of Ali ibn Mamun (1009), the throne of the Khorezmshahs passed to his brother, Abu-l-Abbas Mamun II ibn Mamun. He brought Abu Rayhan Biruni closer to the palace and made him his closest advisor. This opened up great opportunities for the activities of the Mamun Academy.

---

[2] Message from the President of the Republic of Uzbekistan Shavkat Mirziyoyev to the Oliy Majlis // "People's Word", December 30, 2020.

In connection with the study of Abu Rayhan Biruni's works, the scientific community surrounding Abu Abbas Mamun II was carefully examined. It was shown to be similar in many ways to the House of Wisdom (Bayt al-Hikmah) in Baghdad and the academies of that time. It was then called the «Mamun Academy.» According to many scholars, the period when its research began corresponds to 1004.

The main reason for the establishment of the Khorezm Academy of Mamun in Khorezm was that Khorezm Shah Mamun ibn Mamun created a stimulating scientific environment and provided material support for all scientists.

A great impetus to the development of science and culture in Central Asia was the academy under the leadership of King Abu-l-Abbas Mamun ibn Mamun (1009-1017) in Khorezm. It operated in the late 10th and early 11th centuries.

Sufism began to spread widely in Central Asia from the 11th century onwards.

In the 12th century, Sufism spread widely in Khorezm. The Kubrawiyyah movement of Sufism, founded by Najmiddin Kubra (1146-1221), formed and spread widely in Central Asia and other Eastern countries.

During the 9th-12th centuries, Transoxiana (Movarunnahr) was renowned as the most scientifically and culturally developed country in the entire Muslim world. Here, ancient traditions blended with Arab, Persian, partly Indian, and ancient Greek scientific and cultural traditions. Islamic, philosophical, and natural sciences flourished, including astronomy, mathematics, medicine, chemistry, and geography. Famous hadith studies, schools of Islamic jurisprudence (Fiqh), and important works in historiography were created.

From the 12th century to the first quarter of the 13th century, Khorezm became a great kingdom, stretching from the borders of Georgia and Syria to Eastern Turkestan, and from the Indus River (Sind River) to the deserts of the Aral Sea. In this regard, it occupies a central place in sources on the history of the East. The rise of this kingdom, previously located on the periphery of the Muslim world, to such a high level of civilization was indeed unexpected.

Philosophers have always been interested in what the main, leading problem of philosophy is.

Some philosophers saw knowledge of God as the main problem, others knowledge of man, others the definition of the primordial being, and still others knowledge of the world's value dimension.

Are there fundamental problems of philosophy, and if so, what are they?

All philosophical problems can be divided into three main groups, expressed by the following questions:

What is peace?

What is a person?

What is the connection between the world and humanity?

If we take any philosophical problem, it necessarily involves one of these three fundamental problems.

So, the central question of philosophy is humanity's relationship to the world, which arises from its subjective and worldview characteristics.

Here, speaking about the «world-human» system, it should be understood that «world» and «human» are very broad philosophical concepts that mark their opposing sides. Therefore, in this context, these are «I» and «not-I,» «subject» and «object,» «macrocosm» and «microcosm,» «inner world» and «external world,» «soul» and «nature,» «consciousness» and «matter,» «thought» and «being,» «ideal» and «material». Different eras and different philosophical systems reflect human views of the world, which can be seen as binary oppositions.

The content of the «world-human» problem as a central philosophical problem is connected with the content of the leading trends of a particular historical period. When priority problems in society change, the emphasis and focus on the content of this problem also changes. These emphases are an expression of the orientation of philosophers of a particular historical period. In other words, the «world-human» problem has its own historical forms, which represent the direction (paradigm) of philosophical thinking in a particular period.

It must be said that such a process does not develop immediately. In the modern world, the desire to control people through manipulation, intolerance, and imposing harmful ideas on others is becoming increasingly strong.

That is why it is very difficult to prevent such negative situations in the development of humankind, to balance the interests of the parties, and achieve sustainable development. In particular, the development of humanity's intellectual potential affects the growth of its material and spiritual needs. We see that consciousness has a growing need for the formation and development of tolerance, which is the most important factor in taking into account the mutual interests of people.

It should also be taken into account that «...the nation manifests itself through real individuals. It consists of a group of people who share a common spirit of language, customs, traditions, values, and identity»[3].

As Islam Karimov noted during the celebration of the 1,000th anniversary of the Khorezm Academy of Mamun, «Although the Khorezm Academy of Mamun employed scientists from many countries of the East and West, belonging to different nationalities and religions, its founders included Abu Nasr ibn Iraq, Abu Rayhan Biruni, and Ibn Sina. The emergence of mature scholars like Ahmad ibn Hamid Naysiburi, born and raised in this region, fills us all with pride and honor»[4].

The history of the peoples of Central Asia, with its long past, has experienced various events, periods of rise and decline, undoubtedly leaving a certain mark. In particular, the 9th-12th centuries played a significant role in the development of their culture, glorifying them in world culture. Their cultural achievements during this period are an integral part of the development of science.

The 10th-12th centuries constitute a unique period in the history of Khorezm's cultural life. Large schools of religious and secular sciences were created there, and the fame of their representatives spread throughout the world. «We appreciate the significant legacy and contributions to world civilization that they left for future

---

[3] Otamuratov S. Globalization and nation. - Tashkent: Generation of the new century, 2008. - P.62.
[4] Karimov I.A. His speech at the 1000th anniversary of the Khorezm Mamun Academy entitled "The light of knowledge and enlightenment never fades." – People's Word, 2006, November 3.

generations»⁵, «... they bequeathed to us today's history and culture, of which we are the heirs»⁶, said Islam Karimov.

Although the Khorezm Academy of Mamun operated for a short period, from 1004 to 1017, natural sciences such as astronomy, mathematics, medicine, chemistry, geography, mineralogy, history, philosophy, language, law, and other social sciences flourished here.

In particular, research in astronomy led to amendments of ancient astronomical tables, the creation of new instruments, and the calculation of star coordinates. Abu Rayhan Biruni observed a lunar eclipse in June 1004.

In ancient Greek philosophy, Socrates (469-399 BCE) made a great contribution to the idea of the human mind. He explained that the human mind exists in different situations and at different levels, consisting of several layers⁷. Socrates' ideas were further developed by his student Plato (427–347 BCE). When Plato proposed the idea that a man should be a citizen of the state⁸, we can understand that he meant a man should be responsible.

In Khorezm, from ancient times until the time of the Anushteginid dynasty, special attention was paid to philosophical sciences alongside arithmetic, geometry, astronomy, astrology, and many other sciences. The development of philosophical science in Khorezm during the 10th-12th centuries undoubtedly addressed many problems, but it has not been studied as a separate research area until now.

From this point of view, the topic of this monograph is highly relevant. Analyzing the scientific research of Khorezm Academy of Mamun scholars in philosophy and its influence on the work of other foreign scientists remains extremely relevant today. Early mathematical and physical views were explained from a philosophical perspective in science.)

«Plato's Academy» was created in Ancient Greece, and «Mamun Academy» - in Central Asia. Although some progress has been made in the development of scientific

---

[5] Karimov I.A. Without historical memory there is no future. - Tashkent, Uzbekistan, 1999. Volume 7. - P. 148.
[6] Karimov I.A. The homeland will remain forever. - Tashkent, Uzbekistan, 1994. Volume 4. - P. 15.
[7] Ancient rhetoric. Under. ed. A.A. Be quiet. – Moscow: Moscow State University, 1978.
[8] Chernyshevsky N.G. Works in two volumes. Volume 1. – Moscow: Mysl, 1986. – P.220.

knowledge, this is the "embryonic" period before the emergence of science as a separate form of culture. . The study of the natural scientific heritage of scientists of the Khorezm Academy of Mamun can be classified as follows:

Many scientists have conducted scientific research in this area. Among them are B.A.Rosenfeld[9], S.Kh.Sirozhiddinov[10], A.A.Akhmedov[11], G.P.Matviyevskaya[12], P.G.Bulgakov[13], Zh.Kh.Ibodov[14], S.U.Karimova[15], B.A.Abdukhalimov[16],

---

[9] Rosenfeld B.A. On the mathematical works of Nasireddin Tusi//Historical and mathematical research. – Moscow – 1951. – ISSU,e. IV. - pp. 489-512; Rosenfeld B.A. Ibn al-Haytham. A book of commentaries on the introductions of Euclid's book "Elements". Per. and notes // Historical and mathematical research. – Moscow – 1958. – ISSU,e. XI. – P. 743-762; Rosenfeld B.A., Yushkevich A.P. About Nasir ad-Din al-Tusi's treatise on parallel lines // Historical and mathematical research. – Moscow – 1960. – ISSU,e. XIII.– pp. 475-482; Rosenfeld B.A., Krasnova S.A., Rozhanskaya M.M. About the mathematical works of Abu-r-Raikhan al-Biruni // From the history of science and technology in the ranks of the East. – Moscow – 1963. – P. 71-92; Rosenfeld B.A., Yushkevich A.P. The theory of parallel lines in the medieval East of the 9th-14th centuries. – Moscow: Science. 1983. - 125 s; Rosenfeld B.A., Akhmedov A. Unknown treatises of al-Khorezmi. SSU, № 2. – Tashkent: Science. 2984, p. 4-6.

[10] Sirazhdinov S.Kh., Akhmedov A. From the biography of Ibn Sina // Mathematics and astronomy in the works of Ibn Sina, his contemporaries and followers. – Tashkent, 1981. - P. 3-15; Muhammad ibn Musa al-Khwarizmi. Mathematical treatises. Responsible editor S. Sirazhiddinov. - Tashkent: Science. 1983.

[11] Akhmedov A. ISSU,es of substantiation of geometry in the medieval east: Author's abstract. diss. ..cand. physics and mathematics Sci. – Tashkent, 1970. – 23 p.; Akhmedov A Questions of justification of geometry in the medieval Near and Middle East. – Tashkent: Science. 1972. – 131 p.; Abu Rayhan Beruni. Selected Works, Volume V, Book One. - Tashkent: Science. 1973; Volume V is the second book. - Tashkent: Science. 1976; Akhmedov A. "Book on extracting the edge of a cube" by al-Hasan ibn al-Haytham. - In the book: Mathematics and astronomy in the works of scientists of the medieval East. - Tashkent: Science. 1977. p. 113-117; Akhmedov A. About the comments of Abd al-Ali Husayn Birjandi to Ulugbek's "Zij". – In the book: From the history of science of the era of Ulugbek. - Tashkent: Science. 1979, p. 69-109; Abu Rayhan Beruni. Selected works. Volume III, Geodesy. - Tashkent: Science, 1982; Muhammad ibn Musa al-Khwarizmi. Selected works. - Tashkent: Science, 1983; Akhmedov A., Rosenfeld B.A., Sergeeva N.D. Astronomical and geographical works of al-Khorezmi. - On Sat. Muhammad ibn Musa al-Khwarizmi. To the 1200th anniversary of his birth (Ed. A.P. Yushkevich). – M.: Science. 1983, pp. 141-191-; Akhmedov A. Khorazmiy Izhodida mathematician Sciencelar. -Muhammad ibn Muso al-Khwarizmi. Tanlangan asarlar. -T.: Science. 1983, 5-56–bb.; Akhmedov A. Al-Khorezmi - ason and geographer (To the 1200th anniversary of his birth). -In the book Earth in the Universe, № 6, M. 1983, p. 28-32; Akhmedov A. Science of Khorezm and geography. - Muhammad ibn Musa al-Khwarizmi. Selected works. - Tashkent: Science. 1983, 225-291–pp.; Akhmedov A. Theory of planetary motion in "Zij" by al-Khorezmi. SSU,, № 7, Tashkent, Science. 1983, p. 59-64; Akhmedov A Scientific heritage of al-Khorezmi and its place in the history of science and culture. Author's abstract. dis. ..doc. ist. Sci. – Tashkent, 1986; Akhmedov A., Bulgakov P.G. Central Asian-Indian relations in the field of exact sciences. - On Sat. From the stories of cultural relations between the peoples of Central Asia and India. -Tashkent: Science. 1986, p. 24-33; Akhmedov A. Muhammad al-Khorezmi - historian. SSU,. – Tashkent, 1985. – p. 51-55; Ahmedov A.A., Al-Dabbagh J., Rozenfeld B.A. Itanbul Manuscrists of Al-Khwariznu's Treatisas. - Erdem, Ankara, 1987, r. 3, N 7, pp. 163-186; Ahmedov A.A., Al-Dabbagh J., Rozenfeld B.A. Harezmi'mu Eserlerinin Istanbul Yazmalari Geviren: Melek Dosay. - Erdem, Ankara, 1987, p. 3, pp. 7, 187-210.

[12] Matviyevskaya G.P. On the history of mathematics in Central Asia in the 9th-15th centuries. – Tashkent: Publishing House of the Academy of Sciences of the UzSSR. 1962. – 125 pp.; Matviyevskaya G.P. Beruniy va tabiy Sciencelar. – Tashkent: Science. 1963. – 48-b.; Matviyevskaya G.P. The doctrine of number in the medieval Near and Middle East. – Tashkent: Science. 1967. – 341 pp.; Matviyevskaya G.P. The doctrine of number in the Middle Ages. Diss... doc. Phys.Math.Sc. – Tashkent: Science. 1967. –533 pp.; Matviyevskaya G.P. The doctrine of number in the Middle Ages.: Author's abstract. diss.... doc. physical and mathematical sciences. – Tashkent, 1968. – 28 p.; Matviyevskaya G.P. From the history of studying the physical and mathematical heritage of Ibn Sina // Mathematics and astronomy in the works of Ibn Sina, his contemporaries and followers. – Tashkent, 1981. – p. 16-40; Matviyevskaya G.P., Tlashev Kh. Mathematical and astronomical manuscripts of scientists of Central Asia of the X-XIII centuries. – Tashkent: Science. – 1981. – 148 p.; Matviyevskaya G.P. On the history of mathematics in Central Asia in the 9th-15th centuries. – Tashkent Publishing House of the Academy of Sciences of the UzSSR. 1962. – 125 p.

[13] Bulgakov P.G. Life and works of Beruni. – T.: Science. 1972. – 428 pp.; Bulgakov P.G., Akhmedov A. Beruni and al-Kindi on the theory of parallel // Societies. science in Uzbekistan. – 1977. - № 8. – P. 30-36; Rumi Kazi-zade.

Kh.Siddikov[17], M.Akhadova[18], Kh.Muhammadiev[19], O.Fayzullaev[20], O.Boriyev and B.Vakhobova[21], R.Bakhadirov[22], G. Masharipova[24] and others.

Commentary on Chagmini's Compendium of Asonomy. Preface, translation from Arabic and notes by corresponding member of the Ruz Academy of Sciences P.G. Bulgakov. – T.: Science, 1993.

[14] Ibodov Zh.Kh. On a mathematical treatise from the city of Khiva // Mathematics and astronomy in the works of Ibn Sina, his contemporaries and followers. - T.: Science. 1981, pp. 143-154; Ibodov Zh.Kh. Study of four manuscripts with mathematical content//Izv. Academy of Sciences of the UzSSR, series of physical and mathematical sciences. 1983. № 1. P. 69-70; Ibodov Zh.Kh. Mathematical treatises of al-Khububi and al-Sijavandi//From the history of medieval Eastern mathematics and asonomy. - T.: Science. 1983, pp. 72-81; Ibodov Zh.Kh. The work of al-Khorezmi in the assessment of Eastern encyclopedists of the 10th-16th centuries // The great scientist of the Middle Ages al-Khorezmi. - T.: Science. 1985, pp. 265-268; Ibodov Zh.Kh. Physics and mathematics chapters of the encyclopedia "Collection of Sciences" ("Jami ul-ulum") by Fakhr ad-Din ar-Razi. Dep. AT VINITI. Moscow, 1987. № 1066-B87. 14 pp.; Ibodov Zh.Kh. Classification of physical and mathematical sciences in the medieval encyclopedias of Abu Abdullah al-Khorezmi, Fakhr ad-Din ar-Razi, Qutb ad-Din al-Shirazi and Baha ad-Din al-Amili // Abstracts of the XXXIV scientific conference of graduate students and young specialists in the history of natural sciences and technicians of IIE and TRAS. Moscow, 1992. P. 35-36; Ibodov Zh.Kh. "Book of research on algebra" by Hassan ibn Khoris al-Khububi al-Khorezmi // Theses of scientific-theoretical. and tech. conferences professional, lecturer Tashkent State Technical University named after. A. Beruni. Tashkent, 1992, pp. 123-125; Ibodov Zh.Kh. Comparative analysis of the physical and mathematical chapters of the universal encyclopedias "Keys of Sciences" by Abu Abdallah al-Khorezmi (X-XI centuries) and "Collection of Sciences" by Fakhr ad-Din al-Razi. Tashkent State Technical University named after. A.Beruni. 1992. pp. 135-136; Ibodov Zh.Kh., Matviyevskaya G.P. Ahmad al-Fargoniining riyoziyot va falakiyot tarikhidagi yrni. T.: Istiklol, 1998. 89 b.; Ibadov Zh.Kh., Bulgakov P.G. On the history of mathematics of Khorezm at the end of the 10th century. //Social sciences in Uzbekistan. Tashkent, 1988. № 5. P. 62-65; Ibadov J.Kh., Matviyevskaya G.P. Physical and mathematical sciences in the encyclopedia "Keys of Sciences" by Abu Abdallah al-Khorezmi // Izv. Academy of Sciences of the UzSSR. Ser. Physical and mathematical sciences. 1990. № 3. P. 34-39; Ibadov J.KhIbodov Zh.Kh, Matviyevskaya G.P. Exact sciences in the encyclopedia "The Wisdom of the Source (Hikma al-ayn) al-Qazwini"//Izv. Academy of Sciences of the UzSSR. Ser. Physical and mathematical sciences. 1989. pp. 29-31; Ibodov Zh.Kh. Arabic and Persian encyclopedias of the X-XVIII centuries. as sources on the history of exact sciences/Author's abstract. dis. on sois. to the scientist step. Doctor of History Tashkent, 1994. 42 pp.; Ibodov Zh.Kh. Philosophical views of encyclopedists of the Renaissance in Central Asia and discoveries in the field of exact sciences. Tashkent, Mevrius, 2009, 160 pp.; Ibodov J.H. Physics and mathematics chapters of "Keys of Sciences" (Mafotih al-ulum) by Abu Abdallah al-Khorezmi. Tashkent, HERE, 2005, 56 pp.; Ibodov Zh.Kh. Encyclopedias of Central Asian scientists of the 9th-18th centuries as sources on the history of exact sciences. Tashkent, Mevrius, 2010, 174 pp.; Ibodov Zh.Kh. Study of the rich scientific heritage of our country/Problems of improving the quality of personnel training for the field of communications and information technology. Scientific conference TATU. - Tashkent, 2012, volume 1, pp. 105-107.

[15] Karimova S.U. The role of scientists from Maverannahr and Khorasan in the development of chemistry and pharmacology in the medieval east (According to written sources of the 9th-11th centuries). – Author's abstract. dis. ..doc. ist. Sciences – T., 2001, 57 p.

[16] Abdukhalimov B.A. "Bayt al-hikma" and the scientific activity of Central Asian scientists in Baghdad (IX-XI centuries) Natural sciences // Author's abstract. dis. ..doc. ist. Sci. – T., 2001, 47 p.

[17] Siddikov H. Geometry in the works of scientists of Central Asia, the Near and Middle East. - Tashkent: Science. 1981. - 200 p.

[18] Akhadova M.A. Famous mathematicians of Central Asia. - Tashkent: Science. 1964. – 40 p.; Akhadova M.A. Physical and mathematical works of Ibn Sina in the Tajik language: Author's abstract. dis. … sugar. Physical and mathematical sciences. - T.: 1965. - 11 p.; Akhadova M.A. Beruni and his works in mathematics. - Tashkent: Science. 1976. – 32 p.; Akhadova M.A. Famous scientists of Central Asia and their works on mathematics (VIII-XV centuries). – Tashkent: Teacher, 1983. – 216 p.

[19] Muhammadiev Kh. Mathematical chapters of the "Book of Healing" by Ibn Sina // Author's abstract. dis. ..cand. ist. Sci. – Dushanbe, 1967.

[20] Faizullayev A. Scientific creativity of Muhammad al-Khorezmi. – Tashkent, 1983.

[21] Boriyev O., Vakhobova B. Written sources about al-Fergani. - Tashkent, 1998.

[22] Bakhadirov R. From the history of the classification of sciences in the medieval Muslim East. - Tashkent, 2000.

[24] Masharipova G.K. The influence of the natural science, socio-philosophical and spiritual heritage of scientists of the Khorezm Mamun Academy on the development of social thinking. Monography. - Tashkent: Navruz, 2019. - 364 pp.; Masharipova G.K. The role of the scientific, philosophical and spiritual heritage of Abu Ali ibn Sina in the life of society. Monography. – T., Publishing House "Navruz", 2020. – 144 p.; Masharipova G.K. The great discoveries of the Middle Ages are the contribution of Khorezm mathematicians to the development of science. Monography. – Tashkent: Navruz, 2021. – 210 p.

Scientific and cultural processes in the East, especially in Central Asia, in the X-XII centuries are always in the focus of attention not only of scientists of our country, but also of Russian orientalists, issues related to the rise of the political, economic, scientific and cultural life of the peoples of the East of that time, mainly by I.Krachkovsky[25], was discussed in the studies of E.Bertels[26], A.Yushkevich[27], V.Bartold[28], O. Bolshakov[29], B. Rosenfeld[30], A. Khalidov[31].

The study of the development of exact sciences at the Khorezm Academy of Mamun is partially reflected in some studies. For example, P.G. Bulgakov "The Life and Works of Abu Raikhan Beruni" ("The Life and Works of Beruni")[32], S.Kh.Sirodzhiddinov and G.P.Matviyevskaya are co-authors of the article "Towards the study of the history of mathematics in Central Asia"[33], among them is an article by G.P.Matviyevskaya on the history of studying the heritage of Ibn Sina in the field of physical and mathematical sciences[34], 2 Monographys and 2 scientific articles[35] by Zh.Kh.Ibodov.

Among the scientific research related to Abu Rayhan Beruni, the aforementioned monograph by P.G. Bulgakov holds an important place. This book presents conclusions about Beruni's life, detailing his time in Kot (Khorezm), Gurganj (Khorezm), Gurgon, and Ghazna. From the perspective of the history of science, particularly the history of exact sciences, the work analyzes Beruni's

---

[25] Krachkovsky I. Arabic geographical literature // I. Krachkovsky. Selected essays. T. IV. – Moscow-Leningrad, 1957.
[26] Bertels E. History of Persian-Tajik literature // E. Bertels. Favorite works. – Moscow, 1960.
[27] Yushkevich A. History of mathematics in the Middle Ages. – Moscow, 1961.
[28] Bartold V. Culture of Islam // Bartold V. Works. T. IV. - Moscow, 1966. – P. 143-204; Scholars of the Muslim "Renaissance". – P. 617-629; History of the cultural life of Turkestan. T. II. Part 1. – Moscow, 1963.
[29] Bolshakov O. Essays on the history of Arab culture. – Moscow, 1982.
[30] Rosenfeld B., Matviyevskaya G. Mathematicians and astronomers of the Muslim Middle Ages and their works (VIII-XVII centuries). 1-book. – Moscow, 1982.
[31] Khalidov A. Arabic manuscripts and Arabic manuscript tradition. – Moscow, 1985.
[32] Bulgakov P.G. Life and works of Beruni. - Tashkent: Science, 1972.
[33] Sirazhdinov S.Kh., Matviyevskaya G.P. On the study of the history of mathematics in Central Asia./Historical and mathematical research. ISSU,e XX1. - Moscow: Publishing house «Science». 1976. - P.51 – 60.
[34] Matviyevskaya G.P. From the history of studying the physical and mathematical heritage of Ibn Sina. // Mathematics and astronomy in the works of Ibn Sina, his contemporaries and followers. – Tashkent, 1981. - P. 16-40.
[35] Ibodov Zh.Kh. Philosophical views of encyclopedists of the Renaissance in Central Asia and discoveries in the field of exact sciences. Tashkent, Mevrius, 2009, 160 pp.; Ibodov J.H. Physics and mathematics chapters of "Keys of Sciences" (Mafotih al-ulum) by Abu Abdallah al-Khorezmi. Tashkent, TUNTN, 2005, 56 pp.; Ibodov Zh.Kh. Encyclopedias of Central Asian scientists of the 9th-18th centuries as sources on the history of exact sciences. Tashkent, Mevrius, 2010, 174 pp.; Ibodov Zh.Kh. Study of the rich scientific heritage of our country/Problems of improving the quality of personnel training for the field of communications and information technology. Scientific conference TATU. Tashkent, 2012, volume 1, pp. 105-107.

activities in these cities, with a particular focus on spherical trigonometry, geodesy, geometry, and related fields. Based on these disciplines, applied mathematics flourished, leading to the development of measuring instruments, observation devices, and further research in the exact sciences[36].

P.G.Bulgakov goes beyond simply providing information about specific sciences in Khorezm during Beruni's time. He delves into the lives of prominent scientists who worked in the region. These include Abu Rayhan Beruni's teacher, Abu Nasr Mansur ibn Ali ibn Iraq; the court astrologer Abu Mahmud Hamid ibn al-Khidr al-Khojandi (d. c. 1000) who lived in Ray; and the great Eastern polymath Abu-l-Wafa Muhammad ibn Muhammad ibn Yahya. Additionally, Bulgakov mentions Ibn Sina, a physician and philosopher, and Abu Sahl Isa ibn Yahya al-Masihi (d. 1011), a naturalist and medical scientist[36].

The book «Die Mathematiker und Astronomen der Araber und ihre Werke» (The Mathematicians and Astronomers of the Arabs and Their Works) by the renowned Swiss scholar Heinrich Suter is a well-known resource[37]. Published in 1900, it contains concise biographies of 528 Eastern scholars who lived between 750 and 1000 AD, along with information about their works and the location of their manuscripts. Although the work was later expanded upon by other authors in their own style, it remains a valuable source for studying Eastern mathematics and astronomy.

The biobibliographic work of K. Brockelmann, «History of Arabic Literature»[38], can be considered a reliable encyclopedia. It discusses some topics. After this, valuable information can be found in the book «History of the Arabic Manuscript Heritage»[39] by the Turkish scientist F. Sezgin. Meanwhile, the fundamental research of G. P. Matviyevskaya and B. A. Rosenfeld, published in 1983[40], is distinguished by

---

[36] Bulgakov P.G. Life and works of Beruni. - Tashkent: Science. 1972. - P.32-34.
[37] Suter H. Die Mathematiker und Astronomen der Araber und ihre Werke. – Leipzig, 1900.
[38] Brockelmann. C.Geschichte der arabischen Litteratur. 1-2. Leiden, 1898-1902; 2. Ausl. 1-2. Leiden, 1943-1944.
[39] Sezgin F. Geschichte des arabischen Schrifltums. – Leiden, 1974.
[40] Matviyevskaya G., Rosenfeld B. Mathematicians and astronomers of the Muslim Middle Ages and their works (VIII-XVII centuries). In 3 volumes - Moscow, 1983.

its enrichment of a series of biobibliographic works on the history of science of the 9th-12th centuries.

A biobibliographic work published under the title «Stars of Spirituality»[41], containing information about around one hundred great figures, scientists, and writers of Central Asia, can be considered the best and largest of the studies in this category in our country. The book describes the life and scientific heritage of famous people who lived and worked between the 9th and 20th centuries.

Among the important studies produced in recent years are the books The Cambridge History of Arab Literature, Religion, Education and Science in the Abbasid Period[42] and especially the Encyclopedia of the History of Arab Sciences[43], which address important issues related to all spheres of social life of the peoples of the East.

In general, when studying science and culture of the 10th-12th centuries (consider using «from the 10th to the 12th centuries»), scholars such as F.Wustenfeld[44], A. Brown[45], A. Kremer[46], G. Le Strange[47], O. Sayili[48], D. Surdel[49], R.Morelon, J. Saliba, D. King, and studies by foreign scholars such as E. Kennedy, G. Hudonpar-Roni, R. Rashed, Marie-Therese DeBarneau, Donald R. Hill, J.Anawati, E. Savage-Smith, F. Misch, and Mahdi Muhsin[50] serve as an undeniable basis.

In this monograph, great importance was attached to the scientific activities of the Khorezm Academy of Mamun and its successors, as well as scientific research in the field of exact sciences.

---

[41] Stars of spirituality. Publishing house «People's Heritage» named after Abdulla Kadiri. - Tashkent, 1999.
[42] The Cambridge History of Arabic Literature, Relision, Learning and Science in the Abbacid Period. Cambridge, 1990.
[43] Ensyslopedia of the History of Arabic Science/ Ed. B.Rushdi. – London, 1996.
[44] Wustenfeld von F. Die Geschichtschteiber der Araber und ihre Werke. – Gottingen, 1882.
[45] Browne A.A. Literaty History of Persia from Earliest Times until Firdawsi. Vol. 1. – Cambridge, 1902.
[46] Kremer A.V. The Orient under the Caliphs (Translated from von Kremer's Culturgeschihte des Orients) by Khuda Buksh. – Calcutta, 1920.
[47] Le Strange G. Baghdad during the Abbasid Caliphate from Contemporary Arabiv and Persian Sonrses by G. Le Strane/ 2 nd ed. – London, 1920.
[48] Sayili A. The observatory in Islam. – Ankara, 1960.
[49] Sourdel D. Et Sourdel J. La Civilisation de I'slam classique. – Paris, 1968.
[50] See editors of authors from Morelon Regi to Mahdi Muhsin: Ensyslopedia of the History of Arabic Science. Vol. 1. Ed. R.Rushdi. – London, 1996.

The 10th-11th centuries, according to most researchers, were a period of the rise of culture and science of the Middle Ages[51].

In the monograph, along with philosophical knowledge, Khorezm scholars in mathematics, astronomy, geometry, arithmetic, music, philosophy, jurisprudence, logic, and similar sciences conducted scientific research in Khorezm during the 10th-12th centuries.

It is difficult to imagine the science of mathematics, especially algebra, without Muhammad ibn Musa al-Khwarazmi. Therefore, in the process of their scientific work, after studying Euclid's «Elements,» his scientific research in the field of exact sciences is also discussed.

The main problems studied by scientists of the Khorezm Academy of Mamun are examined from the perspective of philosophical sciences.

When discussing the origins of philosophical science development in Khorezm during the 10th-12th centuries, it is necessary to note the existence of a core tradition of scientific continuity and the observed influence of ancient Greek science.

The achievements of ancient Greek science were introduced in Khorezm during the 10th-12th centuries in two ways: the first being directly through the translation and assimilation of works by ancient Greek scientists from Greek into Arabic within Khorezm. For example, Abu Nasr Mansur ibn Iraq, a great scientist who lived and worked in Khorezm and the teacher of Abu Rayhan Biruni, is known to have translated the work of the ancient Greek scientist Menelaus, «Spherics,» from Greek into Arabic.

The second way involved translations into Arabic of works by ancient Greek scientists done by scientists working in Baghdad, the capital of the Arab Caliphate, and their subsequent use by scientists of the Khorezm Academy of Mamun. Thanks to this continuity, some scientific concepts from the works of Greek scientists, including those in the field of philosophical sciences, influenced the development of

---

[51] Khairullayev M.M. Farabi's worldview and its significance in the history of philosophy. - Tashkent: Science. 1967. – P. 112-127; Khairullayev M.M. Farabi and his teachings. - Tashkent: Uzbekistan, 1967. P. 101-116; Bulgakov P. Life and works of Biruni. - Tashkent: Science. 1972. – P. 9-24; Akhmedov A. Mathematicians and astronomers-contemporaries of Abu Ali ibn Sina // Collection of articles for the 1000th anniversary of the birth of Abu Ali ibn Sina. - Tashkent, 1980. – P. 99..

science in Khorezm during the 10th-12th centuries. This can be clearly observed in the work of Abu Rayhan Biruni. In his work, «Geodesy,» he provides information from the Greek scientists Eratosthenes, Hipparchus, and Ptolemy («Geography» and «Almagest»).

Therefore, we can conclude that during the 10th-12th centuries, the achievements of ancient Greek science were creatively used and further developed by introducing corrections and modifications within the scientific environment of Khorezm.

The scientific potential of Khorezm was further enriched by the achievements of Indian science. When Abu Rayhan Biruni wrote his work, «India,» he critically analyzed the results achieved in this area by the ancient Greeks and Indians, including works like «Al-Arkand» and «Correction» by Brahmagupta (associated with the Indian catastrophe, which we have not been able to access), and «Karanatilaka» by Vijayananda. He then introduced some astronomical concepts into the framework of Muslim science within this work.

If we consider the development of science in Khorezm in the X-XII centuries in a broad sense, then from the point of view of continuity, the scientific works created in the Arab Caliphate, especially in its capital Baghdad, are interesting. Muhammad ibn Musa al-Khwarizmi was the greatest scientist in the field of exact sciences of the Baghdad Academy. His works were actively used by scientists working at the Khorezm Academy of Mamun. Abu Rayhon Beruni in his work "Geodesy" analyzed the research of such scientists as Muhammad ibn Musa al-Khwarizmi, Yahya ibn Mansur, Khalid ibn Abdulmalik, al-Makki, al-Fazari from the field of philosophical sciences of the 9th century, so he was well acquainted with their works.

The creation of the decimal system in the field of algebra by Muhammad ibn Musa al-Khwarizmi stimulated the development of mathematical knowledge not only in the East, but also in Europe. This tradition of continuity is manifested in scientific research, and on the basis of this tradition, when we study the development of science in Khorezm in the X-XII centuries, we also use the works of scientists who worked in

Baghdad during the Arab Caliphate, and treatises of ancient Greek scientists translated into Russian and currently published for comparative study.

Abu Rayhon Beruni was well acquainted with the works of al-Battani, al-Saghani, Abu Ali ibn Sina, Abu Mansur ibn Ali ibn Iraq, among the scholars of the 10th century. It should be noted that from the point of view of the history of science, the greatest attention is focused on the scientific heritage of Muhammad ibn Musa al-Khwarizmi and Abu Rayhon Beruni.

A complete description of the works of Abu Ali ibn Sina based on manuscripts from the fund of the Institute of Oriental Studies named after F.A. Abu Raykhan Beruni of the Republic of Uzbekistan was compiled and published by B. Vakhobova in the form of a separate catalog[52]. In this catalog, Ibn Sina's works are divided into two parts: 60 medical and 50 general philosophical sciences.

Another scientifically important aspect of this catalog is that when describing each work, information given about it in other catalogs is also recorded, and thanks to this, it is possible to obtain information about the manuscripts of Ibn Sina's works stored in different libraries around the world.

Manuscripts of Ibn Sina's works in the field of exact sciences are included in the description of general philosophical works in this catalogue.

One of the relevant scientific works for our research is the doctoral dissertation of H. F. Abdullazoda entitled "History of astronomy in Khorasan and Movarunnahr in the Middle Ages (1X – 10th centuries)"[53], based on published works and handwritten sources on this topic, with the aim of highlighting the history of astronomy of this period. Issues such as periodization, the formation of scientific schools, continuity, scientific influences, spherical astronomy and mathematical geography, methods of mathematical modeling of celestial bodies, the study of planetary movements and star catalogs are considered.

Natural Sciences:

---

[52] Vakhabova B.A. Manuscripts of Ibn Sina's works in the collection of the Institute of Oriental Studies of the Academy of Sciences of the Uzbek SSR. - Tashkent: Science, 1982. - P.72.
[53] Abdulla-zadeh H.F. History of astronomy in medieval Khorasan and Transoxiana (1X - 15 centuries). Author's abstract. for the job application scientist step. Doctor of Historical Sciences - Dushanbe, 1990.

Abu Rayhon Beruni «Monuments of ancient peoples». In a broad sense, this work covers the chronology, ethnic status, culture and religious history of the peoples of the East. There is also information related to natural sciences. For example, the formation of thermal energy on Earth from sunlight, the state of water, etc.

In the chapter "Eid al-Fitr and popular days in Iranian months" of this major study, when talking about the days when "the moon meets and looks at the sun," among other things, he expressed the opinion that "on this day the seas recede and the waters are decreasing»[54]. In modern astronomy, this process is called "the phenomenon of the rise and return of sea waters under the influence of the gravity of the Moon and the Sun".

In his description, Abu Rayhon Beruni cited al-Kindi's views on the relationship between the Moon and the Sun, and also wrote about the influence of their gravitational properties on the human body[55]. These views in the twentieth century were confirmed in the research of astronomer A.L. Chizhevsky[56].

In the field of natural sciences, Ibn Sina read a number of treatises and wrote commentaries on Euclid's "Fundamentals" and Ptolemy's "Al-majisti". Important information about this is given in all works on the history of medieval Eastern science[57].

Ibn Sina's greatest work on the natural sciences is Kitab al-Shifa. When he finished writing this book, he was 50 years old. Al-Shifa was written by al-Buwayhi's encyclopedist Shams al-Dawla (d. 412/1021) over a period of ten years in Hamadan.

This work is considered the greatest philosophical work of Ibn Sina and can be called the scientific encyclopedia of its time. It consists of four parts:

1) logical;

---

[54] Beruni A.R. Selected works. - Volume 1, 1968, p. 277.
[55] Ibid., pp. 276-277.
[56] Chizhevsky A.L., Shishina Yu.G. In the rhythm of the Sun. – Moscow, 1969; Chmzhevsky A.L. Earthly echo of solar storms. – Moscow, 1976.
[57] Gartz J. De interpretibus et explanatoribus Euclidis arabicis. - Halae 1823; Klamroth M. Veber den arabischen Euklid. Zeitschr. d. Deutsch Morgenland. Ges. Bd 35. 1881. P. 270-326; Steinsneider M. Euklid bei Arabern. Eine bibliographische Studie. "Zeitschr. fur Math. u. Phys.". Bd 31. 1886. – P. 81-110; Steinschneider M. Die arabischen Ubersetzungen aus dem Griechischen. Zweiter Abschnitt. Mathematik//"Zeitschr. d. Deutsch. Morgenland. Ges.". Bd. 50. 1896. – P. 161-219; P. 337-417; Steinschneider M. Die arabischen Bearbeiter des Almagest//"Bibl. math.", F. 2, p. 6, 1892.

2) natural sciences (minerals, plants, fauna and humans are discussed in separate sections of this part);

3) mathematics subjects are discussed (counting, geometry, astronomy and music);

4) metaphysics or theology. Parts of this work relating to natural sciences and metaphysics were lithographed in Tehran in 1887-88, and the logical part was printed in several volumes in Cairo from 1962.

Only a few sections were published in Latin, Syriac, Hebrew, German, English, French, Russian, Persian and Uzbek languages[58]. Also, along with the medical works of Ibn Sina[59], the third part of the book "Al-Shifa" is what the author calls the third sentence (juz), i.e. series - this series consists only of works related to the mathematical sciences.

In addition to other natural sciences, Abu Ali ibn Sina studied chemistry and wrote works related to it. Since these works were written by him at different times, they clearly reflect the evolution of his attitude towards chemistry. His ideas in the field of chemistry were extremely advanced for the chemistry of his time. At the age of 21, Abu Ali ibn Sina, who had not yet reached the threshold of his scientific career, believed in metallurgy, transmutation, etc., i.e., in the possibility of the chemical transformation of ordinary metals into gold and silver, and under the influence of the books of early alchemists, he wrote "Risola as-sana ilal-baraki» («The Art of Alchemy»), wrote a short work entitled «Treatise on But by the age of 30.» The young scientist, who had accumulated scientific experience, was practically convinced of the futility of attempts in this area and in the work «Risola Alixir «(«Treatise on the Elixir») doubted that pure gold and silver could be obtained

---

[58] Ibn Sina. Medical advice. - Tashkent: Labor, 1991. - 192 p.
[59] Ibn Sina. Book 1: Canon of Medical Sciences. – T.: Science. 1954.-458 pp.; Ibn Sina. Book II: Canon of Medical Sciences. - T.: Science. 1956. - 844 pp.; Ibn Sina. Book IV: Canon of Medical Sciences. - T.: Science. 1960. – 802 pp.; Ibn Sina. Book V: Canon of Medical Sciences. - T.: Science. 1961. – 348 pp.; Abu Ali ibn Sina. Canon of medical sciences. Selecting the third volume. Kh. Khikmatullayev and U. Karimov in cooperation. - T.: Trud, 1993; Khikmatullaev H. Treatise of Abu Ali ibn Sina "Heart Medicines". - T.: Science. 1966. – 181 pp.; Karimov U.I. On the issue of Ibn Sina's views on kimiya // Materials of the scientific session of the Academy of Sciences of the UzSSR. dedicated 1000th anniversary of Ibn Sini. - T., 1953. - P. 13-38.; Karimov U.I. Classification of sciences by Ibn Sina // Materials of the First All-Union Scientific Conference of Orientalists in the city of Tashkent on June 4-11, 1957. - T., 1958. - P. 986-990.

chemically. In Kitab al-Shifa, which he began writing at the age of 40, he tried to theoretically prove that all the efforts of chemists in the field of transmutation were in vain. He believed that each metal known at that time was a separate substance in itself, and not a separate type of metal, as chemists thought. Although he did not know that gold was a separate element, he also understood that it could not be made from things. These theoretical considerations of the scientist played an important role in the development of scientific chemistry in medieval chemistry.

Abu Ali ibn Sina also did a lot of work on botany, since most medicinal substances used in medicine are obtained from plants. He wrote about types of plants, their appearance, nutrition, organs and their functions, and the conditions of reproduction and growth in the section titled «النبات (an-nabāt)» («Plants») of his book «كتاب الشفاء(Kitab ash-shifa)». He also contributed to the creation of scientific terminology.

Abu Sahl Isa ibn Yahya al-Masih was a great natural scientist of his time. He had interests in astronomy, mathematics, philosophy, medicine, and other natural sciences, but he is best known in the history of science as a physician.

According to sources, the Christian scholar Abu Rayhan wrote twelve works for Biruni. The period of their creation corresponds to 389/998 – 395/1004 years, which coincides with the period of Biruni's stay in Jurjan. Masihi sent him these works by letter. His books on mathematics include «كتاب في مبادي الهندسة(Kitab fi mabadi al-handasa)» («Book on Geometric Concepts»), «مقالة في الجذر واختصار كتاب المجسطي» (Makala fi-l-jizri ichtisar kitab al-Majisti)» («On the Derivation of Roots in the Book of Al-Majisti»), and «كتاب في السكون(Kitab fi sukun)» in astronomy. There are also treatises like «الارض او حركتها(al-ard au harakatiha)» («Book on the Movement or Rotation of the Earth»).

Muhammad ibn Ahmad ibn Muhammad ibn Yusuf al-Khwarizmi, as well as Abu Nasr ibn Iraq, Abu Rayhan Biruni, Abu Ali ibn Sina, Abu Abdullah al-Khwarizmi, Muhammad ibn Umar Fakhriddin ar-Razi (1150-1209), Abu Ali al-Hasan ibn Harit al-Khububi, and Mahmud ibn Muhammad ibn Umar al-Chagmini all made significant scientific discoveries in the field of exact sciences.

The topic chosen for the monograph is covered on the basis of written sources, published materials, and scientific research.

Sources:

1. The third series of Kitab al-Shifa by Abu Ali ibn Sina is devoted to mathematical sciences. Usul ilm al-Khandasa was published in Cairo in 1976.

This work was completely translated by the author from Arabic into Uzbek with comments and used in the monograph.

2. Kitab Tahrir Usul li-Uklidis min ta'lifi Nasir ad-Din at-Tusi, written in Arabic, is stored in the manuscript collection of the St. Petersburg Branch of the Russian Academy of Sciences under number 49/672. The work was published in Rome in 1594. Some parts are translated by the author with comments.

3. Nasir ad-Din at-Tusi. Tahrir Uklidis fi 'ilm al-handasa. Tehran, 1881. This work is a Tehran copy of the above-mentioned work by Nasir al-Din al-Tusi (1201-1274). It examines in detail the theorem of Nasir ad-Din al-Tusi on the theory of parallels. In Chapter 3 of the monograph, his theory of parallels is compared with the scientific research of a number of scientists who came before him.

4. Jami' al-Ulum, written by Muhammad ibn Umar Fakhriddin al-Razi, dedicated to Khorezmshah Ala ad-Din Muhammad (1200-1220). A copy stored in the library of the Uzbek scientist Kh. Siddikov was used. The thoughts of Fakhriddin al-Razi on the classification of sciences are scientifically analyzed.

5. The work Mulahas fi al-Hayah by Mahmud ibn Muhammad ibn Umar al-Chagmini is kept in the manuscript collection of the Institute of Oriental Studies named after Abu Rayhan Biruni of the Academy of Sciences of the Republic of Uzbekistan under numbers 10417, 7761/3, 8796/11, 11599/3. There is also a commentary by Qazizada Rumi (1360-1437) on the work of Mahmud al-Chagmini Mulahas fi al-Hayah.

6. Hajjaj ibn Yusuf ibn Matar (late 8th - early 9th century). «Kitab Uqlidis fi al-Usul.» - Kept in the manuscript collection of the Russian Academy of Sciences in St. Petersburg under number C 2145. The treatise of Hajjaj ibn Yusuf ibn Matar was compared with the commentaries of Khorezm scientists on Euclid's «Elements» in

the field of geometry.

7. Nasir al-Din al-Tusi's work «Majmu'a al-rasa'il» was published in Hyderabad (India) in 1358/1939. Information on Nasir al-Din al-Tusi's foundation of sciences was obtained from this work.

8. In the process of writing a study in the manuscript collection of the Institute of Oriental Studies named after Abu Rayhan Biruni of the Academy of Sciences of the Republic of Uzbekistan, the following books were found:

Abu Rayhan Biruni's "Kitab al-Tafhim li Awasi'l Sina'i al-Tanjim" under number 3423.

Abu Ali ibn Sina's «Kunuz al-Ma'rifa» under number 2385/22, «Ganj al-Maruf» under number 3374/5, and «Risala ila Abu Rayhan Muhammad ibn Ahmad al-Biruni» under number 2385/14.

Mahmud ibn Muhammad ibn Umar al-Chaghmini's «Al-Mulahhas fi al-Hay'a» under numbers 10417; 7761/3; 8796/11; and 11599/3. The commentaries on «Al-Mulahhas fi al-Hay'a» include: Ash-Sharh «Al- Mulahhas fi al-Hay'a» № 2655, and Sharh «Al- Mulahhas fi al-Hay'a» № 8217 and 3935 (a total of 20 manuscripts).

Husayn ibn al-Hasan al-Khwarizmi al-Kubrawi's «Nuzhat al-Mulk fi Hayat al-Aflak» numbered 1207/3.

Abu Nasr Farabi's «Risala fi ma yasukh wa ma la yasukh min ahkam an-nujum» numbered 2385/32 manuscripts were used.

Based on the analysis of existing scientific research on the topic «Philosophical Views of Scientists of the Khorezm Academy of Mamun», the following points emerged:

The Scope of Research: This topic has received serious attention from scholars in both Eastern and Western countries.

Focus Areas in Existing Research: Existing research related to the philosophical works of Khorezm scientists from the 10th to 12th centuries falls into three main categories:

Scientific analysis of these works.

Publication of full or partial translations of source materials from this period.

Translation and publication of philosophical works from 10th-12th century Khorezm into various world languages.

Connection to Specific Sciences: The development of irrigated agriculture and urban culture in Khorezm is demonstrably linked to specific scientific disciplines.

Mathematical Achievements: Three problems proved elusive for ancient Greek mathematicians:

Quadrature of the circle (calculating the area of a circle)

Trisection of an angle (dividing an angle or arc into three equal parts)

Doubling the cube (constructing a cube with twice the volume of a given cube)

Pioneering Work in Trigonometry: Historical research confirms that Khorezmian scientist Abu Nasr ibn Iraq was the first to prove the sine theorem for both flat and spherical triangles.

Geographical Scholarship: Comparing geographical coordinates in the works of Abu Rayhan Biruni and al-Khwarizmi reveals some key differences:

Biruni excludes many Western European cities (except Spain) from his tables, focusing instead on cities in Iran, Iraq, the Caucasus, Khorasan, Central Asia, and India.

The coordinates for these regions differ between Biruni and al-Khwarizmi, likely due to the 200-year gap between them. Additionally, Biruni appears to have deliberately omitted coordinates for many cities in Central Asia, Khorasan, and India.

Contributions to Geometry: The theories of parallels proposed by Abu Rayhan Biruni and Ibn Sina differed fundamentally from Euclid's. Notably, N.I. Lobachevsky's work on non-Euclidean geometry built upon these earlier advancements.

Innovation in Mathematics: Abu Ali ibn Sina's extensive use of motion in his works, including «Donishnama,» definitions in «Usul ilm al-Khandasa,» and proofs of theorems, represented a significant innovation and foreshadowed future developments in mathematics.

Ibn Sina's Approach to Geometry: Unlike Euclid, Ibn Sina did not rely solely on abstract reasoning. He employed practical tools like a compass and ruler, enabling him to develop series geometry, which offered alternative proofs to those found in Euclidean geometry. These contributions demonstrate that Ibn Sina's works, «The Book of Healing» (Kitab al-Shifa) and «The Illumination» («Enlightenment»), were not only significant philosophical treatises but also made profound advancements in mathematics and geometry.

Shift in Focus: Following the works of Al-Khwarizmi and Mahmud al-Chaghmini, there appears to be a gap in major mathematical and astronomical studies from Khorezm until the 20th century. This suggests that philosophical inquiry and historiography became the primary focus of later Khorezm scholars. The large-scale mathematical and astronomical research of the 10th-12th centuries evidently represented the peak of scientific achievement in these fields for Khorezm.

CHAPTER I. THEORETICAL AND METHODOLOGICAL BASIS FOR STUDYING THE TOPIC "ROLE IN THE DEVELOPMENT OF CIVILIZATIONS OF THE NATURAL SCIENTIFIC, SOCIO-PHILOSOPHICAL AND SPIRITUAL HERITAGE OF SCIENTISTS OF THE KHOREZM ACADEMY OF MAMUN

1.1. Integral connection of natural science and historical-philosophical heritage in the views of scientists of the Khorezm Academy of Mamun

Among the social problems explored in ancient Eastern and Western philosophy, ethics takes center stage. Wise sayings and phrases created during that period continue to resonate with people today. For instance, Plato's «Dialogues» define concepts like fate, old age, virtue, intelligence, justice, patience, composure, conscientiousness, freedom, modesty, nobility, peacefulness, ease, friendship, kindness, faith, and deep thinking.

According to Aristotle, possessing spiritual and moral qualities like fidelity, thoughtfulness, love of family, honesty, kindness, respect for others' rights, love for parents, vigilance, intelligence, and justice constitutes one of the greatest sources of wealth and power for any society, state, or nation. He argues that the purpose of having something is to use it. Just as a person with eyes doesn't live with them closed but uses them to see the world, the same applies to ears and other senses. He raises the question of whether it's more important for a person simply to have something or to use it. He believes that using something is paramount, as the purpose of having it lies in its application and function[61].

Despite focusing on «The Influence of the Natural Scientific Heritage of Scientists of the Khorezm Mamun Academy on the Development of Human Civilization,» the monograph's content and volume have left a significant mark on the history of science, making it valuable to a wide range of researchers. Science

---

[61] See Boboyev H. Gafurov Z. Development of political and spiritual-educational teaching in Uzbekistan. -T.: Generation of the new century, 2001. - P.85.

flourished in Khorezm during the African, Mamunid, and Anushteginid dynasties. During these centuries, scholars conducted research and authored major works across various scientific fields. Unfortunately, only a portion of these writings have survived, and scientists rely on this remaining heritage to draw conclusions.

The monograph's second chapter delves into «Factors that Influenced the Formation of the Scientific Views of Thinkers Who Worked at the Khorezm Mamun Academy.» Studies within this chapter on the origins of philosophical knowledge development in Khorezm, from ancient times to the 11th century, primarily rely on the results of archaeological expeditions due to the scarcity of written information from antiquity and the early Middle Ages.

The archaeological study of Khorezm began in 1928-1929 with an expedition led by A.Yu. Yakubovsky. This expedition investigated not only early medieval monuments but also Gurganch (Old Urgench), the capital of the Anushteginid state during the period covered by this monograph. These studies continued in subsequent years, culminating in the founding of the Khorezm Archaeological and Ethnographic Expedition in 1937. This expedition's mission was to explore Khorezm's history from the Paleolithic era to the 19th century.

The first major published works on Khorezm's history were written by S.P. Tolstov (1907-1976) [62]. These works directly stemmed from the extensive and complex research conducted in the region by the Khorezm Archaeological and Ethnographic Expedition during its active period (1937-1969).

Yahya Gulomov (1908-1977), a scholar from Uzbekistan, investigated the history of irrigated agriculture and urban culture in Khorezm between 1938 and 1950 as part of the Khorezm Archaeological and Ethnographic Expedition. His works drew upon the expedition's findings[63].

---

[62] Tolstov S.P. Ancient culture of Uzbekistan. - T., 1944.; Tolstov S.P. Ancient Khorezm. Experience in historical and archaeological research. - M., 1948; Tolstov S.P. In the footsteps of the ancient Khorezmian civilization. - M.-L., 1948; Tolstov S.P. In search of ancient Khorezm culture. - T. 1964; Tolstov S.P. Along the ancient delta of Oxus and Jaxartes. - M., 1972.
[63] Gulyamov Ya.G. History of irrigation of Khorezm from ancient times to the present day. - T.: Publishing house of the Academy of Sciences of the UzSSR. - Tashkent, 1957; Gulomov Ya.G. Khorazmning kadimgi sugorilish tarihi. - T.: Science, 1958.

We utilized the scientific conclusions from archaeological expeditions led by S.P. Tolstov and Y. Gulomov in the monograph's second chapter, titled «Ancient Roots of Mathematical and Astronomical Knowledge Development in Khorezm until the 11th Century». These studies reflect the results of excavations conducted at the ruins of ancient Khorezm cities such as Ayozkala, Bazarkala, Jonboskala, Tuprokkala, Koykirilangkala, Kurgankala, Kyzylkala, Kozalikir, and Teshikkala.

Urban planning inherently requires the creation of a project, which necessitates knowledge of specific sciences, particularly geometry. Based on this principle, the expeditions unearthed and introduced into scientific circulation various monuments – inscriptions, images, and material objects – that testify to Khorezm's ancient culture and the development of knowledge. The research findings were published in the form of scientific reports titled «Proceedings of the Khorezm Archaeological and Ethnographic Expedition»[64]. One such study focused on the history of Koykirilgan-kala castle.

Koykirilgan-kala: An ancient mausoleum-castle (4th-3rd centuries BC) lies 22 kilometers northeast of the city of Tortkol in the present-day Republic of Karakalpakstan. The ethnographic expedition documented it in 1938, and archaeological excavations revealed it further between 1951 and 1957. It includes a two-story, round (42 meters in diameter) fire-worshipper temple building dating back to the 4th-3rd centuries BC. Among the various artifacts unearthed at the monument (dishes, ceramic coffins, figurines with colored patterns) were also items used for observing celestial bodies.

From an astronomical perspective, this site was first studied in a collection published as a book in 1967[65]. Subsequently, M.G. Vorobyova, M.M. Rozhanskaya, and I.N. Veselovsky co-authored an article on it in 1969[66]. Their work examined Koykirilgan-kala as an astronomical object, determining that it was used to observe the annual movement of the Sun, the positions of the Moon and stars. They paid

---

[64] Proceedings of the Khorezm archaeological and ethnographic expedition. 1958, vol.2. - P.7-258.
[65] Koi-Krylgan-kala - a cultural mSSU,ment of ancient Khorezm of the 4th century. BC. – IV century AD (Chief editor: S.P. Tolstov, B.I. Weinberg). M., 1967; S.P. Tolstoy. Works of the Khorezm expedition of the USSR Academy of Sciences on excavations of a mSSU,ment of the 4th – 3rd centuries. BC. Koi-Krylgan-kala. Bulletin of Ancient History, 1953, № 1, pp. 160-174.

particular attention to the time of the spring equinox and summer solstice, when the Sun creates the longest day in the Northern Hemisphere.

Astronomical observations stemmed from immediate practical needs. They were deemed essential for organizing agricultural work effectively in ancient Khorezm, particularly determining the Amu Darya's water content and its optimal use.

Timekeeping, which served as a calendar, was not limited to Koykirilgan-kala. Evidence of this can be found in the «Dove» noted in the results of archaeological research at Kavat-kala (12th-13th centuries). Scientific perspectives on this topic are presented in the reports of the Khorezm Archaeological Expedition led by S.P.Tolstov and later in the studies of S.Kh. Azizov. For instance, in his article on the subject, S.Kh. Azizov concluded that «Kaptarkhana» refers to a timekeeping service – a «calculator,» or more precisely, an «observatory»[67] – that functioned as a calendar without interruption.

Muhammad ibn Musa al-Khwarizmi made a great contribution to the theory of cognitive activity. He founded the method of experience-observation and experimentation of cognition. Khorezmi justified the following general didactic principles, methods and forms: independence; creative activity; description of observed facts and events and regular reporting of them; observation experiment; experimental method; the principle of singularity and unity of community in the aspect of induction and deduction; question-and-answer form of training.

A Russian-language study on the history of Khorezm was also published by the famous orientalist V.V.Bartold at the beginning of the twentieth century. P.G.Bulgakov noted in his study that the scientific study of Abu Raykhan Beruni's work "Geodesy" was first carried out by V.V. Bartold in 1926; more precisely, the scientist copied fragments of the history of Khorezm from a single copy of this work. in Istanbul[68]. These passages were translated from Arabic into Russian and published

---

[67] Azizov S.Kh. "Kaptarkhana" in Khorezm - address of the time service / Khorezm Mamun Academy and its place in the development of world science. Materials of the international scientific conference. - Tashkent-Khiva. The science. 2006. – pp. 23-25.
[68] Bulgakov P.G. Life and works of Beruni. - Tashkent: Science. 1972.- P.161-163.

by S.L.Volin in 194[69]. However, most of V.V.Bartold's works in this area are devoted mainly to the history of Khorezm, especially to the problems of the confluence of the Amu Darya into the Aral and Caspian seas[70].

In this work, P.G. Bulgakov examines some problems in the field of exact sciences in the scientific activities of the Khorezm Mamun Academy, including the views of Abu Raikhan Beruni in his field, as well as the study of the scientific heritage of this encyclopedist scientist in science is analyzed. In addition, P. G. Bulgakov published a number of articles on the development of exact sciences in Khorezm in the 10th-12th centuries and published the work of Abu Raikhan Beruni "Geodesy" from Arabic into Russian with a preface and scientific comments[71].

It should be noted that a significant part of the study of the scientific heritage of Abu Rayhon Beruni in world science consists of publications and translations of the scientist's works or the publication of translations of some of his works into other languages. Naturally, these translations also include materials related to specific sciences.

At the end of the 19th century: Italian orientalist I. Fiorini (cartographic projections by Abu Rayhon Beruni); At the beginning of the 20th century, the German scientist G. Zutter, in his works on the history of exact sciences in the East, briefly mentioned the merits of Abu Rayhon Beruni in this field, and also translated his treatises on chords (1910-1911).) and projections of celestial bodies onto a flat surface (1922). In 1908, the Libyan philologist L. Sheikho published the Arabic text of Abu Rayhon Beruni's treatise "The Honorable Sextant". In his research (1911), the Italian scientist C. Nallino analyzed such issues as cosmogony, astronomy, including

---

[69] Volin S. On the history of ancient Khorezm, "Bulletin of Ancient History", 1941. № 1.
[70] Bartold V.V. History of the cultural life of Turkestan. Works, II (1), M., IVL, 1963. - P.167-433; Bartold V.V. History of Turkestan. Works, II (1). M., IVL, 1963. - P.107-166; Bartold V.V. On the iSSU,e of the confluence of the Amu Darya into the Caspian Sea. Essays. T.III. M., 1965. - P.248-251.
[71] Bulgakov P.G. Globe Biruni // Social sciences in Uzbekistan. - Tashkent. 1965. № 1; Bulgakov P.G. Fakhriyev sextant in Biruni's "Geodesy" // Social Sciences in Uzbekistan. - Tashkent. 1963. № 6; Bulgakov P.G. Beruni and his "Geodesy". - In the book: Abu Reyhan Biruni. Favorite works: T.3. Determining the boundaries of places to clarify distances between populated areas ["Geodesy"]. Research, translation and notes by P.G. Bulgakov. - T.: Science. 1966; Bulgakov P.G. Determination of the size of lands in the medieval Muslim East / "Oriental Studies". Vol. 2. - Tashkent: Science. 1991. - P.184. 18-24-p.

Indian concepts of this science, and determining the size of the Earth in the works of Abu Rayhon Beruni.

The German scientist K. Scheu, in his works devoted to the history of mathematics, studied information on geodesy, trigonometry and chords in the work of Abu Rayhon Beruni "Masudi's Law" (1923). J. Sarton, a famous scientist in the history of world science, assessed Abu Rayhon Beruni as the greatest scientist of his time on a global scale[72].

In the first quarter of the 20th century. the great European scientist E. Wiedemann published a number of articles exploring the exact sciences in the works of Abu Rayhon Beruni. For example, determining the size of the Earth, problems related to trigonometry, making an astrolabe, determining the relative weight of substances, information related to mathematics in al-Tafhim, etc.

Foreign research continued in subsequent years: in a collection published in Calcutta in 1951, the works of Abu Rayhon Beruni on the history of geodesy (S.H.Barani)[73], trigonometry of Abu Rayhon Beruni (M.A.Kozim)[74], his methods determination of geographical longitude (I.Kramers)[75]. His method of determining the meridian (E.Kennedy, 1959)[76], mathematical analysis of books III and IV "Qanuni Masudi" (I.I.Ahmad, Cairo, 1959)[77], definition of chords (A.S.Damardash, 1965; Abu Rayhon Arabic the text of Beruni's treatise with extensive scientific comments)[78], the Egyptian scientist Kadri Hafiz Tokan, in his major study on the history of mathematics and astronomy (1963), Abu Rayhon touched upon individual sciences of Beruni's scientific heritage[79]; E.Kennedy, S.Ingle and J.Wamsted

---

[72] Sarton G. Introduction to the histori of science, vol. I-III, Baltimore,1927-1948; vol.I. p.707; Bulgakov P.G. Life and works of Beruni. - Tashkent: Science. 1972. - P.376.

[73] Barani S. H. Muslim Researches in Geodesy // "Al-Biruni – Commemoration Volume", Calcutta, Iran Society, 1951; Bulgakov P.G. Life and works of Beruni. - Tashkent: Science. 1972. - P.381.

[74] Kazim M.A. Al-Biruni and Trigonometry. // "Al-Biruni – Commemoration Volume", Calcutta, Iran Society, 1951; Bulgakov P.G. Life and works of Beruni. - Tashkent: Science. 1972. - P.381.

[75] Kramers G.H. Al-Biruni's Determination of Geographical Longitude by measuring of the distances // "Al-Biruni – Commemoration Volume", Calcutta, Iran Society, 1951; Bulgakov P.G. Life and works of Beruni. - Tashkent: Science. 1972. - P.382.

[76] Kennedi E.S. Biruni's graphical determination of the local Meridian. Scripta Mathematica, XXIV, 1959; Bulgakov P.G. Life and works of Beruni. - Tashkent: Science. 1972. - P.383.

[77] Ahmad I. Al-Biruni's astronomical works, Cairo Universiti Press, Bulletin No 48. Cairo,1959; Bulgakov P.G. Life and works of Beruni. - Tashkent: Science. 1972. - P.383.

[78] Beruni. Istihraj al-Awtar (in Arabic); Bulgakov P.G. Life and works of Beruni. - Tashkent: Science. 1972. - P.387.

[79] Bulgakov P.G. Life and works of Beruni. - Tashkent: Science. 1972. - P.387.

published a study of their knowledge of the Indian calendar (1960)[80].

The scientific heritage of scientists of the East, including scientists of the Khorezm Mamun Academy, in the field of astronomy is covered in the form of scientific research and translations on the pages of the collection "Historical and Astronomical Research", regularly published in Russian since the 50s of the 20th century. These publications also included research by Uzbek scientists (S.D.Jalilov, P.G.Bulgakov, Z.G.Jalilova, G.P.Matviyevskaya, Kh.Tlashev, M.S.Bulatov, O.S.Tursunov, S.Kh.Azizov). The materials published in the collection can be divided into four groups: 1) problems of Muslim eastern astronomy; 2) the scientific heritage of Central Asian scientists; 3) Research related to the activities of the Khorezm Mamun Academy; 4) Translations of works written by Eastern scientists in the field of philosophy.

In studies devoted to the scientific heritage of Central Asian scientists, the treatises of Muhammad ibn Musa al-Khwarizmi "Zij" and "Working with the Astrolabe" were briefly described, and it was also noted that the sine-quadrant was described as a separate astronomical instrument. for the first time in science in the next book[81]; Ahmad al-Farghani's treatises on astronomy provide a more complete description[82]; Several articles are devoted to the activities of Ulugbek, his Samarkand Observatory and the work of scientists therein, containing scientific comments on the achievements of Ulugbek in the field of astronomy[83] and the structure of the observatory he built[84], the life of its scientists (Gazizoda Rumi, Ali Kushchi)[85] and activities[86], as well as the astronomical instrument[87] built in Tashkent in the 9th century.

---

[80] See about this: Bulgakov P.G. Life and works of Beruni. - Tashkent: Science. 1972. - P.388.
[81] Rosenfeld B.A., Sergeeva N.D. On the asonomic tracts of al-Khwarizmi. /Historical and astronomical research. Vol. XIII.- M., 1977. - P.201-218.
[82] Rosenfeld B.A., Dobrovolsky I.G., Sergeeva N.D. On the astronomical treatises of al-Fargani. /Historical and astronomical research. ISSU,e XI. - M., 1972. - P.191-210.
[83] Ventzel M.K. A brief outline of the history of practical astronomy in Russia and the USSR (development of methods for determining time and latitude)./Historical and astronomical research. ISSU,e II. - M., 1956. - P.7-140.
[84] Bulatov M.S. Ulugbek Observatory in Samarkand./Historical and astronomical research. Vol. XYIII -.M., 1986. - P.199-216.
[85] Ibodov Yu.Kh., Matviyevskaya G.P. Ulugbek's student is Ali Kushchi. - T., Science, 1994, p. 36.
[86] Jalalov G.D. Some remarkable statements of asonomists of the Samarkand observatory./ Historical and astronomical research. ISSU,e III. - M., 1957. - P.381-386.

In one of the translations of these collections, the catalog of stars of Abu Rayhon Beruni was translated from Arabic into Russian, and the necessary scientific comments were also given to it[88]. The following translation consists of excerpts from Abu Rayhon Beruni's Qanuni Masudi[389] and Ibn al-Haytham's treatises on astronomy. Scientific works written on the basis of his research and direct observations[90], the Ulugbek Observatory and the scientists who worked in it[91], Ibn Iraq and the scientific heritage of Abdurahman al-Sufi[92], a major representative of Muslim eastern astronomy, are mentioned.

A number of collections entitled "Historical and Astronomical Research" also reflect the activities of the Khorezm Mamun Academy in the field of astronomy. The main part of the materials published in them is devoted to the analysis of the astronomical heritage of Abu Rayhon Beruni. For example, the star catalog of Abu Rayhon Beruni was translated into Russian for the first time, and the star catalogs of Umar Khayyam (1040-1123) and Nasir ad-Din Tusi (1201-1274) were also translated into Russian for the first time; All three works are compared with the data of the Greek scientist Claudius Ptolemy in scientific comments[93].

The catalog of stars of Abu Rayhon Beruni was first published in India as part of the publication "Qanuni Masudi"[94]. B. A. Rosenfeld, who wrote the preface to the Russian edition, expressed the opinion that the catalog of Abu Rayhon Beruni was compiled on the basis of Ptolemy's Almagest and the catalogs of Abulhusayn

---

[87] Tursunov O.S., Azizov S.Kh. An astronomical instrument of the early Middle Ages in the center of Tashkent. /Historical and astronomical research. ISSU,e XXV. - M., 2000. - P.56-60..

[88] Star catalog of al-Biruni with the application of the catalogs of Khayyam and at-Tusi. Translation by S.A. Krasnova, M.M. Rozhanskaya. Ed. B.A. Rosenfeld. /Historical and astronomical research. Vol. VIII. - M., 1962. -P.83-194.

[89] Beruni Abu Rayhan. Selected Works, Vol. 1 book. Canon of Masudi (Article IV). – Tashkent: Science, 1973. – 239 p.

[90] Jalalov G.D. Indian astronomy in Beruni's book "India". /Historical and astronomical research. ISSU,e XUIII. - M., 1962.- P.195-220; P.G. Bulgakov. Biruni's "Geodesy" as a historical and asonomic mSSU,ment. /Historical and astronomical research. ISSU,e XI. - M., 1972. - P.181-190; P.G. Bulgakov. Biruni's early treatise on the Fakhri sextant. /Historical and astronomical research. ISSU,e XI. - M., 1972. - P.211-220; Jalalova Z.G. Al-Biruni's student about the movement of the Sun. / Historical and astronomical research. Vol. XII. - M., 1975. - P.227-236..

[91] Bulatov M.S. Ulugbek Observatory in Samarkand./Historical and astronomical research. Vol. XVIII. - M., 1986. - P.199-216.

[92] Matviyevskaya G.P., Tlashev Kh. On the scientific heritage of the asonomist of the 10th-11th centuries. Abu Nasr ibn Iraq. / Historical and astronomical research. Vol. XIII. - M., 1977. - P.219-234; G.P. Mavievskaya. Abd ar-Rahman al-Sufi and his role in the history of astronomy. /Historical and astronomical research. ISSU,e XVI. - M., 1983. - P.93-138.

[93] Star catalog of al-Biruni with the application of the catalogs of Khayyam and at-Tusi. Translation by S.A. Krasnova, M.M. Rozhanskaya. Ed. B.A. Rosenfeld. /Historical and astronomical research. Vol. VIII. - M., 1962. -P.83-194.

[94] Adu-r-Rayhan al-Biruni/ Al-Qanun' 1 Masudi (Canon Masudicus). - Hayderabad-Dn, Osmania Press, 1954-1956, vol. III. - pp.1014-1126.

Abdurrahman ibn Umar al-Sufi (903-983), who lived in the city of Ray. This translation can be called the first serious study in Russian of the heritage of scientists of the Khorezm Mamun Academy in the field of exact sciences.

In the article by P.G.Bulgakov[95], Abu Rayhon Beruni's work "Geodesy" is noted as an important written monument related to astronomy, and contains issues of practical (geodetic) astronomy (determining the geographic latitude of a place, astronomical instruments made by Abu Rayhon Beruni, determining the deviation of the ecliptic plane to the equator, Honorary Sextant Abu Raihan comes to the conclusion that in Beruni's description one sees a definition of the geographical longitude and size of the Earth, etc.).

he studies of A.K. Tagi-Zade[96] described the quadrants that existed in the East in the Middle Ages; In this area, al-Khwarizmi wrote about the sine quadrant (in the book "Working with the Astrolabe"), and Abu Rayhon Beruni gave detailed information about the quadrant in the books "At-Tafhim", "Qanuni Masudi", "Geodesy", "Honorary Sextant".

The studies of A.K. Tagi-Zadeh describe the quadrants that existed in the Middle Ages in the East; In this area, al-Khwarizmi wrote about the sine quadrant (in the book "Working with the Astrolabe"), and Abu Rayhon Beruni gave detailed information about the quadrant in the books "At-Tafhim", "Qanuni Masudi", "Geodesy", "Honorary Sextant".

Several other articles have been written about Abu Rayhon Beruni's research on Indian astronomy[97], his writings on the zodiacal light in the Qanuni Masudi[98], a treatise on the honorary sextant[99] and his thoughts on the movement of the Sun[100].

---

[95] Bulgakov P.G. "Geodesy" of Biruni as a historical and astronomical mSSU,ment / Historical and astronomical research. Vol. XI. - M., 1972. - P.181-190.
[96] Tagi-Zade A.K. Quadrants of the medieval East / Historical and astronomical studies. Vol. XIII. - M., 1977. - P.183-200.
[97] Jalalov G.D. Indian astronomy in Beruni's book "India" / Historical and astronomical studies. Vol. VIII. - M., 1962. - P.195-220.
[98] Rosenfeld B.A. About the zodical light among the Arabs. /Historical and astronomical research. ISSU,e XV. - M., 1980. - P.290-292.
[99] Bulgakov P.G. Biruni's early treatise on the Fakhri sextant. /Historical and astronomical research. ISSU,e XI. - M., 1972. - P.211-220.
[100] Jalalova Z.G. Al-Biruni's student about the movement of the Sun. /Historical and astronomical research. ISSU,e XII. - M., 1975. - P.227-236.

The study by B. A. Rosenfeld, entitled "Astronomy in Islamic Countries," is written in the form of general information, it briefly touches on the ideas about astronomy that existed among the Arabs in ancient times, and then analyzes research in the field of astronomy in the Baghdad Caliphate, and in it the scientists of the Middle East Asia (Muhammad ibn Musa al-Khwarizmi, Habash al-Khasib, instead of Ahmad al-Fargani, information about the development of astronomy in subsequent centuries in the East - Middle East (Nishapur, Shiraz, Ray), Khorezm, Syria, Arabia, Egypt, Turkey, The history of astronomical knowledge is covered in the Caucasus, India, Maghreb, Spain and during the reign of some dynasties (Ghaznavids, Seljuks, Timurids, Safavids).

In the parts of the article devoted to Khorezm and the Ghaznavids, the author notes that the history of astronomy in Khorezm has ancient roots and that during an archaeological expedition to Koykiril-Kale the remains of an observatory were found. After that, he briefly touched upon the astronomical research of scientists of the Khorezm Mamun Academy (Ibn Iraq, Abu Rayhon Beruni, Mahmud Chagmini); The example of the Ghaznavid dynasty shows the work of Abu Rayhon Beruni[101].

The article by G.P. Matviyevskaya, Kh. Tlashev in the 13th issue of the journal "Historical Astronomical Research"[102] talks about the life and scientific heritage of Abu Nasr ibn Iraq, a major representative of the Khorezm Mamun Academy. Initially, his name was given as Abu Nasr Mansur ibn Ali ibn Iraq and it was indicated that he came from an Iraqi family that belonged to the Khorezmshah dynasty. Further, his works on astronomy and mathematics are given separately with a brief reference and research on the time of their writing, whether they have survived or, if not, in whose work they are mentioned in the works of scientists of the East.

The section on mathematical works mentions that M. Krause translated Ibn Iraq's «Corrections to the Book of Menelaus (Spherical)» into German in 1936. The translation was based on a single copy held in the Leiden University library and

---

[101] Rosenfeld B.A. Astronomy of the san of Islam / Historical and astronomical studies. Vol. XVII. - M., 1984. P.67-122.
[102] Matviyevskaya G.P., Tlashev Kh. On the scientific heritage of the astronomer of the 10th-11th centuries. Abu Nasr ibn Iraq. /Historical and astronomical research. Vol. XIII. - M., 1977. - P.219-234.

published with a detailed philological study. The article authors provide a brief analysis.

Articles devoted to the development of mathematics in the East have also been published in various volumes of the «Historical and Mathematical Research» collection, regularly published in Russian since the second half of the 20th century. A significant portion of these articles focuses on the scientific heritage of Central Asian mathematicians and the Khorezm Mamun Academy. In particular, many articles explore the mathematical work of Abu Rayhan Biruni.

These articles discuss Biruni's methods for creating an ellipse, parabola, and hyperbola in one plane from a circle using an astrolabe (specifically, images of the horizon and almucantarate). Other topics include:

Determining the direction of the Qibla (Vakhabov S.A.)[103], Comparative analysis of methods used by Abu Rayhan Biruni, Mahmud Chagmini, and Kamoliddin of Turkmenistan (11th century) (Atagarriev M.N.)[104], Analysis of Abu Rayhan Biruni's manuscript «Perfect Methods of Making an Astrolabe» («Istiab al-wujuh al-mumkina fi san'a al-asturlob») held at Leiden University Library (Or.591/4) (Vakhabov S.)[105], Abu Rayhan Biruni's «Special Words on the Problem of the Shadow» («Ifrod al-maqol fi amr al-azlal»)[106] and the use of square interpolation (B.A. Rozenfeld)[107].

Two volumes of the collection contain articles on the topics of:

Mathematical knowledge in the history of Central Asian peoples during the 10th-11th centuries (Yushkevich A.P.)[108], The study of the history of mathematics in

---

[103] Vahabov S.A. Projective transformations in al-Biruni's treatise on asolabia. /Historical and mathematical research. Vol. XXXII – XXXIII. - M., Publishing house «Science», 1990. - P.339-344.

[104] Atagarriev M.N. Application of stereographic projection to determine the azimuth of the qibla: al-Biruni, al-Chagmini and at-Turkmoni. /Historical and mathematical research. ISSU,e XXIX. - M., Publishing house «Science», 1980. - P.44-4.

[105] Vahabov S. Two mathematical models of al-Biruni. /Historical and mathematical research. ISSU,e XXV. - M., Publishing house «Science», 1980. - P.328-335.

[106] Rosenfeld B.A. [Some questions of mathematics of variables in al-Biruni's treatise on shadows] /Historical and mathematical studies. Vol. XXIII. - M., Publishing house «Science», 1978. - P.226-231.

[107] Rosenfeld B.A. An attempt at quadratic interpolation by Abu r-Reyhan al-Biruni / Historical and mathematical research. Vol. XII. - M., Publishing house «Science», 1959. - P.421-430.

[108] Yushkevich A.P. On the mathematics of the peoples of Central Asia in the 9th-15th centuries / Historical and mathematical research. ISSU,e IV. M., Publishing house «Science», 1951. - P.455-489.

Central Asia (S.Kh. Sirozhiddinov, G.P. Matviyevskaya)[109] these volumes also consider the development of mathematics in Khorezm.

A.P.Yushkevich's study, mentioned above, challenges the conclusion of Western scholars that mathematics among the Arabs merely repeated the work of ancient Indian and Greek scientists. Yushkevich provides convincing evidence that Eastern scholars made significant changes, corrections, and new contributions to the achievements of ancient Indian and Greek mathematics.

The article also argues that the term «Arabic» science, commonly used in Western science, is inaccurate. It highlights that many people from various regions contributed to scientific advancements during a certain period using the Arabic language. This applies to the field of mathematics as well, with specific examples provided.

Yushkevich emphasizes that mathematical sciences held a significant place in the scientific heritage of Central Asian scientists during the 9th and 10th centuries. He highlights achievements in arithmetic, algebra, and trigonometry, including fundamental discoveries in calculus and combinatorics.

Improvements to the sexagesimal positional system

Discovery of decimal fractions

Development of methods for extracting roots

Application of the binomial formula (now known as the Binomial Theorem) for any natural exponent

Expansion of the understanding of real positive numbers

In algebra, the article discusses the application of numerical algebra in geometry and trigonometry, the discovery of the method of integration, and the creation of a geometric theory for solving cubic equations.

Trigonometric advancements included the creation of a system for plane and spherical trigonometry, allowing for the calculation of highly accurate and precise trigonometric tables.

---

[109] Sirazhdinov S.Kh., Matviyevskaya G.P. On the study of the history of mathematics in Central Asia. /Historical and mathematical research /Historical and mathematical research. ISSU,e XXI. - M., . Publishing house «Science», 1976. P.51-61.

The article approaches the concept of the Central Asian region broadly, encompassing parts of the Middle East.

A more relevant research source compared to our monograph is a short article titled «On the Study of the History of Mathematics in Central Asia»[110], co-authored by S. Kh. Sirodzhiddinov and G.P. Matviyevskaya. The authors note that the systematic study of the history of mathematics in the Near and Middle East, as well as in Central Asia, began in the second half of the 19th century. In Uzbekistan, however, this focus began primarily in the second half of the 20th century.

Research in Uzbekistan extends beyond mathematics, encompassing the history of specific sciences in general. Researchers in this field include A.P. Yushkevich, T.N. Kori-Niyazov, B.A. Rosenfeld, G. P. Jalolov, R. I. Ibodov, N. I. Leonov, G. P. Matviyevskaya, A. Usmanov, E. A. Khatipov, S. A. Akhmedov, Zh. Kh. Ibodov, Kh. Umarov, A. F. Faizullaev, V. P. Shcheglov, and M. A. Sobirov.

Their research has explored topics such as the Ulugbek Observatory, the Ulugbek Zij (astronomical tables), the mathematical and astronomical works of Mahmud Chagmini, and Russian and Uzbek translations of Abu Rayhan Biruni's works. The article positions itself as the first comprehensive analysis of research on the history of mathematics in Uzbekistan.

Since the 1960s, there has been a growing focus on the exact sciences within Abu Rayhan Biruni's scientific heritage in Russian publications. Examples include:

Russian translation of Biruni's mathematical works on the definition of circular areas (S.A. Krasnova and L.A. Karpova, 1963)[111], Russian translation of a book about Indian arithmetic (B.A. Rosenfeld, 1963)[112], «Catalog of Stars» by the encyclopedist al-Biruni in the work of Kanoni Masudi (S.A. Krasnova, M.M. Rozhanskaya,

---

[110] Sirazhdinov S.Kh., Matviyevskaya G.P. On the study of the history of mathematics in Central Asia. /Historical and mathematical research. ISSU,e XX1. - M., "Science", 1976. - P.51 – 60.
[111] Beruni Abu Rayhan. On the definition of chords in a circle; Rosenfeld B.A., Krasnova S.A. Notes to the "Treatise on the Definition of Chords", in collection. "From the history of science and technology in the ranks of the East", III, M., IVL, 1963.
[112] Beruni Abu Rayhan. Book about Indian Rashikas; Rosenfeld B.A. Notes to the "Book of Indian Rashiks", in collection. "From the history of science and technology in the ranks of the East", III, M., IVL, 1963.

1962)[113]. M.M. Rozhanskaya's doctoral dissertation (1968) delved into problems of functional mathematics in Biruni's works, including «Masudi's Law».

In the second half of the 20th century. scientists of Uzbekistan published books, collections, brochures and scientific articles related to the scientific heritage of scientists of the Khorezm Mamun Academy, some of them were devoted to specific sciences; including correspondence between Abu Raykhan Beruni and Ibn Sina (A. Rasulov, M. Abdurakhmanov, 1950), astronomy of Abu Raykhan Beruni (1950), cartographic projections of Abu Raykhan Beruni (G. Jalolov, 1950), his astronomical and mathematical-geographical views include special studies[114].

During this period, some of the works of Abu Rayhon Beruni were translated into Uzbek and Russian and published in Uzbekistan. Exact sciences also have their place in them. In addition to Uzbekistan, scientists from Moscow and Leningrad (St. Petersburg) participated in these publications; in Russian: "Chronology" (1957), "India" (1963), "Mineralogy" (1963); "Geodesy" (1966), in Uzbek: "Monuments of Past Generations" (1968) and these books were republished in 2022 in 9 volumes.

P.G.Bulgakov is a famous foreign scientist from Uzbekistan. In his works he published the text of "Geodesy" by Abu Rayhon Beruni (Cairo, 1962) and the Russian translation (Tashkent, 1966), as well as articles devoted to specific issues of science ("Honorary Sextant of Geodesy", "His Globe"). "The Life of Beruni" and published the Monography "Works" (Tashkent, 1972).

Translations of the works of Abu Rayhon Beruni were published in these scientific works. Their prefaces provide a scientific analysis of each work, and also mention specific sciences.

In the second half of the 20th century, many studies and translations related to the history of science were published in Uzbekistan, some of them were devoted to the history of the development of specific sciences. A.Nosirov (1950), A.A.Semenov (1950), U.I.Karimov (1953, 1957, 1973, 1980), M.Sale (1954), S.P.Tolstov (1960), G.P.Matviyevskaya (1962, 1963, 1967, 1968, 1981). , 1981), M.A.Akhadova (1964,

---

[113] Krasnova S.A., Rozhanskaya M.M. Beruni Star Catalog//From the history of science and technology in the ranks of the East. – M. – 1963. – P. 71-92.
[114] Sadykov Kh.U. Biruni and his works on astronomy and mathematical geography. - M., 1953.

1965, 1976, 1983), Kh.Khikmatullaev (1966), M.M.Khairullayev (1967, 1967, 1994), A.Akhmedov (1972, 1980, 1983, 1984, 1985, 1986), P.G.Bulgakov (1972), A.Irisov (1980), Kh.Siddikov (1981). J.Kh.Ibodov (1981, 1983, 1985, 1987, 1988, 1989, 1990, 1992, 1994, 1998, 2005, 2009, 2011, 2012), S.Kh.Sirojiddinov (1981), I.Abdullaev (1984), S.G.Bagirova (1987), G.K.Masharipova (1994, 1995, 2004, 2019, 2021), Kh.Gamidov (1995), B.A.Abdukhalimov (2001), S.U.Karimova (2001)[115] publications.

Analysis of published works shows that scientific research on the history of oriental science in Uzbekistan began primarily in the 1950s, while research in specific sciences commenced in the 1960s.

During this period, numerous collections on the history of science and materials from scientific conferences (some held for anniversaries) were published. These collections also contained a significant number of articles related to specific sciences.

The existing studies cover a broad range of topics, including bibliography, biographical information about Central Asian scientists, studies related to specific scientific fields, historical analyses of science, and commentaries on primary sources.

Publications relevant to the monograph's subject include articles in collections published in both Uzbek[116] and Russian[117]. These collections were compiled in connection with the celebration of the 1000th anniversary of Abu Rayhan Beruni's birth. The Uzbek collection features articles by A.Akhmedov, K.Norkhodjaev, A.Abdurakhmanov, and A. Rasulov, while the Russian collection includes articles by P.G.Bulgakov, E.G.Kasimova, B.A.Rosenfeld, A.Abdurakhmanov, and G.P.Matviyevskaya.

---

[115] The titles of articles and books written by these scientists are given at the end of the Monographyy.
[116] The collection is dedicated to the 1000th anniversary of the birth of Beruni. - Tashkent: Science. 1973. - P.260.
[117] Beruni. Collection of articles for the 1000th anniversary of his birth. - Tashkent: Science. 1973. - P.204.

Akhmedov's article argues that Abu Rayhan Beruni's work «Kanuni Masudi» explores various aspects of mathematics and spherical astronomy, including the spherical shape of the universe, the location of celestial bodies within these spheres, spherical astronomy, and mathematics (a system of triangles drawn inside a circle). Additionally, the article discusses Beruni's calculations of the value of π (π = 3,14174628) using a table of quantities for radius, cotangent («flat shadow»), tangent («reflected shadow»), and the theorem of sines. It also delves into Beruni's work on spherical astronomy, covering the structure of the astrolabe, spherical coordinates, the greatest deviation of the ecliptic, the rise of twelve constellations, determining the coordinates of places on Earth, finding the azimuths of cities, and the directions of Mecca (qibla)[118]. The author references publications written on this topic in foreign languages[119].

**Norkhodjaev's article provides a brief overview of Abu Rayhan Beruni's contributions to geodesy[120]. He argues against classifying Beruni's work in this field as mathematical geography or astronomy. Instead, Norkhodjaev categorizes Beruni's research in geodesy into five areas:

1. Determining the size of the Earth.

2. Solving problems related to geographic coordinates.

3. Creating geodetic and astronomical instruments.

4. Addressing issues related to engineering geodesy.

5. Cartographic projections (with examples analyzed in Beruni's works).

Abdurakhmanov's article focuses on the topic of trigonometry in the works of Abu Rayhan Beruni, suggesting that this area was a focus of the scientist's early

---

[118] Akhmedov A. Some questions of mathematics and spherical astronomy in Beruni's work "Kanuni Masudi" / Collection dedicated to the 1000th anniversary of Beruni's birth. - Tashkent: Science. 1973. - P.260; 111-122 - p.

[119] The Book of Instruction in the Elements of the Art of Astrology by Abu'l – Rayhan Muhammad ibn Ahmad al-Biruni/ The translation facing the text by R. Ramsay wright, London? 1934. 1V; Loeuvre Dal – Beruni essal bibliographique par D.L. Boilot, Institut dominicain d'etudes orientales du Caire , Melanges 2, Le Caire. Dar al-maaref, 1955, 200 ва бошкалар.

[120] K. Norkhodzhaev Beruni and the science of geodesy / Collection dedicated to the 1000th anniversary of the birth of Beruni. - Tashkent: Science. 1973.B.260; 145-159 - p.

research. The article analyzes examples of tangents and cotangents from Beruni's works «at-Tafhim» and «Qanuni Masudi»[121].

Two articles in the Uzbek language of the collection published on the 1000th anniversary of the birth of Abu Rayhon Beruni contain translations of the works of Abu Rayhon Beruni from Arabic into Uzbek: the first is a list of his works compiled by Abu Rayhon Beruni[122], the second is a projection of the constellation and mapping of places (cartography)[123].

It is worth noting that in the list of works of Abu Rayhon Beruni, the areas of science of Abu Rayhon Beruni are highlighted, and the main place in it is occupied by specific sciences - geodesy, mathematics, astronomy.

The Russian collection published on this occasion also contains articles on specific sciences (P.G. Bulgakov, E.G. Kasimova, B.A. Rosenfeld, A. Abdurakhmonov, G.P. Matviyevskaya, B.V. Lunin)[124]. They examined one of the cases related to spherical astronomy in the work of Abu Rayhon Beruni "Qanuni Masudi" - the question of the position of the ecliptic plane on the horizon (P.G.Bulgakov)[125], the structure and function of the astrolabe, which was part of his scientific heritage in the field of mathematical astronomy - "Istiab treatise called al-wujuh al-mumkina fi san'a al-asturlob" (On all possible methods of making an astrolabe) (B.A.Rosenfeld, A.Abdurakhmanov)[126] and research on spherical trigonometry (E.G.Kasimova)[127], various scientific opinions were expressed as part of the assessment of preliminary research on the study of the scientific heritage of

---

[121] Abdurakhmanov A. Some theorems of trigonometry in the works of Beruni / Collection dedicated to the 1000th anniversary of the birth of Beruni. - Tashkent: Science. 1973. - P. 260; 159-170 - p.

[122] Own list of works by Abu Rayhan Beruni. Translation from Arabic by A. Rasulov / Collection dedicated to the 1000th anniversary of the birth of Beruni. - Tashkent: Science. 1973. - P. 260; 230-244 - p.

[123] On the projection of constellations and moving places (on the map) (Cartography) - translation from Arabic by A. Rusulov / Collection dedicated to the 1000th anniversary of the birth of Beruni. - Tashkent: Science. 1973. - P. 260; 244-259 - p.

[124] Beruni. Collection of articles for the 1000th anniversary of his birth. Tashkent "Science", 1973. - P.204.

[125] Bulgakov P.G. About two fragments from the "Canon of Masud" by Beruni / Beruni. Collection of articles for the 1000th anniversary of his birth. Tashkent "Science", 1973. - P.60-72.

[126] Rosenfeld B.A., Abdurakhmanov A. Beruni's treatises on asolabia / Beruni. Collection of articles for the 1000th anniversary of his birth. Tashkent "Science", 1973. - P.85-90.

[127] Kasymova E.G. Beruni's treatise on spherical trigonometry. / Beruni. Collection of articles for the 1000th anniversary of his birth. Tashkent "Science", 1973. - P.81-85.

mathematics and astronomy (G.P.Matviyevskaya)[128], publications of scientific heritage and published studies dedicated to it (B.V. Lunin)[129].

In connection with the celebration of the millennium since the birth of Abu Rayhon Beruni, the collections published in Uzbek and Russian languages present research on issues related to the fields of geodesy, trigonometry and astronomy, which were included in the works of the scientist, as well as studies of the scientific heritage of Abu Rayhon Beruni. Both collections are of great scientific importance from the point of view of assessing the contribution of Abu Raikhan Beruni to the scientific potential of the Khorezm Mamun Academy.

We consider it necessary to focus on the research of some scientists in this regard. If you think in the field of exact sciences, then among Uzbek scientists in this field, significant studies of the period that we study in the Monography belong to G.P.Matviyevskaya[130], they are connected with the history of mathematics, she continued to develop this direction in her further research and published serious works[131]. The scientist's research deeply scientifically analyzed such topics as the history of mathematics in Central Asia, the counting system in the Middle Ages in the East, the works of Central Asian scientists in mathematics and their influence on Europe.

In the book by G.P. Matviyevskaya on the history of trigonometry (1990)[132] development of this science from ancient times (gnomonics, spherical coordinates), its status among the ancient Greeks (problems of spherical trigonometry in the concepts of Claudius Ptolemy and Menelaus), Indians (siddhantas), Middle Eastern countries and the Middle East. and Europe are discussed. The work pays wide attention to the development of trigonometry in the Muslim East, more precisely, in the countries of the Near and Middle East; Works written on trigonometry in the 9th-

---

[128] Matviyevskaya G.P. From the early history of the study of the mathematical and astronomical heritage of Beruni / Beruni. Collection of articles for the 1000th anniversary of his birth. Tashkent "Science", 1973. - P.173-186.
[129] Lunin B.V. Bibliographic index of Soviet literature about Abu Rayhan Beruni and editions of the texts of his works (1918 - 1972) / Beruni. Collection of articles for the 1000th anniversary of his birth. - Tashkent: Science, 1973. - P.186-202.
[130] Matviyevskaya G.P. Beruni and natural sciences. - Tashkent: Nauka, 1963. - 48 p.
[131] Matviyevskaya G.P. On the history of mathematics in Central Asia in the 9th -15th centuries. – Tashkent, 1962. - P.125.
[132] Matviyevskaya G.P. Essay on the history of trigonometry. - Tashkent:Science, 1990, P. 142.

15th centuries, trigonometry in the scientific heritage of Ptolemy, the influence of Indian science, trigonometry on a flat surface, spherical trigonometry, Menelaus' theorem, theorems of sines and cosines, triangles and trigonometric functions are considered. in separate sections.

This study separately studied the works of Ibn Iraq and Abu Rayhon Beruni from the Khorezm Mamun Academy in the field of trigonometry[133].

In a special article (co-authored with Kh. Tlashev), he studied the commentary of Abu Nasr ibn Iraq (d. 1039) to a work called "Spherics", dedicated to the problems of geometry and spherical trigonometry, written by the Greek scientist Menelaus (1st-2nd centuries)[134]. In the article, Ibn Iraq claims that by simplifying Menelaus' theorem using the theorem of sines, he moved from a system of rectangles to a system of triangles, the ideal shape for a spherical face, that is, he made an important change in the field of trigonometry, and credits Ibn Iraq as one of the scientists who discovered the theorem sines[135].

Regarding the contribution of Abu Rayhon Beruni to trigonometry, it is said that, firstly, his scientific heritage and his research in science, and then in the sections of astronomy from the work "Qanuni Masudi", many practical and theoretical problems of trigonometry are covered[136].

One of the studies directly related to the study of the development of exact sciences in the Khorezm Mamun Academy is an article by G.P. Matviyevskaya on the history of studying the heritage of Ibn Sina in the field of physics and mathematics[137] can be shown. In it, Ibn Sina's legacy in the field of exact sciences is divided into seven parts (classification of exact moments, mathematics, astronomy, physics, mechanics, optics, music theory) and each is analyzed separately, as well as studies in Russian and Western languages shown.

---

[133] Matviyevskaya G.P. Essay on the history of trigonometry. - Tashkent: Science, 1990, pp. 106-125..
[134] Sat. : Mathematics and Astronomy in the works of scientists of the medieval East. - Tashkent: Science. 1977. - P.142. P.81-89.
[135] Collection: Mathematics and astronomy in the works of scientists of the medieval East. - Tashkent: Science. 1977. - P.142, p.85.
[136] Matviyevskaya G.P. Essay on the history of trigonometry. - Tashkent: Science, 1990. P.111-126.
[137] Matviyevskaya G.P. From the history of studying the physical and mathematical heritage of Ibn Sina / Mathematics and astronomy in the works of Ibn Sina, his contemporaries and followers. - T. 1981. 155. P. 16-40.

According to the author of the article, Eastern scientists, continuing the tradition of the ancient Greeks, divided mathematics into four areas - arithmetic, geometry, astronomy and music. However, they approached each area creatively and interpreted its practical aspects in a new way[138], who introduced new classifications of sciences. For example, Ibn Sina divides the field of mathematics into four parts: "'ilm al-adad" (the science of numbers), "'ilm al-handasa" (handasa), "'ilm al-haya" (astronomy), "'ilm al-music".

- In the heritage of Ibn Sina, mathematical sciences have the following branches:

- - calculation, addition and subtraction in Indian ("ilm al-jam' wa-t-tafrik);

- al-jabr wal-muqabala ('ilm al-jabr wa-l-muqabala) (علم الجبر و المقابلة) ;

- discipline belonging to geometry:

- science of measurement ('ilm al-misaha) (علم المساحة) ;

- on moving devices ('ilm al-hiyal al-mutaharrik) (علم الحيل المتحرك);

- shifting of weights ('ilm al-jarr al-askal) (علم الجر الأسقال);

- On weighing and scales ('ilm al-awzan wa-l-mawazin) (علم الاوزان والموازن);

- necessary tools for dissemination ('ilm al-alot al-juziyyah)(علم الآلات الجزئية);

- on optics and the return of light ('ilm al-manozir wa-l-maraya) (علم المناظر والمرايا);

- on the transfer of water from one place to another ('ilm naql al-miya) (علم قل المياه);

- The area of disasters consists of the compilation of disasters (tables) and calendars ('ilm az-zijat wa-t-taqvim) (علم الزيجات والتقويم);

-The music industry involves the manufacture of various instruments.

In other words, Ibn Sina introduced many innovations into the concepts existing among the Greeks in the field of exact sciences and enriched this area.

He mastered Indian calculus, mathematical concepts from the works of the Greek scientists Euclid and Ptolemy, while living in Isfahan, engaged in regular

---

[138] Matviyevskaya G.P. From the history of studying the physical and mathematical heritage of Ibn Sina / Mathematics and astronomy in the works of Ibn Sina, his contemporaries and followers. - T. 1981. 155. P. 17-18.

astronomical practice and founded an observatory in Isfahan, which he led in 1024-1032, carried out observations and wrote several treatises in this area[139].

The scientific heritage of Ibn Sina in the field of mathematics in Western Europe has been recorded since the end of the 18th century (for example, in the book "History of Mathematics" by J.E.Montukla)[140], then G.Libri (1838), F.Vöpke (1859), M.Cantor (1880), P.Tannery (1882)[141], especially K. Brockelmann (1898)[142] and G.Suter (1900)[143] and other studies, Ibn Sina's merits in the field became known mathematics. to the west. If K.Brockelman provided information about the works of Ibn Sina, including in mathematics, then G. Suter gave a list of all his mathematical and astronomical works, and also spoke in detail about his work in this area. We can say that by the beginning of the 20th century, modern science had formed a clear idea of the mathematical heritage of Ibn Sina[144]. These publications consisted of research and translations.

Research in this direction continued in subsequent years. For example, mathematical problems in Ibn Sina's book "Kitab ash-shifa" by Kh.M. Muhammadiev (part of planimetry)[145] and M.S.Sharipova (in the form of a general analysis)[146] studied. B.A.Rosenfeld and N.A.Sadovsky translated parts of the physics and mathematics sections from the treatise "Donishnoma"[147]. M.A.Akhadova,

---

[139] Matviyevskaya G.P. From the history of the study of the physical and mathematical heritage of Ibn Sina / Mathematics and astronomy in the works of Ibn Sina, his contemporaries and followers. - T. 1981. P.20.

[140] Montukly Dj.E. Histoire des mathematiques, vol. 1, Paris, 1758; 1802; Matviyevskaya G.P. Iz istorii izucheniya physiko-mathematicheskogo naslediya Ibn Sini /Mathematika i astronomiya v trudakh Ibn Sini, ego sovremennikov i posledovateley. - T. 1981. 155. S. 20; 39.

[141] Matviyevskaya G.P. From the history of studying the physical and mathematical heritage of Ibn Sina / Mathematics and astronomy in the works of Ibn Sina, his contemporaries and followers. - T. 1981. 155. P. 20-22.

[142] Brockelmann K. Geschichte der Arabischen Literatur. Bd. I, Weimar, 1898. pp. 452-458. (Mathematics and astronomy and the work of Ibn Sina, his contemporaries and followers. - T. 1981. 155. P. 22.

[143] Suter H. Mathematician and Astronomer der Arabern und ihre Werke. Abhandle. tsur Gesh. d. mathematics. Viss. «. H.H. 1900. (Mathematics and astronomy in the works of Ibn Sina, his contemporaries and followers. - T. 1981. P. 155., P. 22; 39.

[144] Matviyevskaya G.P. From the history of studying the physical and mathematical heritage of Ibn Sina / Mathematics and astronomy in the works of Ibn Sina, his contemporaries and followers. – T. 1981. 155. P.22-23.

[145] Kh.M. Muhammadiev. Outline part of «Kitab al-Shifa». Scientific notes of the Leninabad State Pedagogical Institute. ISSU,e XV. Dushanbe, 1962. P.5-8.

[146] Sharipova M.S. Mathematical chapters of the «Book of Healing». Ibn Sini. Abstract of Candidate's Dissertation Dushanbe, 1967 and p.

[147] Ibn Sina. Mathematical chapters of the «Book of Knowledge». Dushanbe, "Irfon", 1967.

S.U.Umarov and B.A.Rosenfeld (in the introduction to the Russian translation) published research[148].

Another direction of the exact sciences - astronomy also came from the legacy of Ibn Sina, and research on it in Europe belongs to E. Wiedemann. He translated and published "Kitab ash-shifa", "Treatise on the refutation of the judgments of the stars", "Book on a method preferable to other methods for making astronomical instruments"[149].

Ibn Sina also researched in the fields of physics, mechanics, optics and music. His "Kitab ash-shifa", "Kitab an-najat", "Donishnama", correspondence of Ibn Sina with Abu Rayhon Beruni, "Tabiyat kiliklari" ("Kurazayi batab"), "Meyar al-ukul" ("Dimension of Consciousness") «, «Makola fi-n-nafs» («Article on the soul»), «Laws of medicine», «Introduction to music theory», etc.

In an article (1977), written jointly by Kh. Tlashev and S.A. Ramazonova, the treatises of Abu Nasr ibn Iraq on the astrolabe were analyzed. The article states that the works of Abu Nasr ibn Iraq were very important for his time from the point of view of theoretical and practical astronomy, and in the field of spherical trigonometry he made conclusions based on a critical analysis of existing ancient and modern sciences[150]. It is also noted that the operating principle of the astrolabe is based on mathematical methods, which is analyzed in detail in the works of Ibn Iraq, and four treatises of Ibn Iraq are devoted to the astronomical instrument - the astrolabe.

M. Akhadova in her article on the history of mathematics[151] Scientists of the Khorezm Mamun Academy stated that the works of Ibn Sina "Kitab al-Shifa", "Kitab

---

[148] Akhadova M.A. Physics and mathematics works of Ibn Sina in Tajik language. Abstract of candidate's dissertation - Tashkent, 1965; Akhadova M.A. Treatise by Abu Ali ibn Sini "The Measure of Reason." - In the book: From the history of exact sciences in the medieval Near and Middle East. - Tashkent: Science, 1972, - P.42-57.

[149] Wiedemann E. Zur Geschichte der Astrologie. «Das Veltail», bldg. 22. 1922. 121-126; Wiedemann E. Uber Ein von Avicenna Herstellertes Beobachtungsinstrument. «Zeitschr., Fur Instrumentenkunde». Bd. 45. 1925, 269–275; Wiedemann E. Einleitung zu dem astronomischen Teil des Kitab al Schifa (Werk der Genesung) von Ibn Sina, "Sitzungsber, d. Phys.-med. Word. In Erlangen», Bd. 58–59, 1926–1927, 225–227. (Mathematics and astronomy and the work of Ibn Sina, his contemporaries and followers. - T. 1981. P. 155. P. 26-28; 40.

[150] Tlashev H., Ramazanova S.A. Treatises of Abu Nasr ibn Iraq on asolabiy / Mathematics and astronomy and works of the upper middle class East. Tashkent "Science", 1977. P.89-97.

[151] M. Akhadova. From the history of mathematics in Bukhara Mathematics in the medieval East. Tashkent «Science». 1978.P.100. P.97-112..

al-Najat", "Donishinma" contain information on mathematics, astronomy and physics.

The article, written by A. Akhmedov in collaboration with B.A.Rosenfeld, cites Abu Rayhon Beruni's book "Cartography", the full title of which is "The Book of Reflection of Constellations on a Flat Surface and Images of Countries on a Flat Surface" ("Risala fi tastih as-suwar wa tabtih al-kuvar») describes the work, it is noted that this is one of the first treatises written by the scientist, and a translation into Russian from the only copy of the work stored in the library is given to the University of Leiden[152]. In the list of works by Abu Raikhan Beruni, given in P.G.Bulgakov's Monography, this work is named as follows: "Istiyab fi tastikh al-kura" - "The final (collection) on lowering a sphere onto a flat surface"[153]. Previously, this work was translated into Uzbek and published by A. Rasulov[154]. Zh.Kh.Ibodov gave information about (32) works on specific sciences in the library of the Muslim Administration of Uzbekistan[155].

Although the book co-authored by G.P.Matviyevskaya and Kh.Tlashev is called "Mathematical and astronomical manuscripts of the teachings of Central Asia (X-XVIII centuries)", for some reason it was mainly written outside the territory of Central Asia, that is, scientists from the Near and Middle East East - Abu-l-Wafa al-Buzhani (10th century), as-Sijovandi (12th century), Imad ad-Din al-Baghdadi (13th century), Sharaf ad-Din al-Masudi (13th century), Nasiruddin Analyzed works Tusi (XIII century), Nizamiddin an-Niisoburi (XIII century), Husainshah al-Simnani (XIII century)[156].

In collections published in Uzbek and Russian languages to celebrate the 1000th anniversary of the birth of Abu Ali ibn Sina[157] and articles on the development of

---

[152] Akhmedov A., Rosenfeld B.A. "Cartography" is one of the first works by Beruni that has reached us. / Mathematics in the medieval East Tashkent "Science", 1978. - P.127-153.
[153] Bulgakov P.G. Life and works of Beruni, Life and works of Beruni. - Tashkent: Science. 1972. - P.309.
[154] Beruniy Abu Raykhon. On the projection of constellations and the transfer of places (on the map) (Cartography), translation from Arabic by A. Rasulov. Beruni. On the 1000th anniversary of his birth. Tashkent, 1973. P. 244-259.
[155] Ibodov Zh.Kh. About mathematical manuscripts from the SADUM library // Collection: Mathematics in the Middle Ages. T.: Nauka, 1978. - P.154-160.
[156] Matviyevskaya G.P., Tlashev H. Mathematical and astronomical manuscripts of the teachings of Central Asia X-XUIII centuries. - Tashkent: Science, 1981. – 148 p.
[157] To the 1000th anniversary of the birth of Abu Ali ibn Sina. (Digest of articles). - Tashkent: Science. 1980. B.200; Abu Ali ibn Sina. To the 1000th anniversary of his birth. - Tashkent: Science, 1980. - P.248.

exact sciences at the Khorezm Mamun Academy. Among the scientists who conducted research in this area is A.Akhmedov[158], P.G.Bulgakov[159], G.Jalolov[160], B.A. Rosenfeld[161], M.M.Rozhanskaya[162], B.V.Lunin[163]. In 163 articles comments are given on the scientific research of Ibn Sina in the field of mathematics (including geometry), astronomy (including applied), mechanics and information on the study of the works of Ibn Sina.

In a collection consisting of an analysis of knowledge in mathematics and astronomy in the heritage of Ibn Sina and his contemporaries (1981)[164] his legacy in the field of physics and mathematics (M.A. Akhadova), his merits in the development of mathematics (A.U. Usmanov), the study of his works in this area (G.P. Matviyevskaya), the astronomical instrument created Ibn Sina (Z.K.Sokolovskaya). This collection contains many articles devoted not only to the legacy of Ibn Sina, but also to various issues of the development of exact sciences in the East as a whole (A.Abdurakhmonov, A.Akhmedov, A.Abdukabirov, G.P.Matviyevskaya, M.A.Abrorova, Kh.Kh. Tlashev, Zh.Kh.Ibodov).

Research on exact sciences at the Khorezm Mamun Academy in this collection consists of articles devoted only to the study of the work of Ibn Sina.

Some studies by Uzbek scientists are devoted to the history of the development of exact sciences in Eastern countries as a whole. The calculus system of G.P.Matviyevskaya in the Near and Middle East, the theories of S.A.Ramazonova about the movement of the Moon and planets in the Middle Ages in the East, the

---

[158] Akhmedov A. Mathematicians and contemporary mathematicians of Abu Ali ibn Sina / To the 1000th anniversary of the birth of Abu Ali ibn Sina. (Digest of articles). - Tashkent: Science. 1980. B. 99-113; Akhmedov A. Ibn Sina and questions of explanation of geometry / Abu Ali ibn Sina. To the 1000th anniversary of his birth. - Tashkent: Science.1980. P.183-189.

[159] Bulgakov P.G. The contribution of ibn Sina and practical asonomies / Abu Ali ibn Sina. To the 1000th anniversary of his birth. - Tashkent: Science, 1980. P. 149-157.

[160] Jalolov G'. A work by Abu Ali ibn Sina called "Al-Hisab" / for the 1000th anniversary of the birth of Abu Ali ibn Sina. (Digest of articles). - Tashkent: Science, 1980. - P. 122-135.

[161] Rosenfeld B.A. On the works of Ibn Sina on mathematics and asonomy / Abu Ali ibn Sina. To the 1000th anniversary of his birth. - Tashkent: Science, 1980. - P. 157-163.

[162] Rozhanskaya M.M. Ibn Sina - mechanic / Abu Ali ibn Sina. To the 1000th anniversary of his birth. - Tashkent: Science, 1980. - P. 163-183.

[163] Лунин Б.В. Жизнь и труды Ибн Сины в отечественной науке / Абу Али ибн Сина. К 1000-летию со дня рождения.- Tashkent: Science, 1980. С. 212-243.

[164] Mathematics and astronomy in the works of Ibn Sina, his contemporaries and followers. - Tashkent: Science, 1981. - P. 155.

work of M.Abrorov on the counting of al-Karji, the articles of A.Akhmedov on the mathematical heritage of Ibn al-Haysam[165] is one of them.

In the article by N.G. Khairutdinova (1969) comparatively analyzed some aspects of trigonometry in the legacy of Farobi and Ibn Sina[166].

Despite the fact that A. U. Usmanov's short article is called "The Merits of Ibn Sina in the Field of Mathematics" (1981), this problem is not expressed in it[167].

The article by A.B. Vildanova (1991) provides brief bibliographic information about the manuscripts of works of Central Asian mathematicians and astronomers in the fund of the UzR FA SHI named after Abu Raikhan Beruni[168]. It is written about three treatises written by Muhammad ibn Abdurashid al-Sijovandi (XII century): "Risala al-Jabr wal muqabala" ("Treatise Al-Jabr wal muqabala"), "Faroisi Sirojiya" ("Right of Inheritance"), "Masoilu samoniya fil halal" ("Eight tasks from the calculation"). All three treatises were rewritten in Arabic in the 17th-18th centuries.

A. Akhmedov, one of the Uzbek scientists, published a number of works in the field of exact sciences, and according to their content they can be divided into two parts: the first is scientific research, the second is the translation of primary sources into language. Uzbek and Russian languages. Most of the scientific articles he published were devoted to the centuries preceding the period that we established as a chronological limit in the Monography, more precisely, to the analysis of the legacy of Muhammad ibn Musa al-Khwarizmi[169] by scientists of the Baghdad Academy. and to the analysis of issues in the history of mathematical knowledge in the East as a

---

[165] Mathematics and astronomy in the Proceedings of the Students of the Medieval East. - Tashkent: Science. 1977. - P.142, P.97-107.

[166] Khairutdinova N.G. Trigonometry and the works of al-Farabi and Ibn Sina.- Volume V. ISSU,e. 3(28). - M., 1969; Mathematics and astronomy in the works of scientists of the medieval East. - Tashkent: Science, 1977. P.142. P.58.

[167] Usmanov A. Disciples of the Medieval East. - Tashkent: Science. 1977. P.142. P.55-58.

[168] Vildanova A.B. Manuscripts of works by Central Asian mathematicians and asonomists in the collection of the IV Academy of Sciences of the UzSSR. - In the book: Materials on the history and history of science and culture of the peoples of Central Asia. - Tashkent: Science, 1991. - P.302-321

[169] Akhmedov A. Al-Khorezmi - astronomer and geographer. - In the book. Earth and universe. № 6. – M., 1983. – P.28-32; Akhmedov A.A., Rosenfeld B.A., Sergeeva N.D. Astronomical and geographical works of al-Khorezmi // Muhammad ibn Musa al-Khorezmi. To the 1200th anniversary of his birth. – M.: Nauka, 1983. – P.141-191; Akhmedov A. Theory of planetary motion in "Zij" by al-Khorezmi // SSU,. № 7. – P.59-64; Akhmedov A. The scientific heritage of al-Khorezmi and its place in the history of science and culture. Abstract of dissertation for doctoral degree in history. – T., 1985. – P.34; Akhmedov A. Muhammad al-Khorezmi – historian // SSU,. – Tashkent, – 1985. - № 11. – P.51-55.

whole[170]. Among his works devoted to the sciences of mathematics and astronomy at the Khorezm Mamun Academy, one can indicate articles in collections published in connection with the 1000th anniversary of the birth of Ibn Sina (1980) and the 1000th anniversary of the Khorezm Mamun Academy (2005)[171].

B. Abdukhalimov's scientific research is devoted to the development of exact and natural sciences in Eastern science and the contribution of Central Asian scientists to this. Information in this direction was first studied in the multi-volume work "Kashf az-zunun" by Haji Khalifa[172]. In terms of their conclusions that the share of Central Asian scientists in the development of exact sciences is large, Abu Abdullah Muhammad ibn Nasr al-Marwazi, Abu Nasr Ahmad ibn Abdullah ibn Sabit al-Bukhari, Abu r-Raja Mukhtar ibn Mahmud az-Zahidi al -Khorezmi, Shamsiddin Muhammad ibn It is noted that the names and works of such Central Asian scientists as Muhammad ibn Mahmud al-Bukhari, Abu Jafar al-Husayni at-Tirmizi, Masud ibn Muhammad al-Gijduvani were first mentioned in the book of Haji Khalifa.

The next major study of the scientist consists of a Monography entitled "Bayt al-hikma" and the scientific activities of Central Asian scientists in Baghdad (exact and natural sciences in the 9th-11th centuries)"173. It has been studied in detail that during the reign of Caliph al-Mamun (813-833) in the territory of the Caliphate, especially in the city of Baghdad, science developed at a high level from the point of view of its time. . The main attention in the Monography is paid to the development of natural and exact sciences - astronomy, mathematics, medicine, chemistry, geography. Scientists of Central Asia who left their mark on science in these areas

---

[170] Akhmedov A. ISSU,es of substantiation of geometry in the medieval Near and Middle East. – T.: Science, 1972. – 372 p.; Akhmedov A. "Book on extracting the edge of a cube" by al-Hasan ibn al-Haytham. – In the book: Mathematics and astronomy in the works of scientists of the medieval East. – T.: Science, 1977. – P.113-117; Akhmedov A. About the comments of Abd al-Ali Husayn Birjandi to Ulugbek's "Zij". – In the book: From the history of science of the era of Ulugbek. – T.: Science, 1979. – P.69-109; Akhmedov A.A., Bulgakov P.G. Central Asian-Indian relations in the field of exact sciences. – From the history of cultural relations between the peoples of Central Asia and India. – T.: Science, 1986. – P.24-33.

[171] Akhmedov A. Mathematicians and astronomers-contemporaries of Abu Ali ibn Sina // Collection of articles for the 1000th anniversary of the birth of Abu Ali ibn Sina. - T.: Nauka, 1980. - 99 p.; Khorezm Mamun Academy. - Tashkent: Science, 2005.

[172] Abdukhalimov B.A. "Kashf az-zunun" as a source on the history of the exact sciences of Transoxiana and Khorasan. Author's abstract. dis. for the job application uch. step. PhD. ist. Sci. Tashkent, 1994.

(Yahya ibn Mansur, Muhammad Musa al-Khorezmi, the scientific activity of Khalid al-Marwarrudi is analyzed, Abul Abbas al-Jawahari, Ahmed al-Sarakhsi, etc.).

The relevance of the work for this Monography lies in the fact that it states that the works of the Beit al-Hikma scientists in the field of natural and specific sciences were reflected in the works of the scientists of the Khorezm Mamun Academy according to the tradition of continuity in science, especially Abu Rayhon Beruni creatively used it

In the article by S.U. Karimova, published in the National Encyclopedia of Uzbekistan[174], talks about the life and scientific heritage of Ibn Sina, and also mentions his achievements in the field of specific sciences. A description of the manuscripts of Ibn Sina's works, stored in the treasury of the Institute of Oriental Studies of the Russian Academy of Sciences, is also given in the volume of the "Catalog of Oriental Manuscripts", co-authored by Kh. Khikmatullaev and S. Karimova, which includes works related to medicine, but it describes only works related with medicine[175].

In the Khorezm Academy of Mamun, in general, the topic of the history of astronomy in Khorezm is almost not studied in this study, and only some examples are given from the works of Abu Raikhan Beruni (mainly "Qanuni Masudi").

In the collection "Astronomy in Central Asia in the 20th century," published in the first year of Uzbekistan's independence,176 the development of astronomy in ancient Khorezm was highlighted in the primer of the archaeological site Koykiril-Kala and the work of Abu Raikhan. Beruni «Monuments left by ancient peoples.» Then general conclusions are presented about the development of astronomical knowledge in Khorezm, in particular, the Khorezm Mamun Academy for the Middle Ages. The scientific heritage of Muhammad ibn Musi al-Khorezmi, Abu Abdullah Muhammad ibn Ahmad al-Khorezmi, Ibn Iraq, Abu Sahl al-Masihi, Abu Rayhon Beruni, Ibn Sini is shown as a source. Then there are general conclusions about the development of astronomical knowledge in Khorezm, in particular, the Khorezm

---

[174] National Encyclopedia of Uzbekistan. 4. Tashkent "National Encyclopedia of Uzbekistan", 2002. - P. 703. 53-59 - p.
[175] Collection of oriental manuscripts of the Academy of Sciences of the Republic of Uzbekistan. Medicine

Mamun Academy for the Middle Ages, and the sources are Muhammad ibn Musa al-Khorezmi, Abu Abdullah Muhammad ibn Ahmad al-Khorezmi, Ibn Iraq, Abu Rayhon al-Abu Rayhon Beruni, Ibn Sina, as well as a striking example of the scientific heritage of Abu Sahli al-Masihi.

A number of scientific articles were published in the collection "Oriental Studies", which has been prepared and published since 1990 at the Institute of Oriental Studies of the Academy of Sciences of the Republic of Uzbekistan. They contain information on various aspects of Oriental studies - source studies, history of science, astronomy, mathematics, medicine, chemistry, geography, Islam, mysticism, literature, music, historiography. The Eastern written heritage and scientists, the history of the Timurids and Baburi, documents on the history of Uzbekistan, the new history of the countries of the East, scientific information and other information of various contents are presented.

Some articles published by scientists of the Institute of Oriental Studies of the Russian Academy of Sciences in the issues of this collection are devoted to the history of the development of science in Khorezm in the 11th - 12th centuries, some of them also belong to the field of exact sciences. As an example, we can cite articles by P.G.Bulgakov[177], A.Akhmedov[178], B.Abdukhalimov[179], S.Karimova[180], O.Boriev[181], A.Khabibullaev[182], G.Masharipova[183], I.Abdullaeva[184], Zh.Khazratkulov[185], M.Khasaniya[186], O.Korieva[187] quoted. Among them, articles by A.Akhmedov, B. Abdukhalimov, O.Boriev, G.Masharipova, A.Khabibullaev are directly related to the topic of this Monography.

---

[177] Bulgakov P.G. Activities of Central Asian scientists in Baghdad./ "Oriental Studies", 1. - P.19 – 28; A. Akhmedov. Ulugbek and his "Zij"/"Oriental Studies" № 5. - P.10-17.

[178] Akhmedov A. Beruni "On preparing a reliable basis for explaining the concept of the passage of light." / "Oriental Studies" № 12. - P.58-63.

[179] Abdukhalimov B. About Hadji Khalifa Beruni/ "Oriental Studies" № 4.- P.82-89.

[180] Karimova S. About Al-Khorezmi al-Kasi and his work "Ain al-sana"/"Oriental Studies" № 8. - P.58 - 62..

[181] Boriev O. Continuity of the scientific heritage of Ahmad al-Fargani and Abu Raikhan Beruni / "Oriental Studies. № 12. - P.63-71.

[182] Khabibullayev A. Beruni's works in Oxford/»Oriental Studies» № 8. - P.89-95.

[183] Masharipova G. Work of Abu Ali ibn Sina "Fundamentals of Geometry"/"Oriental Studies" № 5. - pp. 41-49.

[184] Abdullayev I. New information about Al-Saalibi/»Oriental Studies» № 1. - P.28-37.

[185] Khazratkulov J. Rashid Vatvot – writer/ "Oriental Studies" № 8. - P. 189 – 196..

[186] Hasani M. Beruni and Ibn Sina: poetry and medicine/ Oriental Studies № 12. - P.71-76.

[187] Kariyev O. Problems of marriage in "Hindistan" by Beruni and "Khidaya" by Marginani/»Oriental Studies». № 5. - P. 49-54.

A. Akhmedov analyzed this work in the article "Abu Rayhon Beruni "On the preparation of a reliable basis for explaining the concept of the passage of light" based on the only existing manuscript in the Bankipur library in India, based on the edition of Abu Rayhon Beruni. Collection in Hyderabad 1948–188 It says that this treatise is devoted to the passage of luminaries through certain points of the celestial sphere, and is also partly related to astrology. In this study, the encyclopedist also used the achievements of ancient Greek and Indian astronomy and thought about studying the work in science.

In the article by B. Abdukhalimov "About Haji Khalifa Abu Rayhon Beruni," the information related to the scientific activities of Abu Rayhon Beruni in the work of Haji Khalifa "Kashf az-zunun" is fully studied.

In particular, in this book his name is mentioned 24 times, his scientific works - (آثار الباقية) "Asor al-Baqiya", (ارشاد في أحكام النجوم) "Irshad fi ahkom an-nujum", (الاستشهاد باختلاف الأرساد) "al-Istishhad bi ichtilaf al -arsad», (الاستعاب) "al-Istiab», كتاب) (العمل بالاسترلاب) «Kanuni Mas» udi», It is said to contain information on (منيرالاجية) «Mineralogy» and other subjects.

In the article by O. Boriev "Ahmad al-Fargani and Abu Raykhan Beruni", it is comparatively studied that Abu Raykhan Beruni in his works analyzed data on the disasters of Ahmad al-Fargani and gave them a positive assessment, and also wrote a work on this topic ("Tahzib fi usul al-Farghani»), scientific conclusions are given.

One article by the author, G.K. Masharipov, was published in a collection of oriental studies, including an analysis of the work of Abu Ali ibn Sina "Fundamentals of Geometry," which relates to the field of exact sciences. The article discusses vageometry, which is said to be a comparative study of the book "Fundamentals" by the ancient Greek scientist Euclid (IV century BC) Ibn Sina, who supplemented it in an abbreviated form with changes using his Arabic comments to the data of the third. parts of his work "Kitab al-Shifa" (كتاب الشفا).

Historiography includes an article entitled "The Works of Abu Rayhon Beruni in Oxford," published by A. Khabibullaev in the eighth issue of the collection, which provides information about the works of Abu Rayhon Beruni, stored in the Bodleian

Library of the University of Oxford, Great Britain; Nine manuscripts of seven of his works are reported to exist, and a brief description of them is appended. Among them are "Qanuni Masudi", (كتاب في استرلاب الوجوه الممكنة في صنعة الاسترلاب) "Kitab fi istiab al-wujuh al-mumkina fi sanat al-asturlab" («A book describing possible methods for making asturlab»), (كتاب الدرر في سطح العكر) «Kitab ad-durar fi sat al-ukar» («The Book of the Durars, which tells about the surface of the earth»), (مقالات في سير سحمي السعادة و الغيب) «Makolatu fi sayr sahmay as-sa'oda wa-l-ghayb» (mqalat fy syr shmy alsʿada w alghyb) ("An article about the journey of copies of disappearance and happiness"), about astrology: (كتاب زهة النفوس والأفكار في حواس المواليد الثلاث المعدن والنبات والأحجار) "Kitab nuzhat an-nufus wa-l-afkor fi hawass al-mawalid kak-salos al-ma'dan wa-n-nabat wa-l-ahjor" «Three things - metals, plants, and a book that brings joy to the mind and heart about the properties of stones»), about mineralogy (تسحيل التصحيح الاسترلاب والعمل بمركبته من الشمال والجنوب) «Tashil at-tashih al-asturlob wal amal bi maqabakatihi min ash-Shimal «Southern Shaft» ("Promoting the correction of asturlobes, working with asturlobes consisting of northern and southern species"); (كتاب التفهيم) "Kitab at-tafhim" are included.

In general, the above articles published in this collection are of direct importance in terms of additional information for our Monography.

Even during the years of independence, research related to the history of exact sciences continued in Uzbekistan, several articles and books were published. One of the major scientific studies in this area is the doctoral Monography (1994)[189] by Zh.Kh.In this regard, he also published several scientific articles[190].

---

[189] Ibadov J.Kh. Arabic and Persian encyclopedias of the X-XVIII centuries. as sources on the history of exact sciences / Abstract of thesis...doc.historical sciences. – T., 1994. – 42 p.

[190] Ibadov J.Kh. Classification of physical and mathematical nunuks in the medieval encyclopedias of Abu Abdullah al-Khorezmi, Fakhr ad-Din ar-Razi, Qutb ad-Din al-Shirazi and Baha ad-Din al-Amili // Abstracts of the XXXIV scientific conference of graduate students and young specialists in the history of natural sciences and technical books of IIE and T RAS. – M., 1992. – P.35-36; Ibodov Zh.Kh. "Book of research on algebra" by Hassan ibn Haris al-Khububi al-Khorezmi // Abstracts of scientific-theoretical and technical conferences of professionals, lecturer of Tashkent State Technical University named after A. Beruni. – T., 1992. – P.123-125; Ibodov Zh.Kh. Comparative analysis of the physical and mathematical chapters of the universal encyclopedias "Keys of Sciences" by Abu Abdallah al-Khorezmi (X-XVI centuries) and "Collection of Sciences" by Fakhr ad-Din al-Razi. – Tashkent State University named after A. Beruni, 1992. – P.135-136.

Some of the scientist's studies on the history of the exact sciences were published even before independence[191], and further studies are their organic continuation. Some studies published by Zh.Kh.Ibodov are related to the history of the development of exact sciences in the Khorezm Mamun Academy[192], they talk about scientists who worked in the field of exact sciences and the mentioned problems related to mathematics. in his works, history of mathematics, etc.

A scientific collection was published in connection with the celebration of the 1000th anniversary of the Khorezm Mamun Academy (2005)[193]. This collection contains a number of studies on the activities of the Academy: the beginning of the word (B.Abdukhalimov), the formation of the Academy (A. Akhmedov), mathematics and astronomy (A. Akhmedov), chemistry (S.U. Karimova), medicine (S.U.Karimova), geography (O.Boriev), social sciences - philosophy (A.Sharipov), history (A.Akhmedov), literature (I.Elmurodov), linguistics (Z.Islamov), current activities of the Academy (K. Safarov).

The section on mathematics and astronomy provides brief information about Hasan ibn Hammar, Hasan al-Khububi, Isa al-Masih, Abu Nasr ibn Iraq, Ibn Sina,

---

[191] Ibodov Zh.Kh. On a mathematical treatise from Khiva // Mathematics and sonomy in the works of Ibn Sina, his contemporaries and followers. – T.: Science, 1981. – P.143-154; Ibodov Zh.Kh. Mathematical treatises of al-Khububi and as-Sijavandi / From the history of medieval eastern mathematics and astronomy. – T.: Science, 1983. – P.72-81; Ibodov Zh.Kh. Study of four manuscripts of mathematical content // Izvestia AN UzSSR. Series of physical and mathematical sciences. 1983. № 1. – P.69-70; Ibodov Zh.Kh. The creativity of al-Khorezmi in the assessment of Eastern scientists-encyclopedists of the X-XVI centuries. // The great scientist of the Middle Ages al-Khorezmi. – T.: Science, 1985. – P.265-268; Ibodov Zh.Kh. Physics and mathematics chapters of the encyclopedia "Collection of Sciences" ("Jami ul-ulum") by Fakhr ad-Din ar-Razi. Dep. IN VINITI. – M., 1987. № 1066. – B87. – 14 s.; Ibadov J.Kh., Bulgakov P.G. On the history of mathematics of Khorezm at the end of the 10th century// Social Sciences in Uzbekistan, 1988. № 5. – P.62-65; Ibadov J.Kh., Matviyevskaya G.P. Exact sciences in the encyclopedia "The Wisdom of the Source (Hikma al-ayn) al-Qazwini" // Izv. AN UzSSR. Ser. Phys.-Math. Sciences, 1989. – P.29-31; Ibadov J.Kh., Matviyevskaya G.P. Physical and mathematical sciences in the encyclopedia "Keys of Sciences" by Abu Abdallah al-Khorezmi // Izv. AN UzSSR. Ser. Phys.-Math. Sciences, 1990. № 3. – P.34-39..

[192] Ibadov J.Kh. Mathematical treatises of al-Khububi and al-Sijavandi // From the history of medieval eastern mathematics and astronomy. – T.: Science, 1983. – P.72-81; Ibodov Zh.Kh. Physics and mathematics chapters of the encyclopedia "Collection of Sciences" ("Jami ul-ulum") by Fakhr ad-Din ar-Razi. Dep. IN VINITI. – M., 1987. № 1066. – B87. – 14 s.; Ibadov J.Kh., Bulgakov P.G. On the history of mathematics of Khorezm at the end of the 10th century// Social Sciences in Uzbekistan, 1988. № 5. – P.62-65; Ibodov J.H. Physics and mathematics chapters of "Keys of Sciences" (Mafotih al-ulum) by Abu Abdallah al-Khorezmi. Tashkent, TUNTN, 2005, 56 pp.; Ibodov Zh.Kh. Encyclopedias of Central Asian scientists of the 9th-18th centuries as sources on the history of exact sciences. Tashkent, Mevrius, 2010, 174 pp.; Ibodov Zh.Kh. Study of the rich scientific heritage of our country/Problems of improving the quality of personnel training for the field of communications and information technology. Scientific conference TATU. Tashkent, 2012, volume 1, pp. 105-107.

[193] Khorezm Mamun Academy. - Tashkent: Science, 2005.

some of their works in the field of exact sciences, as well as the services of Abu Rayhon Beruni in this area are discussed in detail[194].

The materials of the international scientific conference dedicated to this date (November 2-3, 2006, Khiva-Tashkent)[195] were also published. Articles devoted to specific scientific issues were also published in the Khorezm Mamun Academy. For example, in the dissertations of K. Abdurimov[196], in general, the formation of exact sciences in Central Asia is divided into five stages, with the first stage occurring in AD. average. Calculated from 2000 years. Several places are given as examples of archaeological finds from ancient Khorezm. However, the questions and conclusions are preliminary.

Other articles on specific sciences in the collection: astronomy, In other articles on exact sciences in the collection - astronomy, including the problem of calendars - «Kaptarkhan» as the address of the time service (S.Kh. Azizov)[197], knowledge in the Khorezm Academy of Mamun, in including the number of scientific conclusions on the exact sciences. sciences, are positive for the development of science in later periods, the influence of (B.Abdukhalimov)[198], geographical knowledge in the Khorezm Mamun Academy, including issues of mathematical cartography (O.Boriev)[199], the works of Ibn Sina and the Khorezm Mamun (S.Karimov)[199], including his work on geometry (G.Masharipova)[201], and the status of the Swiss

---

[194] Khorezm Mamun Academy. - Tashkent: Science, 2005, 33-86 - p.
[195] Khorezm Mamun Academy and its role in the development of world science. Materials of the international scientific conference. Tashkent-Khiva "Science", 2006.- P.215.
[196] Abdurimov K. Origins of the Khorezm Academy of Mamun: calculation, observation technology and culture of Central Asia, their invariants / Khorezm Academy of Mamun and its place in the development of world science. Materials of the international scientific conference. Tashkent-Khiva "Science", "2006. - P.25-27.
[197] Azizov S.Kh. "Kaptarkhana" in Khorezm - address of the time service / Khorezm Mamun Academy and its place in the development of world science. Materials of the international scientific conference. Tashkent-Khiva "Science", 2006, 23-25 – p.
[198] Abdukhalimov B.A. Khorezm Academy of Mamun and its influence on the development of medieval science / Khorezm Academy of Mamun and its place in the development of world science: Proceedings of the international scientific conference. Tashkent-Khiva "Science", 2006, pp. 163-165.
[199] Boriev O. Geographical knowledge in the Khorezm Academy of Mamun and its role in the revival of the Timurids / Khorezm Academy of Mamun and its role in the development of world science. Materials of the international scientific conference. Tashkent-Khiva "Science", 2006, 27-32-p.
[199] Boriev O. Geographical knowledge in the Khorezm Academy of Mamun and its role in the revival of the Timurids / Khorezm Academy of Mamun and its role in the development of world science. Materials of the international scientific conference. Tashkent-Khiva "Science", 2006, 27-32- p.
[201] Masharipova G. Postulates and axioms in mathematics of Abu Ali Ibn Sina / Khorezm Mamun Academy and its role in the development of world science. Proceedings of the international scientific conference. Tashkent-Khiva "Science", 2006, 76-78-p.

scientist I.Toman includes comments by Abu Mansura ibn Iraq on the Shiite calendar method[202].

This monograph draws conclusions based on existing scientific research on the topic «The Influence of the Natural Scientific Heritage of Scientists of the Khorezm Mamun Academy on the Development of Social and Philosophical Thinking.» The first noteworthy aspect is the broad scope of research, with scholars in both Eastern and Western countries devoting serious attention to this topic.

It has now come to light that scientific works on specific subjects, written by Khorezm scientists during the 10th to 12th centuries, have been studied by researchers around the world in three primary areas: firstly, scientific analysis; secondly, publication of full or partial translations of source materials from this period; and thirdly, the translation and publication of scientific works created in Khorezm during the 10th to 12th centuries into various world languages.

Archaeological and ethnographic expeditions conducted in Khorezm over many years have played a central role in identifying the ancient roots of scientific development in the region. These expeditions have provided crucial materials for this field of study.

Examining research on this topic chronologically, we see that it began in the 19th century, primarily in Europe. A more rigorous and systematic study of the development of exact sciences in Khorezm during the 10th-12th centuries emerged in the second half of the 20th century, with a significant number of studies published in Russian. Some of these studies are drawn from various issues of the collections «Historical and Astronomical Research» and «Historical and Mathematical Research».

The achievements of Khorezm scholars in the field of philosophical sciences during the 10th-12th centuries received systematic study in Uzbekistan during the second half of the 20th century. Local scholars played an increasingly prominent role in this research. This tradition has continued into the post-independence period.

---

[202] Johannes Thomann. Abu Mansur b. Iraq's criticism of the Shi'a calendarical methods F Khorezm Ma'mun Academi fnd its role in the development of world science. - Tashkent-Khiva "Science", 2006, 111-112-p.

Research findings have been published in a variety of formats, including studies, scientific articles, popular science brochures, individual monographs, and collections.

If we draw a conclusion to the ongoing scientific research from the perspective of the problem's essence, we can see that work in the field of philosophical sciences in Khorezm during the 10th-12th centuries arose from the need for the history of science. In other words, along with general analyses, scientific research related to specific areas of philosophy was published. This included articles devoted to the study of particular scientific problems, the activities of scientists from that time, and their contributions to science. Some of these articles were written in the historiography style.

Some studies emphasize the issue of continuity in the history of science. Scientific works created during the ancient Greek, Indian, and Arab caliphates, especially in its capital Baghdad, occupy a certain place in the development of philosophical sciences in Khorezm during the 10th-12th centuries. Scientists of the Khorezm Mamun Academy creatively used the existing scientific heritage in philosophy, supplemented it, and, if necessary, pointed out its shortcomings. For example, Ibn Iraq revised Menelaus' Spherica.

On the other hand, there is a large number of published works devoted to the scientific activities of Abu Rayhan Biruni in the field of philosophical sciences and social relations. Researchers have addressed various problems in the field of history of science.

It was also noted that in Khorezm during the 10th-12th centuries, there was an increased focus on philosophical sciences. This was primarily associated with everyday practical needs. In other words, scientific research in this direction was linked to factors such as the development of irrigated agriculture in Khorezm, the expansion of trade relations, and the rise of cultural and spiritual life.

One of the important issues related to the topic of this monograph is the celebration of the millennium of scientific activity of the Khorezm Mamun Academy. In this regard, scientific collections and materials from international conferences were published, with most of the articles relating to the field of philosophy. Thanks to this event, the study of the history of scientific activities of the Khorezm Mamun Academy was raised to a new and relevant level.

In summarizing the published works, it was found that the works of some scientists who worked in Khorezm during the 10th-12th centuries in the field of philosophical sciences (for example, Abu Rayhan Biruni) have been much better studied, while the work of others remains relatively unexplored.

1.2. The main directions of research into the sources of scientists of the Khorezm Mamun Academy, their natural science and historical and philosophical analysis

In studies devoted to the scientific heritage of Central Asian scientists, the treatises of Muhammad ibn Musa al-Khwarizmi "Zij" and "Working with the Astrolabe" were briefly described, and it was also noted that the sine quadrant was described for the first time in science as a special cataststrophic instrument - in the following book[203]. More complete information is given in the work of Mahmud al-Shagmini "Al-mulahas fi-l-haya" (الملخص في الهيئة)[204]. Several articles are devoted to the work of Ulugbek, his Samarkand Observatory and the work of scientists in it, which describe Ulugbek's achievements in the field of catastrophic disasters[205], the structure of the observatory he built[206], the life and work of its scientists (Gazizoda Rumi, Ali Kushchi)[207] and activities[208], as well as the instrument of the disaster, built in Tashkent in the 9th century[209].

---

[203] Rosenfeld B.A., Sergeeva N.D. On the astronomical treatises of al-Khwarizmi. /Historical and astronomical research. Vol. XIII. - Moscow, 1977. - P.201-218.
[204] Rosenfeld B.A., Dobrovolsky I.G., Sergeeva N.D. On the astronomical treatises of al-Fargani. /Historical and astronomical research. ISSU,e XI. - Moscow, 1972. - P.191-21.
[205] Ventzel M.K. A brief outline of the history of practical astronomy in Russia and the USSR (development of methods for determining time and latitude)/Historical and astronomical research. ISSU,e II. - Moscow, 1956. - P.7-140.
[206] Bulatov M.S. Ulugbek Observatory in Samarkand // Historical and astronomical studies. Vol. XYIII - Moscow, 1986. - P.199-216.
[207] Ibodov Dj.Kh., Matviyevskaya G.P. Ulugbek's student is Ali Kushchi. - Tashkent: Science, 1994, p. 36.
[208] Jalalov G.D. Some remarkable statements of astronomers at the Samarkand Observatory // Historical and astronomical studies. ISSU,e III. - Moscow, 1957. - P.381-386.
[209] Tursunov O.S., Azizov S.Kh. Astronomical instruments of the early Middle Ages in the center of Tashkent // Historical and astronomical studies. ISSU,e XXV. - Moscow, 2000. - P.56-60.

In one of the translations of these collections from Arabic into Russian, the catalog of stars of Abu Rayhon Beruni was translated, and the necessary scientific comments were also given to it[210]. The following translation consists of excerpts from "Qanuni Masudi" by Abu Rayhon Beruni and "Al-Mulahas fi-l-haya" by Ibn al-Haytham[211]. In the studies of Uzbek scientists published in these collections, there are more questions related to the scientific activities of Abu Rayhon Beruni, including scientific works written on the basis of research and direct observations of specialists in specific sciences in the field of knowledge of catastrophic disasters[212]. It mentions the Ulugbek Observatory and the scientists who worked there[213], Ibn Iraq and the scientific legacy of Abulhusayn Abdurrahman ibn Umar al-Sufi, a major representative of the Muslim eastern catastrophe[214].

A number of editions of collections entitled "Historical and Astronomical Research" also reflect the activities of the Khorezm Mamun Academy in the field of astronomy. The main part of the materials published in them is devoted to the analysis of the legacy of Abu Rayhon Beruni in the field of astronomy. For example, the star catalog of Abu Rayhon Beruni was translated into Russian for the first time, and the star catalogs of Umar Khayyam (1040-1123) and Nasir ad-Din Tusi (1201-1274) were also translated into Russian for the first time; All three works are

---

[210] Star catalog of al-Biruni with the appendix of the catalogs of Khayyam and at-Tusi. Translation by S.A. Krasnova, M.M. Rozhanskaya. Ed. B.A. Rosenfeld. /Historical and astronomical research. Vol. VIII. – Moscow, 1962. -P.83-194.

[211] Rosenfeld B.A. About the zodical light among the Arabs./Historical and astronomical studies. ISSU,e XV. – Moscow, 1980. - P.290-292; Ibn al-Haytham. Treatises on burning mirrors (preface by B.A. Rosenfeld, translation by I.O. Mohammed and N.V. Orlova, notes by N.V. Orlova and B.A. Rosenfeld). - Historical and astronomical research. ISSU,e XV. - Moscow, 1980. - P.305-338.

[212] Jalalov G.D. Indian astronomy in Beruni's book "India" // Historical and astronomical studies. ISSU,e XUIII. – Moscow, 1962.- P.195-220; P.G. Bulgakov. "Geodesy" of Biruni as a historical and astronomical mSSU,ment // Historical and astronomical studies. ISSU,e XI. - Moscow, 1972. - P.181-190; P.G. Bulgakov. Biruni's early treatise on the Fakhri sextant // Historical and astronomical studies. ISSU,e XI. – Moscow, 1972. - P.211-220; Jalalova Z.G. Al-Biruni's student about the movement of the Sun // Historical and astronomical studies. Vol. XII. – Moscow, 1975. - P.227-236.

[213] Bulatov M. S. Ulugbek Observatory in Samarkand // Historical and astronomical studies. Vol. XVIII. – Moscow, 1986. - P.199-216.

[214] Matviyevskaya G.P., Tllashev Kh. On the scientific heritage of the astronomer of the 10th-11th centuries. Abu Nasr ibn Iraq // Historical and astronomical studies. Vol. XIII. - Moscow, 1977. - P.219-234; G.P. Mavievskaya. Abd ar-Rahman al-Sufi and his role in the history of astronomy. /Historical and astronomical research. ISSU,e XVI. - Moscow, 1983. - P.93-138.

compared with the data of the Greek scientist Claudius Ptolemy in scientific comments[215].

The star catalog of Abu Rayhon Beruni was first published in Indian science as part of the Qanuni Masudi[216]. B.A.Rosenfeld, who wrote the preface to the Russian edition, expressed the opinion that the catalog of Abu Rayhon Beruni was compiled on the basis of Ptolemy's "Almagest" and the catalogs of Abulhusayn Abdurrahman ibn Umar al-Sufi (903-983), who lived in the city of Ray. This translation can be called the first serious study in Russian of the heritage of scientists of the Khorezm Mamun Academy in the field of exact sciences.

In the article by P.G.Bulgakov[217], Abu Rayhon Beruni's work "Geodesy" is noted as an important written monument related to astronomy, which addresses issues of practical (geodetic) astronomy (determining the geographical latitude of a place, astronomical instruments made by Abu Rayhon Beruni, determining the deviation of the plane ecliptic to the equator, honorary sextant. In the description of Abu Rayhon Beruni, he concludes that the geographical longitude and determination of the size of the Earth, etc.

The research of A.K.Tagi-Zade[218] described the quadrants that existed in the Middle Ages in the East. In this area it is said that al-Khwarizmi wrote about the quadrant of the sine (in the book "Working with the Astrolabe"), and Abu Rayhon Beruni gave detailed information about the quadrant in the books "At-Tafhim", "Qanuni Masudi", "Udy", and "Geodesy," "Honorary Sextant".

Several other articles have been written about Abu Rayhon Beruni's research on Indian astronomy[219], his writings on the zodiacal light in the Qanuni Masudi[220], the treatise Fakhri Sextant[221], and his thoughts on the movement of the Sun[222].

---

[215] Star catalog of al-Biruni with the appendix of the catalogs of Khayyam and at-Tusi. Translation by S.A. Krasnova, M.M. Rozhanskaya. Ed. B.A. Rosenfeld // Historical and astronomical studies. Vol. VIII. – Moscow, 1962. - P.83-194.
[216] Abu-r-Rayhan al-Biruni // Al-Qanun' l Masudi (Canon Masudicus). - Hayderabad-Dn, Osmania Press, 1954-1956, vol. III. - P.1014-1126.
[217] Bulgakov P.G. "Geodesy" of Biruni as a historical and astronomical mSSU,ment // Historical and astronomical studies. Vol. XI. - Moscow, 1972. - P.181-190.
[218] Tagi-Zade A.K. Quadrants of the Middle Ages // Historical and astronomical studies. Vol. XIII. - Moscow, 1977. - P.183-200.
[219] Jalalov G.D. Indian astronomy in Beruni's book "India" // Historical and astronomical studies. Vol. VIII. - Moscow, 1962. - P.195-220.

The study by B. A. Rosenfeld, entitled "Astronomy in the Countries of Islam," is written in the form of general information. It briefly touches on the ideas about astronomy that existed among the Arabs in antiquity, and then analyzes research in the field of astronomy in the Baghdad Caliphate, which separately evaluates Central Asian scientists (Muhammad ibn Musa al-Khwarizmi, Habash al-Khasib, Ahmed al-Fargani). Then, in subsequent centuries, information is provided about the development of astronomy in some of its countries in the East - the Middle East (Nishapur, Shiraz, Ray), Khorezm, Syria, Arabia, Egypt, Turkey, the Caucasus, India, Maghreb, Spain, during the reign of some dynasties (Gaznavids, Seljuks, Timurids, Safavids) the history of astronomical knowledge is covered.

In the parts of the article devoted to Khorezm and the Ghaznavids, the author notes that the history of astronomy in Khorezm has ancient roots. An archaeological expedition in Koykirilgan discovered the remains of an observatory. After that, the author briefly touches upon the astronomical research of scientists from the Khorezm Mamun Academy (Ibn Iraq, Abu Rayhan Biruni, Mahmud Chaghmini). The example of the Ghaznavid dynasty showcases the work of Abu Rayhan Beruni[223].

In the 13th issue of «Historical and Astronomical Research» by G.P.Matviyevskaya, the article by Kh. Tlashev[224] discusses the life and scientific legacy of Abu Nasr ibn Iraq, an important representative of the Khorezm Mamun Academy. His name was originally given as Abu Nasr Mansur ibn Ali ibn Iraq and it was shown that he came from an Iraqi family belonging to the Khwarazmshah dynasty. Each of his astronomical and mathematical works is then listed separately, with a brief reference and exploration of when they were written, whether they have survived or, if not, which oriental scholars are mentioned in their works.

---

[220] Rosenfeld B.A. About the zodical light among the Arabs // Historical and astronomical studies. ISSU,e XV. - Moscow, 1980. - P.290-292.
[221] Bulgakov P.G. Biruni's early treatise on the Fakhri sextant // Historical and astronomical studies. ISSU,e XI. – Moscow, 1972. - P.211-220.
[222] Jalalova Z.G. Al-Biruni's student about the movement of the Sun // Historical and astronomical studies. ISSU,e XII. – Moscow, 1975. - P.227-236.
[223] Rosenfeld B.A. Astronomy of Islamic countries // Historical and astronomical studies. Vol. XVII. – Moscow, 1984. - P.67-122.

The section on mathematical works also includes «Islah Kitab Manalus» (اصلاح كتاب منالوس) («Corrections to the Book of Menelaus («Spherical»)») by Ibn Iraq. Its text is reported to have been translated into German by M. Krause in 1936, from a single copy kept in the library of the University of Leiden, and published with a detailed philological study, a short study being given by the authors of the article.

Articles devoted to the development of mathematics in the East were also published in various volumes of the collection «Historical and Mathematical Research», which has been published regularly in Russian since the second half of the 20th century. An important part of it is the scientific heritage of the scientists from Central Asia and Khorezm of the Mamun Academy. In particular, there are many articles reflecting the work of Abu Rayhon Beruni on mathematics. They used the methods of Abu Raikhan Beruni to create an ellipse, parabola and hyperbola on a plane from a circle using an astrolabe, more precisely, images of the horizon and almucantarate in the form of an ellipse, parabola, hyperbola (Vakhabov S.A.)[225], determining the direction of Abu Raikhan's Qibla Beruni, Mahmud Chagmini and Kamoliddin Turkmani (11th century) comparative analysis of the methods mentioned in the works (Atagarriev M.N.)[226], Abu Raikhan Beruni «Perfect methods for making astrolabes» («Istiab al-wujuh al-mumkina fi san'a al - asturlob»). asturlob») (استعاب الوجوه الممكنة في صنعى الاسترلا) Analysis of his work based on the manuscript in the library of Leiden University (Or. 591 /4) (Vakhabov S.)[227], «Selected words on the problem of shadows» by Abu Rayhon Beruni (افراد المقال في أمر الأظلال) («Ifrod al-maqol fi amr al-azlal»)[228] and the use of quadratic interpolation (Rosenfeld B.A.)[229] are analysed.

---

[225] Vakhabov S.A. Projective transformations in al-Biruni's treatise on astrolabes // Historical and mathematical studies. Vol. XXXII-XXXIII. - Moscow: Science, 1990. - P.339-344.
[226] Atagarriev M. N. Application of stereographic projection to determining the azimuth of the qibla: al-Biruni, al-Chagmini and at-Turkmoni // Historical and mathematical studies. ISSU,e XXIX. - Moscow: Science, 1980. - P.44-47.
[227] Vakhabov S. Two mathematical models of al-Biruni // Historical and mathematical studies. ISSU,e XXV. - Moscow: Science, 1980. - P.328-335.
[228] Rosenfeld B.A. [Some questions of mathematics of variables in al-Biruni's treatise on shadows] // Historical and mathematical studies. Vol. XXIII. - Moscow: Science, 1978. - P.226-231.
[229] Rosenfeld B.A. An attempt at quadratic interpolation by Abu r-Reyhan al-Biruni // Historical and mathematical studies. Vol. XII. - Moscow: Science, 1959. - P.421-430.

In two volumes of the collection there are articles on mathematical knowledge in the history of the peoples of Central Asia in the 9th-15th centuries. (A.P.Yushkevich)[230] and the study of the history of mathematics in Central Asia (S.Kh.Sirodzhiddinov, G.P.Matviyevskaya)[231], which also examines the development of mathematics in Khorezm.

The above-mentioned study by A.P. Yushkevich, devoted to the contribution of the peoples of Central Asia to the development of mathematical knowledge in the 9th-15th centuries, is based on convincing evidence that the conclusion of Western scientists that mathematics among the Arabs was merely a repetition of the heritage of ancient Indian and Greek scientists is incorrect. In the East it was found that only the achievements of ancient Indian and Greek science were subject to changes, corrections and new considerations.

The article also states that the term «Arab», which has become a tradition in Western science, is a mistake, that many peoples created the Arabic language during a certain period of time, and this situation also applies to the field of mathematics. and specific examples are given.

A.P.Yushkevich emphasised that mathematical sciences occupy an important place in the scientific heritage of Central Asian scientists of the 9th-15th centuries, highlighting achievements in the field of arithmetic, algebra and trigonometry, as well as fundamental discoveries; in arithmetic and combination - improving the hexadecimal position system, discovering decimal fractions, developing methods for deriving numbers from roots, applying Newton's binomial formula for any natural exponent, expanding the understanding of real positive numbers; in algebra - the application of numerical algebra to geometry and trigonometry and the discovery of the method of integration, the creation of a geometric theory for solving cubic equations; such as the creation of a system of plane and spherical trigonometry, the calculation of accurate and perfect trigonometric tables.

---

[230] Yushkevich A.P. On the mathematics of the peoples of Central Asia in the 9th-15th centuries // Historical and mathematical studies. Issue IV. - Moscow: Science, 1951.- P.455-489.
[231] Sirazhdinov S.Kh., Matvievskaya G.P. On studying the history of mathematics in Central Asia. Historical and mathematical research // Historical and mathematical research. Issue XXI. - Moscow: Science, 1976. - P.51-61.

The article explores the concept of the «Central Asian region» in a broader sense, partly including the Middle East.

More relevant research compared to the monograph is a small article «On the study of the history of mathematics in Central Asia»[232], co-authored by S.Kh.Sirodzhiddinov and G.P.Matviyevskaya. Its authors note that the consistent study of the history of mathematics in the Near and Middle East, as well as in Central Asia, began in the second half of the 19th century, and in Uzbekistan - mainly in the second half of the 20th century. It must be said that research in Uzbekistan is not only about mathematics, but also about the history of specific sciences in general. Researchers in this field include A.P.Yushkevich, T.N.Kori-Niyazov, B.A.Rosenfeld, G'.Y.Jalolov, R.I.Ibodov, N.I.Leonov, G.P.Matviyevskaya, A.Usmanov, E.A.Khatipov, S.A.Akhmedov, Y.H.Ibodov, Kh.Umarov, A.F.Faizullaev, V.P.Shcheglov, M.A.Sobirov. They say that the research reflects the observatory of Ulugbek, Ulugbek «Zij», the activities of Mahmud Chagmini related to mathematics and astronomy, translations of the works of Abu Rayhon Beruni into Russian and Uzbek.

In general, this article can be considered the first retrospective analysis of the study of the history of mathematics in Uzbekistan.

Since the 60s of the 20th century, in studies published in Russian, attention to issues of exact sciences in the scientific heritage of Abu Rayhon Beruni has increased. The Russian translation of the mathematical work of Abu Raikhan Beruni «Definition of circles» (S.A.Krasnova and L.A.Karpova, 1963)[233], the Russian translation of a book about Indian lovers (B.A.Rosenfeld, 1963)[234], the encyclopaedia «Catalogue of stars in the work of the scientist «Kanuni Masudi» (S.A.Krasnova, M.M.Rozhanskaya, 1962)[235] is one of them. M.M.Rozhanskaya devoted her

---

[232] Sirazhdinov S.Kh., Matviyevskaya G.P. On the study of the history of mathematics in Central Asia // Historical and mathematical studies. ISSU,e XX1. - Moscow: Science, 1976. - P.51-60.
[233] Beruni Abu Raihan. On the definition of chords in a circle; Rosenfeld B.A. , Krasnova S.A. Notes to the "Treatise on the Definition of Chords" // From the history of science and technology in the countries of the East, III. - Moscow: IVL, 1963.
[234] Beruni Abu Raihan. Book about Indian Rashikas; Rosenfeld B.A. Notes to the "Book about Indian Rashikas" // From the history of science and technology in the countries of the East, III. - Moscow: IVL, 1963.
[235] Krasnova S.A., Rozhanskaya M.M. Beruni's star catalog // From the history of science and technology in the countries of the East. – Moscow, 1963. - P. 71-92.

candidate's thesis to the problems of functional mathematics in her works, including «Kanuni Masudi» (1968).

In the second half of the 20th century, scientists of Uzbekistan published various books, collections, pamphlets and scientific articles related to the scientific heritage of the scientists of the Khorezm Mamun Academy, some of them devoted to specific sciences, including the correspondence of Abu Raykhan Beruni and Ibn Sina (A.Rasulov, M. Abdurakhmonov, 1950), Astronomy of Abu Raykhan Beruni (H.U.Sadikov, 1950), Cartographic Projections of Abu Raykhan Beruni (G. Jalolov, 1950), his research is devoted to astronomy and mathematical-geographical views[236].

During this period, some of Abu Rayhon Beruni's works were translated into Uzbek and Russian and published in Uzbekistan. More precise sciences also had their place. Besides Uzbekistan, scientists from Moscow and Leningrad (St. Petersburg) took part in these publications in Russian: «Chronology» (1957), «India» (1963), «Mineralogy» (1963); the books «Geodesy» (1966) and «Yodgorliklar» (1968) were published in Uzbek. In 2022, 8 volumes of Abu Rayhon Beruni were republished in Tashkent: «Monuments of Past Generations» (Osor al-Bakiya) (Volume I), «India» (Volume II), «Establishing Address Boundaries to Determine Distances (Between) Residential Buildings» (Volume III), «Law of Masudi (Articles 1-5)» (Volume IV), Law of Masudi (Articles 6-11)» (Volume V), Explanatory Book on the Basics of the Art of Astrology «Tafhim» (Volume VI), «Mathematical and Astronomical Treatises» (Volume VII), Saidana (Volume IX).

P.G. Bulgakov is a famous foreign scientist from Uzbekistan. He wrote a Russian translation (Tashkent, 1966) of the text of Abu Rayhon Beruni's book «Geodesy» (Cairo, 1962) and articles on issues of exact sciences («Geodesy», «Honorary Sextant», «His Globe»). «The life and work of Beruni. A monograph was published (Tashkent, 1972).

These scientific works published translations of the works of the encyclopaedist Abu Reyhan Beruni. The prefaces provide a scientific analysis of each work and also mention specific sciences.

---

[236] Sadykov Kh.U. Biruni and his works on astronomy and mathematical geography. – Moscow, 1953.

In the second half of the 20th century, many studies and translations of the history of science were published in Uzbekistan, some of them devoted to the history of the development of specific sciences. A.Nosirov (1950), A.A.Semenov (1950), U.I.Karimov (1953, 1957, 1973, 1980), M.Sale (1954), S.P.Tolstov (1960), G.P.Matviyevskaya (1962, 1963, 1967, 1968, 1981). 1981), M.A.Akhadova (1964, 1965, 1976, 1983), Kh.Khikmatullayev (1966), M.M.Khairullayev (1967, 1967, 1994), A.Akhmedov (1972, 1980, 1983, 1984 , 1985, 1986), P.G.Bulgakov (1972), A.Irisov (1980), Kh.Siddikov (1981). Y.K.Ibodov (1981, 1983, 1985, 1987, 1988, 1989, 1990, 1992, 1994, 1998, 2005, 2009, 2011, 2012), S.K.Siroyiddinov (1981), I.Abdullaev (1984) , S.G. Bagirova (1987), G.K. Masharipova (1994, 1995, 2004, 2019, 2021, 2022, 2023), Kh. Gamidov (1995), B.A. Abdukhalimov (2001), S.U. Karimova (2001), including[237] publications.

The subject matter of this study is broad: bibliography, biographical information on Central Asian scientists, studies related to a specific field of science, analysis of the history of philosophy, commentaries on source materials, etc.

Publications related to the subject of the monograph include articles in collections published in Uzbek[238] and Russian[239] in connection with the celebration of the 1000th anniversary of the birth of Abu Rayhon Beruni; articles by A. Akhmedov, K. Norkhodjaev, A. Abdurakhmonov, A. Rasulov in the Uzbek collection, P. G. Bulgakov, E. G. Kasimova, B. A. Rosenfeld, A. Abdurakhmanov, G. P. Matviyevskaya in the Russian collection.

In connection with the celebration of the 1000th anniversary of the birth of Abu Rayhon Beruni, the collections published in Uzbek and Russian languages present researches on geodesy, trigonometry and astronomy from the works of the scientist, as well as researches on the scientific heritage of Abu Rayhon Beruni. Both collections are of great scientific importance from the point of view of assessing the

---

[237] The titles of articles and books by these scientists are given in full in the list of references at the end of the Monographyy.
[238] Collection dedicated to the 1000th anniversary of the birth of Beruni. – Tashkent: Science, 1997. – 260 p.
[239] Beruni. Collection of articles for the 1000th anniversary of his birth. - Tashkent: Science, 1973. - 204 p.

contribution of Abu Raikhan Beruni to the scientific potential of the Khorezm Mamun Academy.

We think it is necessary to focus on the research of some scientists in this regard. If we think in the field of exact sciences, then among the Uzbek scientists in this field, significant studies of the period we are studying in the dissertation belong to the pen of G. P. Matviyevskaya[240], they are connected with the history of mathematics, she continued to develop in this area in her further research and published serious works[241]. In the research of the scientist, such topics as the history of mathematics in Central Asia, the system of counting in the Middle Ages in the East, the works of Central Asian scientists related to mathematics and their influence on Europe were thoroughly scientifically analysed.

The book by G.P. Matviyevskaya on the history of trigonometry (1990)[242] examines the development of this science from ancient times (gnomonics, spherical coordinates), its development among the ancient Greeks (problems of spherical trigonometry in the views of Claudius Ptolemy and Menelaus), Indians (siddhants), countries of the Near and Middle East and their position in Europe. The work pays great attention to the development of trigonometry in the Muslim East, more precisely in the countries of the Near and Middle East; works written on trigonometry in the 9th-15th centuries, trigonometry in the scientific heritage of Ptolemy, the influence of Indian science, trigonometry on a flat surface, spherical trigonometry, Menelaus' theorem, theorems of sines and cosines, triangles and trigonometric functions discussed in separate sections.

This study separately examined the works of Ibn Iraq and Abu Rayhon Beruni, scholars of the Khorezm Mamun Academy, in the field of trigonometry[243].

In a special article (co-authored with Kh. Tlashev) he studied the commentary of Abu Nasr ibn Iraq (d. 1039) on a work called «Spherics», dedicated to the problems of geometry and spherical trigonometry, written by the Greek scientist Menelaus (1st-

---

[240] Matviyevskaya G.P. Beruniy and natural sciences. - Tashkent: Science, 1963. - 48 p.
[241] Matviyevskaya G.P. On the history of mathematics of Central Asia in the 9th-15th centuries. - Tashkent, 1962. – 125 p.
[242] Matviyevskaya G.P. Essays on the history of trigonometry. - Tashkent: Science, 1990. - 142 p.
[243] Matviyevskaya G.P. Essays on the history of trigonometry. - Tashkent: Science, 1990. - P.106-125.

2nd century)[244]. In the article, Ibn Iraq emphasises that Menelaus' theorem was simplified by the theorem of sines from a system of rectangles to an ideal shape for a spherical surface - a system of triangles, i.e. he made an important change in the field of trigonometry. He credits Ibn Iraq as one of the scientists who discovered the theorem of sines[245].

Regarding the contribution of Abu Rayhon Beruni to trigonometry, it is said that first of all his scientific heritage and his research in science, then in the sections of astronomy of the work «Qanuni Masudi» many practical and theoretical problems of Abu Rayhon Beruni in trigonometry are discussed[246].

One of the largest scientific studies in the field of exact sciences in Uzbekistan is the doctoral thesis of J. H. Ibodov on the topic «Exact sciences in Arabic and Persian encyclopaedias of the X-XVIII centuries» (1994)[247]. He also published several scientific articles in this field[248].

The scientist's research on the history of exact sciences was published even before independence[249]; further research is an organic continuation of it. Some of the

---

[244] Collection: Mathematics and astronomy in the works of scientists of the Middle Ages. - Tashkent: Science, 1977. – 142 p. P.81-89.

[245] Collection: Mathematics and astronomy in the works of scientists of the Middle East. - Tashkent: Science, 1977. - P. 85, 142.

[246] Matviyevskaya G.P. Essays on the history of trigonometry. - Tashkent: Science, 1990. - P.111-126.

[247] Ibadov J.Kh. Arabic and Persian encyclopedias of the X-XVIII centuries. as sources on the history of exact sciences // Author's abstract of thesis...doc.historical sciences. - Tashkent: Science, 1994. - 42 p.

[248] Ibadov J.Kh. Classification of physical and mathematical sciences in the medieval encyclopedias of Abu Abdullah al-Khwarizmi, Fakhr ad-Din al-Razi, Qutb ad-Din al-Shirazi and Baha ad-Din al-Amili // Abstracts of the XXXIV Scientific Conference conferences for graduate students and young specialists in the history of natural sciences and IIE and T RAS technicians. – Moscow, 1992. - P.35-36; Ibodov Zh.Kh. "Book of research on algebra" by Hasan ibn Haris al-Khububi al-Khorezmi // Abstracts of scientific theories and technical conferences of professors, lecturer at Tashkent State Technical University. A. Beruni. - Tashkent: Science, 1992. - P.123-125; Ibodov Zh.Kh. Comparative analysis of the physical and mathematical chapters of the universal encyclopedias "Keys of Sciences" by Abu Abdallah al-Khwarizmi (X-XVI centuries) and "Collection of Sciences" by Fakhr ad-Din ar-Razi. - Tashkent State Technical University named after A. Beruni, 1992. - P.135-136.

[249] Ibadov J.Kh. About the mathematical treatise from the city of Khiva // Mathematics and sonomy in the works of Ibn Sina, his contemporaries and followers. - Tashkent: Science, 1981. - P.143-154; Ibodov Zh.Kh. Mathematical treatises of al-Khububi and al-Sijavandi // From the history of medieval eastern mathematics and astronomy. - Tashkent: Science, 1983. - P.72-81; Ibodov Zh.Kh. Study of four manuscripts with mathematical content // Izv. AN UzSSR. Series of physical and mathematical sciences. 1983. № 1. - P.69-70; Ibodov Zh.Kh. The creativity of al-Khorezmi in the assessment of Eastern scientists-encyclopedists of the 10th-16th centuries. // The great scientist of the Middle Ages al-Khorezmi. - Tashkent: Science, 1985. - P.265-268; Ibodov Zh.Kh. Physics and mathematics chapters of the encyclopedia "Collection of Sciences" ("Jami ul-ulum") by Fakhr ad-Din ar-Razi. Dep. IN VINITI. – Moscow, 1987. № 1066. - B87. - 14 s.; Ibadov J.Kh., Bulgakov P.G. To the history of mathematics of Khorezm at the end of the 10th century. // Social sciences in Uzbekistan, 1988. № 5. - P.62-65; Ibadov J.H., Matviyevskaya G.P. Exact sciences in the encyclopedia "The Wisdom of the Source (Hikma al-ayn) al-Qazwini" // Izv. AN UzSSR. Ser.Phys.-Math.Sciences, 1989. - P.29-31; Ibadov J.H., Matviyevskaya G.P. Physical and mathematical sciences in the encyclopedia "Keys of Sciences" by Abu Abdullah al-Khwarizmi // Izv. AN UzSSR. Ser.Phys.-Math.Sciences, 1990. № 3. - P.34-39; Ibadov

researches published by J.H. Ibodov are related to the history of development of exact sciences in the Khorezm Mamun Academy[250], they talk about scientists who worked in the field of exact sciences and the mentioned problems related to mathematics. in his works, history of mathematics, etc.

The questions of Abu Rayhon Beruni Ibn Sina (18 in all) and the answers to them have come down to us in the form of a separate treatise. The fact that they discuss specific sciences, including astronomy, is directly related to the subject of our research. Ten questions were asked about Aristotle's work entitled The Book of the Heavens (celestial sphere, motion of the celestial spheres, dimensions of a flat surface, etc.)[251]. Ibn Sina develops Aristotelian views on the concept of «infinity».

The works are called in scholarship «Answers to ten questions to Sheikhur-Rais (Ibn Sina)» («Ajubaan ashara masail saala anho ash-Sheikh ar-Rais»)[252]. This treatise can also be found under other names: «Letter to Abu Rayhon Muhammad ibn Ahmad al-Abu Rayhon Beruni» («Risala ila Abu Rayhon Muhammad ibn Ahmad al-Beruni»)[253]. The following eight questions relate to some of the questions in Aristotle's Physics. This correspondence was translated into Russian and published by Yu.N. Zavadovsky (1957, republished in 1973)[254].

J.H., Matviyevskaya G.P. Physical and mathematical sciences in the encyclopedia "Keys of Sciences" by Abu Abdullah al-Khwarizmi // Izv. AN UzSSR. Ser.Phys.-Math.Sciences, 1990. № 3. - P.34-39.

[250] Ibodov Zh.Kh. Mathematical treatises of al-Khububi and al-Sijavandi // From the history of medieval eastern mathematics and astronomy. - Tashkent: Science, 1983. - P.72-81; Ibodov Zh.Kh. Physics and mathematics chapters of the encyclopedia "Collection of Sciences" ("Jami ul-ulum") by Fakhr ad-Din ar-Razi. Dep. IN VINITI. – Moscow, 1987. № 1066. - B87. - 14 s.; Ibadov J.Kh., Bulgakov P.G. To the history of mathematics of Khorezm at the end of the 10th century. // Social sciences in Uzbekistan, 1988. № 5. - P.62-65; Ibodov Zh.Kh. Philosophical views of encyclopedists of the Renaissance in Central Asia and discoveries in the field of exact sciences. - Tashkent-Mevrius: 2009. - 160 pp.; Ibodov J.H. Physics and mathematics chapters of "Keys of Sciences" (Mafotih al-ulum) by Abu Abdullah al-Khorezmi. - Tashkent: TUNTN, 2005. - 56 p.; Ibodov Zh.Kh. Encyclopedias of scientists of Central Asia of the 9th-18th centuries as sources on the history of exact sciences. - Tashkent-Mevrius: 2010. - 174 p.; Ibodov Zh.Kh. Studying the rich scientific heritage of our country // Problems of improving the quality of personnel training for the field of communications and information. Scientific conference TATU. - Tashkent: 2012, volume 1. - B. 105-107.

[251] Vakhabova B.A. Manuscripts of Ibn Sina's works in the collection of the Institute of Oriental Studies of the Academy of Sciences of the Uzbek SSR. - Tashkent: Science, 1982. - P.38-39.

[252] Manuscript of the Abu Rayhan Beruni Institute of Oriental Studies, № 2385/XLVI; There is also information that these questions were asked by Abulkasim Jurjani (or al-Kirmani) (B.A. Vakhabova. Manuscripts of Ibn Sina's works in the collections of the Institute of Oriental Studies of the Academy of Sciences of the UzSSR. - Tashkent: Science, 1982. - 32 p.).

[253] Manuscript of the Abu Rayhan Beruni Institute of Oriental Studies, №2385/XIV.

[254] Al-Biruni and Ibn Sina. Ten questions from Biruni regarding Aristotle's "Book of Heaven" and Ibn Sina's answers. Biruni's eight questions regarding Aristotle's "Physics" and Ibn Sina's answers. Per.Yu.N.Zavadovsky. - In the book: Materials on the history of progressive social and philosophical thought in Uzbekistan. - Tashkent, 1957. - P.128-162; Beruni and Ibn Sina. Correspondence. Per. Y.N.Zavadovsky. - Tashkent: Science, 1973.

Ibn Sina's treatise entitled «The Essence of Letters» (Sharh Khuruf at-taji) is partly related to practical issues of astronomy, examining the characteristics of each letter of the Arabic alphabet[255].

In the theoretical part of Ibn Sina's treatise on the classification of philosophical sciences («Risala fi aqsam al-hikmah»), the lower, middle and upper classes of sciences were considered, and the middle class was defined as the field of mathematical knowledge[256].

«Kitab ash-shifa» is an encyclopaedic work by Ibn Sina, a complex of scientific and philosophical knowledge: it consists of four parts (jumla) and 18 volumes. The first is logic (al-ilm al-mantiqi), the second physics (al-ilm al-tabiy), the third mathematical sciences (al-ulum ar-mathematician), the fourth metaphysics (al-ulum al-mathematician). al-alihiyya). Therefore, this work emphasises the mathematical sciences.

There have been several scholarly studies of the Kitab al-Shifa. For example, F.Vöpke (1863), K.Lokoch (1912), Kh.Muhammadiev[257], M.S.Sharipova[258], G.Jalolov[259], G.Masharipova[260] and others.

Another study, «Risala fi tahqiq az-zawiyya» («Treatise on the Determination of Angles»), is also by Ibn Sina, it is somewhat related to mathematics, it talks about acute angles.

Risola fi tahqiq az-zawiyya (Treatise on the Determination of Angles) translated into Russian by A. T. Grigoryan and M. M. Rozhanskaya (1974)[261].

---

[255] Manuscript of the Institute of Oriental Studies named after Abu Rayhan Beruni of the Academy of Sciences of the Republic of Uzbekistan, № 2385/XIII, in Persian; B. A. Vakhabova. Written by Ibn Sina and the collection of the Institute of Oriental Studies of the Academy of Sciences of the Uzbek SSR. Tashkent: Science, 1982. - P.50.

[256] Manuscript of the Institute of Oriental Studies named after Abu Raikhan Beruni of the Academy of Sciences of the Republic of Uzbekistan, No. 2213/III; B. A. Vakhabova. Written by Ibn Sina and the collection of the Institute of Oriental Studies of the Academy of Sciences of the Uzbek SSR. - Tashkent: Science, 1982. - P.23-24.

[257] Muhammadiev Kh. Mathematical chapters of the "Book of Healing" by Ibn Sina: Author. dis.candidate of historical sciences. – Dushanbe, 1967. - 22 p.

[258] Sharipova M.S. Mathematical chapters of the "Book of Healing" by Ibn Sina. (Planimetric chapters). - "Scientific notes of the Dushanbe State Pedagogical Institute", ISSU,e 56. - Dushanbe, 1967; Sharipova M.S. Questions of number theory in the "Book of Healing" by Ibn Sina. - "Scientific notes of the Dushanbe State Pedagogical Institute", ISSU,e 71. – Dushanba, 1970. - P.3-30; Sharipova M.S. Mathematical chapters of the "Book of Healing" by Ibn Sina. Author's abstract of candidate's dissertation Dushanbe, 1967 and others.

[259] Jalolov G'. The work of Abu Ali ibn Sina entitled "Al-Hisab" // Collection of articles "On the 1000th anniversary of the birth of Abu Ali ibn Sina". - Tashkent: Science, 1980. - P. 122-134.

[260] Masharipova G.K. "Fundamentals of Geometry" by Abu Ali ibn Sina // Sharkshunoslik, № 5. – Tashkent, 1994. – P. 41-49.

The scientific collection (2005)[262], published in connection with the celebration of the 1000th anniversary of the Khorezm Mamun Academy, contains a number of studies on the activities of the Academy: the beginning of the word (B.Abdukhalimov), the foundation of the Academy (A.Akhmedov), mathematics (A.Akhmedov). Akhmedov), mathematics and astronomy (A. Akhmedov), chemistry (S.U.Karimova), medicine (S.U. Karimova), geography (O. Boriev), social sciences - philosophy (A.Sharipov), history (A.Akhmedov), literature (I.Elmurodov), linguistics (Z. Islamov), current activities of the Academy (K.Safarov).

The section on mathematics and astronomy provides brief information on Hasan ibn Hammar, Hassan al-Khububi, Isa al-Masih, Abu Nasr ibn Iraq, Ibn Sina, some of their works in the field of exact sciences, as well as the achievements of Abu Rayhon Beruni. are discussed in detail in this section[263].

The materials of the international scientific conference (2-3 November 2006, Khiva-Tashkent)[264] dedicated to this date have also been published. It included articles devoted to questions of the exact sciences of the Khorezm Mamun Academy. For example, in the dissertations of K. Abdurimov[265] the formation of the sciences in Central Asia is generally divided into five stages, the first of which falls on the year 2000. A number of sites are cited as examples of archaeological finds from ancient Khorezm. However, the questions and conclusions are provisional.

Among other articles on exact sciences in the collection - astronomy, including the problem of calendars - «Kaptarkhana» is taken as the address of the time service (S.Kh. Azizov)[266], knowledge of the Khorezm Mamun Academy, including the development of science in later periods of scientific conclusions in the exact sciences,

---

[261] Grigoryan A.T., Rozhanskaya M.M. Mechanics and astronomy in the Middle Ages East. - Moscow: Science, 1980.
[262] Khorezm Mamun Academy. - Tashkent: Science, 2005.
[263] Khorezm Mamun Academy. - Tashkent: Science, 2005. - P.33-86.
[264] Khorezm Mamun Academy and its role in the development of world science. Proceedings of the international scientific conference. - Tashkent-Khiva: Science, 2006. - 215 p.
[265] Abdurimov K. Origins of the Khorezm Academy of Mamun: calculation, observation technology and culture of Central Asia, their invariants / Khorezm Academy of Mamun and its role in the development of world science. Proceedings of the international scientific conference. - Tashkent-Khiva: Science, 2006. - P.25-27.
[266] Azizov S.Kh. "Kaptarkhana" in Khorezm - the address of the time service // Khorezm Mamun Academy and its place in the development of world science. Proceedings of the international scientific conference. - Tashkent-Khiva: Science, 2006. - P. 23-25.

positive influence (B. Abdukhalimov)[267], geographical knowledge in the Khorezm Academy of Mamun, including issues of mathematical cartography (O. Boriev)[268], works of Abu Ali ibn Sina in the Khorezm Academy of Mamun (C. Karimov)[269], concerning the works of Ibn Sina on geometry (G. Masharipova)[270], in the article of the Swiss scientist I. Thomann, comments of Abu Mansur ibn Iraq on the Shiite style of the calendar[271] were included.

Taking into account the size of this collection, the weight of materials related to exact and philosophical sciences is not so great. However, the scientific problems raised in the existing articles are distinguished by their importance for the history of the Khorezm Mamun Academy.

Conclusions under paragraph 1.2.

1. The materials published in the collections dedicated to the heritage of the scientists of the Khorezm Mamun Academy can be divided into four groups: 1) problems related to specific sciences in the heritage of the Muslim scientists of the East; 2) the scientific heritage of the Central Asian scientists; 3) researches related to the activities of the Khorezm Mamun Academy; 4) translations of scientific and philosophical works of the Oriental scientists.

2. It is known that the achievements in the field of philosophical sciences made in Khorezm in the 10th-12th centuries were systematically studied in Uzbekistan in the second half of the 20th century, and the weight of local scientists in these studies was increasing. . Published in the form of studies, scientific articles, popular scientific pamphlets, individual monographs and collections.

---

[267] Abdukhalimov B.A. Khorezm Academy of Mamun and its influence on the development of medieval science // Materials of the international scientific conference on the topic «Khorezm Academy of Mamun and its place in the development of world science.» - Tashkent-Khiva: Science, 2006. - P. 163-165.

[268] Boriev O. Geographical knowledge in the Khorezm Academy of Mamun and its role in the revival of the Timurids // Materials of the international scientific conference on the topics «Khorezm Academy of Mamun and its place in the development of world science.» - Tashkent-Khiva: Science, 2006. - P. 27-32.

[269] Karimova S.U. Scientific activity of Abu Ali ibn Sina at the Khorezm Academy of Mamun // Materials of the international scientific conference on the topic «Khorezm Academy of Mamun and its place in the development of world science.» - Tashkent-Khiva: Science, 2006. - P. 168-170.

[270] Masharipova G. Postulates and axioms in the mathematics of Abu Ali ibn Sina // Materials of the international scientific conference on the topics «Khorezm Mamun Academy and its place in the development of world science». - Tashkent-Khiva: Science, 2006. - P. 76-78.

[271] Johannes Thomann. Abu Mansur b. Iraq's criticism of the Shi'a calendarical methods // Materials of the international scientific conference on the topic "Khorezm Mamun Academy and its place in the development of world science". - Toshkent-Khiva: Science, 2006. – P. 111-112.

3. Summarising the published works, it was noted that the works of some scientists who worked in Khorezm in the X-XII centuries in the field of philosophical sciences (for example, the scientific legacy of Abu Raikhan Beruni) have been much better studied, but at the same time their works have been little studied. Similarly, the works of Abu Ali ibn Sina have been studied in various fields by the scholars of the Khorezm Mamun Academy, but they have been little studied from a philosophical point of view.

1.3. Classification of the natural science and historical-philosophical heritage of scientists of the Khorezm Mamun Academy

According to the aims and objectives of the monograph, an important source was, on the one hand, the Eastern sources, including the works in the field of philosophical sciences created in Khorezm in the 10th-12th centuries and which have come down to us, and, on the other hand, the archaeological research materials.

Speaking about the origins of the development of philosophical sciences in Khorezm in the X-XII centuries, it is necessary to note, first of all, the existence of a tradition of continuity in science, in which the influence of ancient Greek science can be observed.

The achievements of ancient Greek science were introduced in Khorezm in the 10th-12th centuries in two ways: the first - directly through the translation and assimilation of the works of ancient Greek scientists from Greek into Arabic. For example, it is known that Abu Nasr Mansur ibn Iraq, a great scientist who lived and worked in Khorezm, teacher of Abu Rayhon Beruni, translated the work of the ancient Greek scientist Menelaus from Greek into Arabic.

The second is the translation and development of the works of ancient Greek scientists into Arabic by scientists working in Baghdad, the capital of the Arab Caliphate, and their use by the scientists of the Khorezm Mamun Academy. Thanks to this continuity, some scientific concepts in the works of Greek scientists, including in the field of philosophical sciences, influenced the development of science in

Khorezm in the 10th-12th centuries. Examples of this can be clearly seen in the work of Abu Rayhon Beruni. In his work «Geodesy» he provides information from the Greek scientists Eratosthenes, Hipparchus and Ptolemy («Geography» and «Almagest»). Thus, we can say that in the 10th-12th centuries, the achievements of ancient Greek science were creatively used in the scientific community of Khorezm and developed with corrections and changes.

At the same time, the achievements of Indian science also took place in the scientific community of Khorezm. When Abu Rayhon Beruni wrote the work «India», he used the results achieved in this field by the ancient Greeks and Indians, including «Al-Arkand» and «Tuzatish» by Brahmagupta, «Karana-tilaka» by Vijayananda, which have not reached us, and critically analysed them, introducing in this work some concepts of astronomy into the field of Muslim science.

Considering the development of science in Khorezm in the X-XII centuries in a broad sense, the scientific works produced in the Arab Caliphate, especially in its capital Baghdad, are relevant from the point of view of continuity. Muhammad ibn Musa al-Khwarizmi was the greatest scientist in the field of exact sciences of the Baghdad Academy. His works were actively used by scientists working at the Khorezm Mamun Academy. Abu Rayhon Beruni in his work «Geodesy», so he was well acquainted with their works.

The creation of the decimal system in the field of algebra by Muhammad ibn Musa al-Khwarizmi stimulated the development of mathematical knowledge not only in the East but also in Europe. This tradition of continuity was shown in scientific research, and on the basis of this tradition we studied the development of science in Khorezm in the X-XII centuries, the works of scientists who worked in Baghdad during the Arab Caliphate, and the treatises of ancient Greek scientists translated into Russian and published when necessary for comparative study.

Abu Rayhon Beruni was well acquainted with the works of al-Battani, al-Saghani, Abu Ali ibn Sina, Abu Mansur ibn Ali ibn Iraq, among the scholars of the 10th century. It should be noted that from the point of view of the history of science, the greatest attention is paid to the scientific legacy of Muhammad ibn Musa al-Khwarizmi and Abu Rayhon Beruni.

It is known that in 1036 he wrote a work entitled «Fihrist of the Books of Muhammad ibn Zakariya ar-Razi» and attached to it a list of his works. In this list, he divided his works into 13 thematic groups in which a total of 113 names are mentioned. In this list, eight topics are discipline-specific:

- Spherical astronomy and constellations (18 works);
- Geodetic mathematics and geodesy (15);
- Counting (8);
- Astrological astronomy (4);
- Astrolabe and its use (5);
- Problems with time (5);
- About meteors and comets (5);
- Astrological (7)[272].

Of course, this list does not include works written by the encyclopaedist before the end of his life. P.G. Bulgakov compiled such a complete list and gave it in the form of an appendix at the end of his monograph, the total number of which is 162 (the titles of the works are given in Russian translation, the Arabic name is in the notes within the monography). book)[273]. Unfortunately, only some of the works in this list have reached us.

Abu Rayhon Beruni. "Monuments to past generations"

The work covers the chronology, ethnic status, culture and religious history of the peoples of the East. There is also information on the natural sciences. For example, the formation of thermal energy on earth from sunlight, the state of water, etc.

---

[272] Bulgakov P.G. - S. -313; Their names (in Russian translation) and other details are also written here.
[273] This source. - B. 420-424.

In this great study, in the chapter «Eid al-Fitr and famous days in the months of the Iranians», when talking about «the days of the meeting of the moon and the turning of the sun», he expressed, among other things, the opinion that «on this day the seas recede and the waters decrease»[274]. In modern astronomy this process is called «the phenomenon of the rising and receding of the sea waters under the influence of the gravitational forces of the Moon and the Sun».

In his description, Abu Rayhon Beruni also quoted al-Kindi's thoughts on the relationship between the Moon and the Sun and wrote about the influence of their gravitational properties on the human body[275]. These ideas were confirmed by the research of the astronomer A.L.Chizhevsky[276] in the 20th century.

From the point of view of the exact sciences, the history of the calendar is given, which is closely related to the question of theoretical astronomy. Lunar and celestial calculations, the history of the determination of epochs, theories of calendars, lunar positions and the theory of projections are outlined. Abu Raikhan Beruni's information on the peoples of Central Asia, including the Khorezm and Sugdian calendars, leap years, and Khorezm ideas about astronomy, is based directly on local sources. For example:

- a word about day and night, the nature of their connection and the beginning (time) of both;

- the nature of months and years, consisting of days and nights;

- Jewish years and periods of other years, beginnings, moods and leaps of years and months;

- On the famous days of the Khorezm period;

- About the addresses of the moons, their rising, setting and shapes, etc.

From the point of view of the history of mathematics, the works on geometric projections in Osor al-Baqiya are important, and it can be said that Abu Rayhon Beruni discovered the cylindrical projection in this work.

---

[274] Beruni A.R. Selected works. - Volume 1. – Tashkent: Science, 1968. – 277 p.
[275] Beruni A.R. Selected works. - Volume 1. - Tashkent: Science, 1968. - P. 276-277.
[276] Chizhevsky A.L., Shishina Yu.G. In the rhythm of the Sun. – Moscow, 1969; Chmzhevsky A.L. Earthly echo of solar storms. – Moscow, 1976.

Abu Rayhon Beruni's book «Asar al-Bakiya» contains many maps of different kingdoms and dynasties of different periods, including the Macedonian Btlimus (Ptolemies), Roman, Christian, ancient Iranian, Sasanian, Arab caliphs (Umayyads and Abbasids). They are derived from such accurate sources that the times of the reigns of the kings are almost exactly indicated and fully proven when compared with other historical books.

They disagree with the opinions of previous scientists on some issues. For example: 1) Is the speed of the Sun constant throughout the zodiac? Ptolemy answered in the affirmative, but Abu Rayhon Beruni answered in the negative. The question is whether the ecliptic rotates or not. He later distinguished between the ideas of Kepler and Copernicus;

2) Is it possible to determine the year by the movement of the moon and therefore by the unit of the moon? Abu Rayhon Beruni does not agree with the conclusion of Hipparchus and Ptolemy;

3) Abu Rayhon Beruni proves that Abu-l-Faraj's story about the fire seen by Kalvozade is a fiction; 4) Hamza ibn Hasan says that Muhammad ibn Musa ibn Shakir's story about Nowruz is wrong. But Abu Rayhon Beruni vindicates Muhammad ibn Musa al-Khwarizmi.

He examines scientific disputes between scientists living in different centuries. These include differences between the opinions of Thabit ibn Qurra and Jolin, al-Razi and Tammor. Abu Ali ibn Sina objects to some of the opinions in the book of Anwa.

One of his questions to Ibn Sina, the question of compulsion, is also included in «Asor al-Baqiya».

He also shows the duration of the solar year with precise calculations in his work «Memorials of Ancient Peoples». He gives information about its position and the equinoxes. He then explains the problem of the apogee of the sun. He criticised the errors of his predecessors in determining the length of the solar year.

The method of qiyas (analogy) is often used by Abu Rayhon Beruni. Analogy is used to avoid rejecting the idea of life and body. There is a lot of such information.

Those who haven't seen it know it by heart. Abu Rayhon Beruni pays special attention to the method of comparing knowledge[277].

The method of qiyas (analogy) is often used by Abu Rayhon Beruni. Analogy is used to avoid rejecting the idea of life and body. There is a lot of such information. Those who haven't seen it know it by heart. Abu Rayhon Beruni pays particular attention to the method of comparing knowledge[278].

As noted in the work of the encyclopaedist, the Khorezmians used lunar addresses. They were used to make judgements about astronomy. Those who remembered the names of the addresses. Later, those who knew the mood to observe them disappeared, says Abu Rayhon Beruni[279]. The inhabitants of Khorezm divided the addresses of the moon into 12 constellations and called them by their own names in their own language. Abu Rayhon Beruni gives the names of the constellations (zodiac) in Arabic, Persian, Syriac, Hebrew and Indian languages.

The question of the calendar raised by Abu Rayhon Beruni has not yet been properly resolved. The question of changing to a new calendar has been raised several times since 1834. The Economic and Social Council of the United Nations also considered the calendar question in 1954.

A number of issues raised in the encyclopaedist's work «Monuments of Ancient Peoples» are of great importance in shedding light on the development of natural science and philosophical thought.

ABU RAYKHAN BERUNI. «INDIA»

The second volume of the «Selected Works» of Abu Rayhon Muhammad ibn Ahmad Beruni was called by the scientist himself «Kitab tahrir ma li-l-Hind min makhula makhbula fi-l-'aql au marzula», which is the name of «India». Henceforth we shall refer to it by this short name. In the later periods of the Middle Ages, the

---

[277] Abu Rayhan Beruni. MSSU,ments to past generations. – Tashkent: Science, 1968. – Pp.24-25.
[278] Abu Rayhan Beruni. MSSU,ments to past generations. – Tashkent: Science, 1968. – 29 p.
[279] Abu Rayhan Beruni. MSSU,ments to past generations. – Tashkent: Science, 1968. – 30 p.

work was also called «History of India», but this name was not established in science. This work was republished by Ashraf Akhmedov in 2022[280].

The German orientalist E. Zachau first published the Arabic text of this work in London in 1887, and then an English translation there in 1888.

The manuscript of the work was found by L. in the early 20s of the 20th century. Massinon was found in the Koprulu Library in Istanbul under the number 11589[281]. In 1930, I. Hauer wrote about this manuscript. Hauer wrote about this manuscript. Later, G. Ritter dealt with it and in 1955 published an article in Persian in a collection dedicated to Ibn Sina in Teheran. In 1956, the same scholar published the complete Arabic text of this work in the journal Oriens (Leiden).

«India» was hardly mentioned by Arab writers; even Yakut Hamavi did not write about it in his work. Only al-Idrisi in «Nuzhat al-Mushtaq» and Rashididdin in «Jami al-Tawarikh» quote chapter XVIII in full. Some Persian authors (Gardizi, Auffi) give only small quotations from it. This situation also indicates that the manuscripts of the work were not widely distributed. It is a fortunate event that the work has survived to the present day, moreover, it arrived in the form of an ancient copy copied from the original on the 4th day of Jumad-ul-Awal 554 AH / 24 May 1159 AD. Three other later copies arrived (one from Paris, the other from Istanbul). All written traditions of this work and even quotations from it by Eastern authors go back to the manuscript in its composition on which Schäfer based his edition.

E. Zahau worked on his publication for 20 years, with some interruptions, and it was a truly important publication. His publications and translations, his detailed acquaintance with Beruni, his time and his works, his comments and indicators were rightly recognised by the community and took their rightful place in scholarship. Both editions were later reprinted in 1910 and 1925 without the stereotypes.

Publications in Uzbekistan:

---

[280] Abu Rayhan Beruni. Selected works. India. T.2. Translation from Arabic by A. Akhmedov and [Abdufattah Rasulov]. The authors of the preface, comments and indicators are A. Akhmedov and M. Khandamova. – Tashkent: "Uzbekistan", 2022.
[281] L. Massignon. Essaisur les origins du lexique de la mustique musulmane, Paris, 1922, p. 79; 2-нашр, Paris, 1954, p. 97

Abu Rayhon Biruni. Selected works. «India» translated by A.B. Khalidov and Yu.N. Zavadovsky. T. II. Tashkent. Publishing House of the Academy of Sciences of the USSR, 1963;

Abu Rayhon Beruni. Selected works. «India». T. II. Translated from the Arabic by A. Rasulov, Y. Khakimjonov and G. Djalolov. Tashkent, «Science», 1965;

Abu Rayhon Beruni. Selected works. India. J.2. Translation from the Arabic by A. Akhmedov and [Abdufattah Rasulov]. The authors of the preface, comments and notes are A. Akhmedov and M. Khandamova. Tashkent, «Uzbekistan», 2022.

Abu Rahman Beruni's book India mentions seven treatises on India, and their number is estimated to be more than[282]. Some of them are devoted to specific sciences. In terms of content, they covered topics such as the Indian accounting system, concepts of solar and lunar eclipses, 'position of the moon', 'fixed stars' and 'astrological' concepts.

India, the largest work on the history of the Indians by the encyclopaedist Abu Rayhon Beruni, also contains information on specific sciences. The main attention is given to the analysis of books on Indian astronomy:

Chapter 14: Surya-siddhanta, Vasishtha-siddhanta, Romaka-siddhanta, Pulisa-siddhanta, Brahma-siddhanta;

Chapter 15 deals with the Indian system of units of measurement;

Chapter 16 deals with accounting;

Chapter 18 contains a geographical description of India, distances;

Astronomy and time measurement in chapter 19;

Questions of astronomy and geography in chapters 20 and 21;

Time measurement in chapters 32-45;

Astronomy in chapters 45-48;

The concepts of «chronology» in Chapters 49-53;

Astronomy in Chapters 54-55;

Lunar addresses in chapter 56;

Chapter 57 is the time of the rising stars;

---

[282] Abu Reyhan Biruni, India. - Moscow: 2008. – 202 p.

Astronomy in chapter 59;

Chapter 60 is devoted to the lunar eclipse.

India was first published from Arabic into German (1888, reprinted 1910) by the German orientalist Eduard Zachau, who undertook extensive research into the sources. Publications of «India» continued in the following years (Arabic text, Hyderabad, 1958); translation into Russian, 1963 (translators - A.B. Khalidov, Yu.N.Zavadovsky); translation from Arabic text into Uzbek, 1965 (edited by translators - A. Rasulev, Y. Khakimjonov, G. Djalolov, A. Irisov).

Many scientific studies have been carried out on the work «India». Including in the field of exact sciences. For example, mathematical problems of the work were first studied in Europe in the work of B. Boncompany (1869).

WORK OF ABU RAYKHAN BERUNI «GEODESY»

The scientific study of «geodesy» began in the 20th century. In 1913, O.Rescher gives general information about the only manuscript of the work, which is kept in the Sultan Fatih Library in Istanbul under the number № 3386. 1930 H.Ritter gives a brief description of the work.

In 1962, P. G. Bulgakov published a critical text of the work in Arabic, based on a photocopy of the Istanbul manuscript of «Geodesy» in Cairo. In the same year, the Turkish historian of science M.T.Tanci independently publishes a critical text of this manuscript in Ankara.

In 1966, P.G. Bulgakov published a Russian translation of «Geodesy» based on the Arabic text he had published, with a detailed introductory article and philological and historical-geographical notes. On the basis of the Arabic text published by Bulgakov, Jamil Ali published a complete English translation of Geodesy without notes in Beirut in 1967. In 1973 E.S. Kennedy wrote Geodesy on the basis of this translation. I will publish his notes as a separate book. So the publications from Uzbekistan are in the following order:

Abu Rayhon Biruni. Selected works. «Geodesy», T. III. Research, translation and application of P.G.Bulgakov. Tashkent. Publishing house «SCIENCE» UzSSR, 1966;

Abu Rayhon Beruni. Selected works. «Geodesy», author of the introduction, translation and comments A.Akhmedov. T. III. Tashkent, «SCIENCE», 1982;

Abu Rayhon Beruni. Selected works. Geodesy. Volume 3. Translators - A.Akhmedov and B. Abdullaev. The author of the preface is A.Akhmedov. Notes and indicators A.Akhmedov, compiled by B.Abdullaev and U.Kuranbaeva. Tashkent, «Uzbekistan», 2022[283].

In 1926, the only copy of the work in Istanbul was studied by V.V. Bartold, from which extracts of the part concerning the history of Khorezm were copied and translated into Russian by S.L. Volin in 194[284].

The first scientific study related to the exact sciences from this work was published in Calcutta in 1951 and was devoted to the history of the measurement of the longitude of the Earth's meridian. The scientific-critical text of the work was first prepared and published in 1962 by at-Tanji in Ankara and then in the same year in Cairo by P.G.Bulgakov. P.G.Bulgakov translated the work into Russian and published it in Tashkent in 1966, together with a preface and scientific comments, which amounted to a large volume of research[285].

«Geodesy» by Abu Rayhon Beruni consists of a large introduction, five chapters devoted entirely to questions of geodesy, that is, a major work in the field of philosophical sciences. In it we will mathematically determine the latitude by the height of the stars and the height of the Sun, measure the angle of deviation of the ecliptic, find the maximum deviation and show the study of these issues in the history of science, highlight the concept of «geographical longitude» in the historical aspect, gives an idea of the prime meridians, measuring the size of the Earth, deep scientific

---

[283] Akhmedov A. Contents of the work "Geodesy" and the scientific iSSU,es presented in it // Beruniy Abu Raikhan. Determination of address boundaries to determine distances (between) residential buildings (Geodesy) // Selected works. Volume III. - T.: NMIU "Uzbekistan", 2022.
[284] Bulgakov P.G. Life and works of Beruni. - Tashkent: Science, 1972. - P.161-163.
[285] Bulgakov P.G. Life and works of Beruni. - Tashkent: Science, 1972. – 164 p.; Abu Reyhan Biruni. Selected works, T.111. Determination of the boundaries of places to clarify distances between populated areas ("Geodesy"), research, translation and notes by P.G. Bulgakov. - Tashkent: Science, 1966.

problems of that time, such as measuring the distances between settlements on Earth based on their geographical coordinates, determining the direction of Qibla. Both practical and theoretical aspects of the problem are covered. The scientific conclusions in Geodesy are based directly on the results of observations and calculations made by Abu Rayhon Beruni himself, in other words, on geodetic and astronomical observations. In this work, Abu Rayhon Beruni separated geodesy from astronomy and established it as a separate science.

One of the important problems solved by Beruni in his «Geodesy» is the measurement of the Earth's radius. He made these measurements at Nandna Fort during one of Mahmud Ghazni's campaigns in India around 1020.

Beruni first used important trigonometric formulae in his work 'Geodesy', written much earlier than his other major works. Abu Rayhon Beruni invented important rules of spherical trigonometry in his Geodesy.

Abu Rayhon Beruni "Tamhid al-mustakar or tahqiq maan al-mamarr" (تمهيد المستقر لتحقيق المعني الممر) Treatise (Preparation of a reliable basis for clarifying the concept of transition [of lights]»)

The treatise highlights the astronomical problem of the passage of luminaries through certain points of the celestial sphere. It is also interpreted from an astrological point of view. The treatise lists the names of famous but little known scientists of the ancient Greek, Indian and Middle Eastern written heritage in the field of exact sciences[286].

The full title of the treatise «Cartography» is «The Book of Reflection of Constellations on a Flat Surface and Images of Countries on a Flat Surface» («Risala fi tastih al-suwar wa tabtih al-kuwar»). It is described in an article by A. Akhmedov in collaboration with B. A. Rosenfeld, which is noted as one of the first works of the scientist. A translation into Russian of the only copy of the treatise kept in the library

---
[286] Akhmedov A. Beruniy "On the preparation of a reliable basis for clarifying the concept of the passage of lights" // Sharqshunoslik. №. 12. - Tashkent, 1994. - P.58 - 63.

of the University of Leiden is also provided[287]. It is described in the monograph by P.G. Bulgakov. In the list of works of the scientist-encyclopedist it is called «Istiyab fi tastih al-qura» (استعاب في تسطيح الكرة) - «The last (collection) on the lowering of a sphere on a flat surface»[288].

Previously, this work was translated into Uzbek and published by A.Rasulov[289].

Some works written in the field of philosophical sciences in Khorezm in the 10th-12th centuries belong to the pen of Abu Ali ibn Sina. Although Ibn Sina is best known in the field of medicine, he is a scientist who worked in the field of exact sciences. For example, his Arabic Kitab ash-shifa, Kitab al-najot and Donishnoma, written in Persian, also deal separately with issues related to mathematics and physics.

In general, there are many works attributed to Ibn Sina, and it is known that their list was compiled by Abu Ubayd Abdulwahid al-Juzhani, a student of the scientist. The manuscript containing the list of works attributed to Ibn Sina, which is kept in the treasury of the Abu Rayhon Beruni Institute of Oriental Studies[290], contains the names of 148 works. K. Brockelman listed 250[291] works in his catalogue, J.S.Kanawati listed 276 works in his catalogue, and the Iranian scholar Said Nasafi listed 456 works (of which 242 have reached us)[292]. Ibn Sina's works expressed scientific views related to a number of areas of exact sciences - classification of exact sciences, mathematics, astronomy, physics, mechanics, optics, music theory.

When writing the monograph, we used the works of scientists who contributed to the study of the development of philosophical sciences and social relations in Khorezm in the 10th-12th centuries - Ibn Iraq, Abu Raikhan Beruni, Ibn Sina and

---

[287] Akhmedov A., Rosenfeld B.A. "Cartography" is one of the first works of Beruni that have come down to us // Mathematics in the Middle Ages East. - Tashkent: Science, 1978. - P.127-153.
[288] Bulgakov P.G. Life and works of Beruni. - Tashkent: 1972. – 309 p.
[289] (Beruni). On the projection of constellations and the movement of places (on the map) (Cartography), translation from Arabic by A. Rasulov // To the 1000th anniversary of the birth of Beruni. - Tashkent: 1973. - P. 244-259.
[290] Manuscript of the Institute of Oriental Studies of the Academy of Sciences of the Republic of Uzbekistan, №2385/X1, "Fehrist kutub al-Sheikh ar-rais." For more details, see also: B.A.Vakhabova. Manuscripts of Ibn Sina's works in the collection of the Institute of Oriental Studies of the Academy of Sciences of the Uzbek SSR. - Tashkent: Science, 1982. - P.72; Collection of oriental manuscripts AN Ruz. Medicine. Compiled by: Kh. Khikmatullaev, S.U. Karimova. - Tashkent: 2000. - 302 p.
[291] Brockkelman C. Geschicte der Arabishen Literatur, 1. – Berlin, 1902. - P.452- 458.
[292] Vakhabova B.A. Manuscripts of Ibn Sina's works in the collection of the Institute of Oriental Studies of the Academy of Sciences of the Uzbek SSR. -Tashkent: Science, 1982. - P.3-4.

others. It should be noted that parts (chapters) of their works related to philosophical sciences, or major works, were translated into Russian and published, and we referred to these translations during the study.

G.P. Matviyevskaya published a special article studying information, translations and related research in the works of Ibn Sina[293].

Ibn Sina's treatise «Donishnomai Alai» (other names: «Kitobi Alai», «Hikmati Alai») was written in honour of Aluddavla Abu Jafar Muhammad ibn Dushmanzar (398/1007 - 483/1041). This is because Ibn Sina lived in his palace for some time.

The «Donishnama» consists of five treatises, each devoted to a branch of science of the time: logic, physics, ilm al-haya, music, and the supernatural sciences, i.e. metaphysics[294].

This work also included mathematical knowledge, which was initially lost, but after Ibn Sina's death was recovered by his disciple[295]. Thus, it can be said that Ibn Sina's scientific comments on astronomical and mathematical knowledge were taken from this treatise.

It is known that Ibn Sina's work «Donishnama» was translated into Russian[296] and in the West - into French[297]. Based on this, some parts were translated into Russian and published. In particular, the parts related to mathematics were translated by B.A. Rosenfeld and N.A. Sadovsky (1967)[298].

One of the scholars of the Khorezm Mamun Academy is Abu Nasr ibn Iraq. He is believed to have been born between 961 and 965 and died between 1034 and 1036; G.P.Matviyevskaya, Kh.Tlashev are co-authors of the article «The Scientific Heritage of Ibn Iraq»[299], his full name is given as Abu Nasr Mansur ibn Ali ibn Iraq, and it is

---

[293] Matviyevskaya G.P. From the history of studying the physical and mathematical heritage of Ibn Sina // Mathematics and astronomy in the works of Ibn Sina, his contemporaries and followers. – Tashkent, 1981. - P. 16-40.

[294] Manuscript of the Institute of Oriental Studies of the Academy of Sciences of the Republic of Uzbekistan, № 2385/XVII - XIX.

[295] Vakhabova B.A. Manuscripts of Ibn Sina's works in the collection of the Institute of Oriental Studies of the Academy of Sciences of the Uzbek SSR. – Tashkent: Science, 1982. - P.30-31.

[296] Ibn Sina. "Danish-name." Translation and introductory article by A.M. Bogoutdinov. - Dushanbe, 1957.

[297] Avicenne. Le ivre de science, t.1. – Paris: 1955; t.II. (Physique - mathematiques), trad.par. M. Achena et H.Masse. - Paris,1958.

[298] Ibn Sina, Abu Ali. Mathematical chapters of the "Book of Knowledge" (Donishnoma). – Dushanbe: Irfon, 1967.

[299] Matviyevskaya G.P., Tllashev Kh. On the scientific heritage of the astronomer of the 10th-11th centuries. Abu Nasr ibn Iraq // Historical and astronomical studies. ISSU,e XIII. - Moscow, 1977. - P.219-234.

indicated that he came from a family of Iraqis belonging to the Khorezm Shah dynasty. Ibn Iraq lived first in the city of Qat and then in Gurganj, the capital of the Khorezm Shahs. After Mahmud Ghaznavi conquered Khorezm in 1017 and took the scientists to Ghazna, he lived in Ghazna.

In the article mentioned above, it is stated that 25 works belong to the pen of Ibn Iraq, most of which have come down to us, and some of which are known from other works, and a list of these works is also given. In this list, each of his works on astronomy and mathematics is listed separately, with a brief indication of the time when they were written, whether they have survived, or if not, which Orientalist is mentioned in the work, and the study was written. Some of Ibn Iraq's treatises were published as a separate collection in 1943-1947 in Hyderabad, India.

In her book on the history of trigonometry, G.P. Matviyevskaya gives a brief summary of Ibn Iraq's works on astronomy and mathematics[300].

«Al-Majisti al-Shahi» («Shahi al-magest») is the main work of Ibn Iraq. It has not survived and some of its fragments can be found in the treatises of Abu Rayhon Beruni and Nasriddin Tusi[301].

Ibn Iraq is known to have written commentaries on the works of a number of scholars who lived before him. For example, «Treatise on Proofs of Abyssinian Calculations Using Correction Tables» or «Table of Minutes» (رسالة في جدول الدقائق), which write about trigonometric functions used in solving problems of spherical astronomy. This work was studied by K. Jensen (1971), who concluded that the method of calculation in it corresponds to Greek science, more precisely to the period of Claudius Ptolemy[302].

In a work entitled «Treatise on the Evidence of the Narratives of Muhammad ibn al-Sabah», Ibn Iraq again points out the errors made by al-Sabah regarding the deviation of the ecliptic from the celestial equator[303].

Ibn Iraq also has works on the manufacture of astrolabes. The article by Kh. Tlashev and S.A. Ramazonova notes that four treatises of the scientist are devoted to

---

[300] Matviyevskaya G.P. Essays on the history of trigonometry. - Tashkent: Science, 1990. - P.106-110.
[301] Matviyevskaya G.P. Essays on the history of trigonometry. - Tashkent: Science, 1990. – 108 p.

the astronomical instrument - the astrolabe, and some examples are given: 1) «Treatise on the Astrolabe» («Treatise-asturlab»); 2) «Treatise on the Dispute between Abu Hamid al- Saghani and the astronomer Ray about working with the astrolabe» (مقالة في منازعة الأعمال الاسترلاب التي وقعت بين أبي حميد الساغا ي و بين منجمي الرى); 3) «Treatise on the intersection (finding points) of azimuthal circles on an astrolabe (plane)» («Risala davoir as-sumut fi al-asturlab») (رسالة دوائر السموت في الاسترلاب), in other words, this treatise on the intersection of azimuth circles with the horizon and the equator, devoted to the problem of finding points on the astrolabe plane; 4) «Treatise on the Production of Astrolabes by a Practical Method» («Risala fi san'at al-asturlob bit-t-tarik al-sanai») (رساة في صنعة الاسترلاب بالطريق الصناعي)[304].

His mathematical works are more related to spherical astronomy, more precisely to trigonometry. In particular the interpretation of the work «Spherics» by the Greek scientist Menelaus using the method of trigonometry («Maqola fi islah shakl Manalus fi kuriyyat») (مقالة في اصلاح شكل مناوس في الكرية) in the scientific literature «Islah shakl kitab Manalus fi ashkol»al- quriyyat» (اصلاح شكل كتاب منالوس في أشكال الكرية) «Islah kitab Manalus fil Ashkol al-quriyyat» (also written in the form اصلاح كتاب منالوس في الأشكال الكرية) is his new approach. The text of the work was translated into German in 1936 by M. Krause from a single copy in the library of the University of Leiden and published with a detailed philological study[305].

This work consists of three chapters in which we talk about spherical triangles, the position of parallel circles on the surface of a sphere, and lemmas about basic relations[306].

«Risala fi-l-jawab masa'il al- handasa» by Ibn Iraq (رسالة في الجواب مسائل الغياميترية) («Answers to Questions on Geometry») and «Theorem of sines on plane and spherical surfaces and its application to rectangular and oblique surfaces», «Risala fi

---

[304] Tllashev Kh., Ramazanova S.A. Treatises of Abu Nasr ibn Iraq on asolabia // Mathematics and astronomy in the works of scientists of the Middle Ages East. - Tashkent: Science, 1977. - P. 89-97; 142.
[305] Krause M. Die Sphärik von Abu Nasr Mansur b. 'Ali b. Iraq, mit Untersuchungen zur Geschichte des Textes bei den islamischen Mathematiker // Berlin, 1936. – 10 c.; Matviyevskaya G.P., Tllashev H. On the scientific heritage of the astronomer of the 10th-11th centuries. Abu Nasr ibn Iraq // Historical and astronomical studies. ISSU,e XIII. – Moscow, 1977. – 219 p.
[306] Matviyevskaya G.P., Tllashev Kh. On the scientific heritage of the astronomer of the 10th-11th centuries. Abu Nasr ibn Iraq // Historical and astronomical studies. ISSU,e XIII. – Moscow, 1977. - P.223-230.

tastih, ma wa ka li Abu Jafar al-Khazin min as-sahw fi zij as-safaih» (رسالة في تسطيح ما وقع لأبي جعفر الحازن من السهو في زيج السفائح), («Abu Jafar al-Khazin in his «Zij» treatise on the correction of the forgotten»), his next two works were studied by G. Sutter and M.T.Debarno[307].

Abu Abdullah Muhammad ibn Ahmad ibn Yusuf al-Khwarizmi (d. 997) was born and raised in Khorezm, educated (mainly in Kat), then lived in various cities of the Samanid state (Nishapur, Bukhara), minister of the Samanids, in Nishapur (977-982) Abulhasan al - worked as a secretary in the military service[308]. His knowledge in the field of classification of sciences was formed under the influence of ancient Greek scientists, as well as the works of al-Kindi, Abu Nasr Farabi, Abu Bakr al-Razi, and later he became an important encyclopaedist in this direction[309].

The most important work in the field of classification of sciences is «Mafatih al-ulum» (مفاتيح العلوم) («The Key of Sciences») - an encyclopaedic work that provides information about the science and culture of the Muslim countries of the East of its time and covers almost all the fields of that time: jurisprudence, philosophy, logic, poetry, arithmetic, geometry, chemistry, etc., 93 chapters in all. According to tradition, Abu Abdullah divides the sciences into two groups, the «sciences of the Sharia» and the «sciences of the laity».

The work is divided into two parts, which in turn are divided into fifteen sections.

The first part covers jurisprudence, speech, grammar, writing, the theory of poetry and history; the second part provides information on philosophy, logic, medicine, arithmetic, geometry, astronomy, music, mechanics and chemistry.

Specific sciences in the work are discussed in the works of G.P.Matviyevskaya[310], B.A.Rosenfeld[311], M.M.Rozhanskaya[312], Kh.Gasanov[313]. In

---

[307] Matviyevskaya G.P. Essays on the history of trigonometry. – Tashkent: Science, 1990. – 30 p.
[308] Krachkovsky I.Yu. Selected works. T.IV. – Tashkent, 1967. – 240 p.
[309] Khairullayev M.M., Bakhadirov R.M. Abu Abdullah al-Khwarizmi. - Moscow: Nauka, 1988. – 144 p.; R.M.Bakhadirov. From the history of the classification of sciences in the medieval Muslim East. – Tashkent: Science, 2000. – 244 p.
[310] Matviyevskaya G.P. Arabic medieval encyclopedias as sources on the history of mathematics and astronomy of the Near and Middle East / Mathematics in the Middle East. - Tashkent, 1978. - P.88-96; Matviyevskaya G.P. The doctrine of number in the medieval Near and Middle East. - Tashkent: Science, 1967. - 341 p.

his research R.M.Bakhadirov separately described the fields of calculation, geometry, astronomy, music and mechanics[314].

In the part of Abu Abdullah al-Khwarizmi's Mafatih al-Uloom relating to the exact sciences, much attention is paid to theoretical accounting, which occupies four of the five chapters devoted to accounting in this work; the fifth chapter is devoted to practical accounting. Information on accounting was studied by G.P. Matviyevskaya[315]. Zh.Kh.Ibodov translated chapters on exact sciences from Arabic into Russian with comments[316].

In Mafatih al-Uloom, the section on geometry consists of four chapters: the first chapter is about the theoretical part, the second chapter is about lines, the third chapter is about flat geometric figures, the fourth chapter is about the geometric shapes of bodies (cube, cone, sphere).

The astronomical part of the treatise consists of four chapters: 1) the position of the fixed and variable stars in the constellations; 2) the position of the stars in the sphere of the universe, on the surface of the earth, its climate and other elements of mathematical geography; 3) the basics of astrology; 4) astronomical instruments are discussed.

An important source for writing the monograph were manuscripts related to certain sciences kept in the treasury of the Institute of Oriental Studies of the Academy of Sciences of the Republic of Uzbekistan named after Abu Rayhon Beruni. Manuscripts related to specific sciences are included in the eleven-volume catalogues of manuscripts published in Russian by the Institute of Oriental Studies of the Faculty of Uzbekistan named after Abu Rayhona Beruni. Abu Rayhona Beruni[317]

---

[311] Matviyevskaya G.P., Rosenfeld B.A. Mathematicians and astronomers of the Muslim Middle Ages and their works (VIII-XVII centuries). – Moscow, 1983. Book. 1, 2, 3.
[312] Rozhanskaya M.M. Mechanics in the Middle Ages East. – Moscow, 1976.
[313] Khasanov H. Geographers and tourists of Central Asia. - Tashkent, 1964.
[314] Khairullayev M.M.: Bakhadirov R.M. Abu Abdullah al-Khwarizmi. - Moscow: Science, 1988. - P.90-102; 144; R.M. Bakhadirov. From the history of the classification of sciences in the medieval Muslim East. Tashkent: Science, 2000. - pp. 94-98, 244.
[315] Matviyevskaya G.P. The doctrine of number in the medieval Near and Middle East. – Tashkent: Science, 1967. – 341 p.
[316] Ibadov J.Kh. Physics and mathematics chapters of the encyclopedia "Keys of Sciences" (Mafatih al-ulum) by Abu Abdullah al-Khorezmi. – Tashkent: TATU, 2005. - 54 p.
[317] Collection of eastern manuscripts of the Academy of Sciences of the Republic of Uzbekistan.T.I-XI. - Tashkent: Science, 1952-1987.

and «Catalogue of Oriental Manuscripts of Academy of Sciences of the Republic of Uzbekistan». It is described in Russian in a separate book «Exact and Natural Sciences» (1998)[318]. We have used these publications. In the collection, which is devoted to the philosophical and natural sciences, the Oriental manuscripts are described in Arabic, Persian and Turkish in the order of scientific directions. It is also divided into the fields of arithmetic, algebra, geometry, astronomy and astrology, astronomical instruments, calendars, geography: the dictionaries are also divided, with chapters on both philosophy and the exact sciences.

Only a few of the works mentioned above are relevant to our study. These are «At-Tafhim» by Abu Rayhon Beruni[319], «Kunuz al-ma'rifa» by Ibn Sina[320] and «Ganj al-maruf»[321], «Correspondence of Abu Rayhon Beruni and Ibn Sina»[322], Mahmud al-Chag' mini «Al-Mulahhas» fi-l-haya»[323] and consists of manuscripts written by Ali al-Jurjani[324], Ghazizad Rumi[325] and commentaries in Persian[326] written by Husayn al-Kubrawi.

The above-mentioned collections also describe a manuscript of the Central Asian scientist Abu Nasr Farabi's treatise «Astronomy and Astrology» entitled «Treatise on Reliable and Unreliable Things According to the Stars»[327]. This treatise examines the corresponding, rather hard-to-believe realities associated with the

---

[318] Collection of oriental manuscripts of the Academy of Sciences of the Republic of Uzbekistan. Exact and natural sciences. Composer A.B. Vildanova. – Tashkent: Science, 1998. – 248 p.

[319] Beruni Abu Rayhan. At-tafhim li wali sinaa at-tanjim: Manuscript of the Academy of Sciences of the Republic of Uzbekistan. Institute of Oriental Studies named after Abu Rayhan Beruni, № 3423, in Persian.

[320] Ibn Sina Abu Ali. Kunuz al-Marifa. Academy of Sciences of the Republic of Uzbekistan. Institute of Oriental Studies named after Abu Rayhan Beruni, № 2385/22, in Persian.

[321] Ibn Sina Abu Ali. Ganj al-Maruf. Academy of Sciences of the Republic of Uzbekistan. Institute of Oriental Studies named after Abu Rayhan Beruni № 3374/5, in Persian.

[322] Risola ila Abu Rayhan Muhammad ib Ahmad al-Biruni. Manuscript of the Academy of Sciences of the Republic of Uzbekistan. Institute of Oriental Studies named after Abu Rayhan Beruni, 2385/XIV, in Arabic.

[323] Al-Chagmini Mahmud ibn Muhammad ibn Umar. Al-mulahas fil haya. Manuscripts of the Academy of Sciences of the Republic of Uzbekistan. Institute of Oriental Studies named after Abu Rayhan Beruni, 10417; 7761/III; 8796/II; 11599/III.

[324] Ash-Sharkh "Al-mulahhas fil haya." Manuscript of the Academy of Sciences of the Republic of Uzbekistan. Institute of Oriental Studies named after Abu Rayhan Beruni, №. 2655.

[325] Commentary "Al-mulahhas fil haya" Manuscripts of the Academy of Sciences of the Republic of Uzbekistan. Institute of Oriental Studies named after Abu Rayhan Beruni: № 8217, " 3935 and p. /20 total).

[326] Al-Kubrawi Hussein ibn al-Hasan al-Khwarizmi. Nuzhat al-mallok fi hayat al-aflok. Manuscript of the Academy of Sciences of the Republic of Uzbekistan. Institute of Oriental Studies named after Abu Rayhan Beruni, No. 1207/III.

[327] Farabi Abu Nasr. Risala fi mo yasukh wa mo lo yasukh min ahkom an-nujum: Manuscript of the Institute of Oriental Studies named after Abu Raikhan Beruni of the Academy of Sciences of the Republic of Uzbekistan, № 2385/XXXIII.

position of the stars, the description of celestial bodies, and issues of their interrelationship.

Most of the works on specific sciences described in the collection come from outside Central Asia.

Katib Chalabi, real name Mustafa ibn Abdullah (1017/1609 -1065/1657), Turkish geographer and historian, author of more than 20 works, including «Jahonnama» («Mirror of the World»), historical and geographical, «Kashf al-Zunun». Author of famous bibliographical treatises.

We have used the bibliographical work of Haji Khalifa in writing the monography.

In its entirety, the work is called «Kashf az-zunun an asami al-kutub wa-l-funun» (كشف الظنون عن أسامي الكتب والفنون) («Removing doubts about the names of books and sciences»). It consists of an introduction, general information on the subject, a bibliography and a conclusion. The main part - the bibliography - contains information on 15,000 works, 10,000 authors and more than 300 fields of science.

«Kashf az-zunun» was published by G. Flügel in 1835-1858 with an Arabic text and a Latin translation in seven volumes[328] and later served as a basic book for many scholars; in the following years the work was published several times in Turkey and Lebanon[329].

In Haji Khalifa's work, Kashf az-zunun, many names of Khorezm scholars are mentioned. Including bibliographical information about Khorezm scientists who worked in the field of exact sciences and their scientific heritage. For example, Muhammad ibn Musa al-Khorezmi, Abu Ali al-Hasan ibn Haris al-Khorezmi al-Khububi, Abu Ali ibn Sina, Abu Rayhon Beruni and others.

Chapter summaries:

Analysing the above sources, we can draw the following conclusions:

---

[328] Haji Khalfa. Lexicon encyclopedicum et bibliographicum./ Primum edidit Latine yertit et commenterto indificibusque G.Fluegel.- Leipzig - London, 1835-1858. 1 - 7 vol.
[329] Abdukhalimov B.A. "Kashf az-zunun" by Hadji Khalifa as a source on the history of the exact sciences of Maverannahr and Khorasan. Abstract for the degree of candidate of historical sciences. - Tashkent, 1994.

1. In the X-XII centuries, in Khorezm, from the point of view of their time, very large scientific researches were carried out in the field of exact sciences. For example, scientific works written during the reign of Mamun Khorezm Shah can be cited as evidence of the scientific achievements of that period.

2. In Khorezm in the X-XII centuries, the attention to concrete and philosophical sciences increased comparatively, and it should be noted that this arose primarily from everyday practical needs, i.e. scientific research in this direction was connected with such factors as the development of irrigated agriculture in Khorezm, the expansion of trade relations, the rise of cultural and spiritual life. Astronomical observations arose from immediate practical needs and were considered necessary for the correct organisation of agricultural work in ancient Khorezm, for determining the water content of the Amu Darya and its effective use.

3. It is possible to draw conclusions about the achievements in the field of natural and exact sciences on the basis of the monuments of the time, i.e. the written heritage. To this end, work was carried out such as the publication of critical texts of existing sources, their translation into other languages, or the printing of individual parts in the form of tablets with scientific annotations. Among the scientists who worked in Khorezm in the X-XII centuries and wrote works in the field of various sciences, the works of Abu Raikhan Beruni, Abu Ali ibn Sina, Abu Nasr ibn Iraq, Mahmud Chagmini, etc. can be mentioned.

4. With the publication of primary sources, more opportunities for scientific research appeared, including the study of the history of science and philosophy.

5. An analysis of the sources on the subject shows that only some of them are currently in scholarly circulation, and much work remains to be done in this direction.

6. Among the studies devoted to the natural and philosophical sciences, the studies consisting in the analysis of the scientific problems mentioned in the sources are more important than the translation of the sources.

7. The achievements of ancient Greek science were introduced in Khorezm in the X-XII centuries in two ways: the first - directly through the translation and assimilation of the works of ancient Greek scientists from Greek into Arabic in

Khorezm. It is known that Abu Nasr Mansur ibn Iraq translated the work of the ancient Greek scientist Menelaus «Sphere» from Greek into Arabic. The second is the translation and development of the works of ancient Greek scientists into Arabic by scientists working in Baghdad, the capital of the Arab Caliphate, and their use by the scientists of the Khorezm Mamun Academy. This can be clearly seen in the work of Abu Rayhon Beruni. In his work «Geodesy», he provides information from the Greek scientists Eratosthenes, Hipparchus and Ptolemy («Geography» and «Almagest»). Thus, we can say that in the X-XII centuries, the achievements of ancient Greek science were creatively used in the scientific environment of Khorezm, developed by making corrections and changes.

8. A collection of scientific and philosophical knowledge in the encyclopaedic work of Abu Ali ibn Sina «Kitab ash-shifa»: consists of four parts, the first is logical (al-ilm al-mantiqi), the second is physics (al-ilm at-tabii), the third is mathematical sciences (al-ulum ar-mathematician), the fourth - metaphysics (al-ulum al-alihiyya) consists of details, and its information is of great importance today.

CHAPTER II. DEVELOPMENT OF SOCIAL AND PHILOSOPHICAL THINKING IN NATURAL SCIENTIFIC APPROACHES OF KHOREZM MAMUN ACADEMY

The origins of the development of philosophical knowledge in Khorezm from ancient times to the 11th century, the formation of the Khorezm Ma'mun Academy, the scientists who worked in it, the development of mathematical sciences, disasters, calculations and geometry in the Khorezm Ma'mun Academy: this chapter scientifically discusses postulates, axioms and theories of development of parallels, their influence on social life. The progress made so far in the field of philosophical knowledge also proves to us that the formation of geometry as a science began in ancient Greece. However, however developed the geometrical ideas of the peoples of the ancient world were, they were not able to systematise them and bring them into a single form, as in Euclid's work «Fundamentals». Nevertheless, the history of geometry begins in the distant past of the ancient world. Information about it is given by the ancient historians Eudemus (4th century BC), Plutarch (50-120), Diogenes Laertius (3rd century), Proclus (410-485), Herodotus (414-425), Xenophanes (430-385) and other works. According to them, geometry passed from Sumer-Babylon to Ancient Greece.

In Ancient Greece, the exact sciences developed together with philosophy. This system separated geometry from practical matters in the time of Plato, only Archimedes (287-212 BC) combined its theoretical structure with practice according to the needs of the time. During the 7th-5th centuries BC in Ancient Greece, a lot of information was collected in the field of geometry; it was necessary to systematise it and put it in a strict order. This work was done by Euclid in his Principles in the 4th century BC.

Central Asia is one of the ancient centres of civilisation. In the 8th and 9th centuries, Central Asia was part of the Arab Caliphate. During this period, culture and science flourished in the centres of the Caliphate - Baghdad and Damascus.

In the VI-XII centuries. Great progress was made in the fields of central processing, horticulture and animal husbandry. Especially the IX-XII centuries were a period of great growth of the peoples of this country. Especially the IX-XII centuries were a period of great growth of Khorezm. During the reigns of the caliphs al-Mansur (754-776), Harun al-Rashid (786-809) and Mamun (813-833), interest in translations of Indian and Greek literature increased. philosophers studied. At the beginning of the 9th century, Dar ul-Hikmat - the House of Knowledge - was founded in Baghdad. In this dargah, scholars invited from different cities of the caliphate studied astronomy, medicine, history, geography, chemistry, philosophy and other sciences in detail. Al-Mamun was a scientist and the initiator of frequent scientific discussions in the Bayt al-Hikmah. This led to a sharp increase in the number of scientists, translators and various types of scholars[330]. The peoples of Central Asia have a great history. In this land, from the 9th century BC to the 7th century BC, the culture of cities developed continuously.

At the beginning of the 9th century, the Soman state was first established, but in the 20s of the 13th century, the Khorezm state was subject to continuous attacks from the Mongols. However, despite centuries of warfare, culture, science, art and literature continued to develop in Central Asia. The features of the Khorezm Mamun Academy, the process of its formation, the development of science in various fields, its application in practice, science during the Anushteginid-Khorezm Shah period, the restoration of the Khorezm Mamun Academy in Uzbekistan, the development and prospects of its world science is one of the most pressing problems.

2.1. Creation of the Khorezm Mamun Academy, turning it into a natural scientific and socio-philosophical center

In the 9th and 10th centuries, several independent states arose on the territory of our country, and from the point of view of political and economic development,

---

[330] Abdukhalimov B. Bayt al-Hikma and the scientific activities of Central Asian scientists in Baghdad. - Tashkent: Tashkent Islamic University. - 2004. - 34 p.

Khorezm had a greater advantage than other countries. Gurganch flourished in the 10th century. It was surrounded by the strong walls of a white castle six metres high. Newly constructed fine buildings add to the beauty of the city. Muqaddasiya (10th century) writes: «Gurganch is expanding day by day, there is nothing in Khorasan that can compare with the gates of the palace built by Mamun in front of the Khojaj Gates. Mamun's son Ali built a palace before him. «In front of the palace there is a square like in Bukhara»[331].

Ali ibn Mamun built hospitals, mosques and madrassas in Gurganj. The streets of the city are clean and orderly. During this period, cleanliness was taken seriously. The laying of polished stones on the streets and the excellent organisation of city life led to a special order of streets in the 9th-12th centuries. Also in the 10th century, Khorezm Shah Ali ibn Mamun carried out many landscaping works in Khorezm and provided direct material support to scientists.

Cities had internal rules that all inhabitants had to follow. According to a written source, their implementation was controlled by a special government official - a specialist. In particular, he was responsible for monitoring the cleanliness of the streets[332].

Scientists of the time travelled to other countries to engage in scientific creativity and improve their knowledge. However, not all rulers liked their free thinking and truthfulness. This forced the followers of science to leave their homeland and seek refuge from the rulers of other countries.

Sometimes the gathering of scientists in one place happened much faster. The same thing happened in the 9th and 11th centuries, when scientists of different abilities and interests moved in different directions. Although scattered across different regions, they gathered in the palaces of rulers who offered them a comfortable life in exchange for their knowledge. In those turbulent times, it was not easy to find such a comfortable place for creative activities. At the end of the 10th

---

[331] Romanova B. R. Pedagogical thoughts of Khorezm poets-educators of the late XIX - early XX centuries: Author. diss.... PhD. ped. science - Tashkent, 1978. - 22 p.
[332] Alimzhanov H. Study of Beruni's activities. Public education. - Tashkent, 1994. - №. 1-2. – 69 p.

and the beginning of the 11th century, Gurganch was free from such upheavals and conditions were favourable for the followers of science.

At the academy of Khorezmshah Ma'mun ibn Ma'mun («Majlisi Ulema») Abu-l-Khair Hammar (X-XI century), Abu Muhammad ibn Khidra al-Khojandi (X-XI century), Ma'mun ibn Ma'mun (d. 1017), Abu Rayhon Beruni, Abu Sahl Isa ibn Yahya al-Jurjani al-Masihi (d. 1011), Abu Nasr ibn Iraq, Abu Sa'id ibn Ahmad ibn Muhammad ibn Miskawaih (d. 1030), Ahmad Muhammad al-Sakhri (d. 1015), Zainuddin Jurjani (10th-11th century), Abulkarim Zirgali (10th-11th century), Abu Ali ibn Sina, Abu Abdullah al-Biyan al-Naysaburi (d. 1004), Ahmad ibn Muhammad al-Sakhri al-Khwarizmi (d. 1015), Abu Mansur al-Salibi (961-1038), Abu Abdullah Ilaqi (d. 1038) and other scholars. They studied various fields of science such as mathematics, astronomy, psychology, alchemy, logic, medicine, philosophy, history, linguistics, pedagogy (education), literature, music, geography, topography, mechanics, geodesy.

The work of the historian and poet Abu Bakr Muhammad ibn al-Abbas al-Khwarizmi (935-993), who was fruitfully active before the establishment of the Khorezm Mamun Academy, also deserves attention.

Abu Bakr Khorezmi occupies a special place among the scientists of the 10th century. Born and raised in Khorezm, he later lived in Aleppo, Bukhara and Nishapur. Despite the hardships of life and conflicts in the palaces of various rulers, he spent his entire life in the pursuit of knowledge. In addition to his creative activities, Alloma mentored many young people and taught students. Thanks to his work with young people, his works are imbued with educational and moral ideas.

Every thinker was a supporter of people with good character and positive qualities. According to him, everyone will be respected by their actions and will rise to the top. This shows that it's everyone's duty to do good to others, to be generous and kind. According to I. Abdullayev: «Goodness is like fame. No matter how much people harm him, a good man will gain glory»[333].

---

[333] Abdullayev I. Poetry in Arabic in Central Asia and Khorasan of the 10th - early 11th centuries. - Tashkent: Science, 1984. - 294 p.

When analysing the history of spiritual and educational development, it is absolutely impossible not to consider the political and economic conditions. In order to study the legacy of the scientists of the Mamun Academy and use it effectively in educational practice, it is necessary to turn to the history of the Khorezm state of that time and analyse the events that took place there.

Abu Mansur ibn Khidr al-Khojandi was a great scientist who worked in the fields of catastrophology and mathematics. He was the first to make a sextant, an instrument used to measure the distance between the earth and the sky. This instrument, known as the «Khojandi Sextant», was the main equipment of the Samarkand Observatory, founded four centuries later by the great astrologer Mirzo Ulugbek, and made it possible to measure the coordinates of luminaries with great accuracy. Later, many observatories in Eastern countries were built on the model of this observatory. The scientific heritage of Al-Khojandi is described in the works «Book on the Universal Instrument», «Problems of Geometry», «Treatise on Calculation», «Book on Southern Azimuth».

Abu Nasr Mansur Ali ibn Iraq - a great mathematician and astrologer, mentor of Abu Rayhon Beruni. The famous poet and scientist Omar Khayyam called him «the greatest of those who studied mathematics». Ibn Iraq's works «Al-Majisti al-Shahi» («King al-Magesti»), «Risala fi zadba masa'il al-Khandasa» («Answers to Khandasa's Questions») and others are well known.

Abu Sahl Isa ibn Yahya al-Jurjani al-Masihi is a great scholar who studied medicine, ethics, psychology and philosophy at the Mamun Academy. He trained many students during his life and scientific work. His works «One Hundred Questions on Medicine», «The Book of the Mind», «The Book of General Medicine» are well known.

According to Abu Usaybia, Masihi was a close friend of Ibn Sina and was his mentor in the field of medicine. Ibn Sina also wrote works dedicated to Sultan

Mahmud Ghaznavi. He died at the age of 40 in 401/1010 while fleeing to Khorasan with Ibn Sina after refusing Sultan Mahmud's invitation to Ghazna[334].

Abul Hakim Al-Qosi is a scientist at the Academy who studied chemistry. His «The Essence and Help of Art» (عين الصنعة و عين الصناعة) («Ain al-sana and ayn as-sana») corresponds to the level of scientific research in Europe in the 13th-14th centuries, and its translation into English in 1905 shows the high level of his knowledge. The Uzbek scientist S. Karimova conducted scientific research on this work of Al-Qosi.

Abu Mansur Abdulmalik ibn Muhammad ibn Ismail al-Salibi is one of the most prolific founders of the Academy, with knowledge in the fields of history, literature, logic and linguistics. Alloma, the author of many works on the problems of human ethics and etiquette, left us a rich legacy. He is the author of «Masterpieces of the Era on the Virtues of the People of the Century», «Best Manners», «Linguistic Laws and Secrets of the Arabic Language», «Amazing Information» and other works.

Abu Ubayd Abd al-Wahid al-Jujani - judge, disciple of Ibn Sina. He studied philosophy, medicine and law. Jujani set an example of dedication in preserving the legacy of his mentor. His famous work is the «Biography of the Chief Scholar (Ibn Sina)». In addition to studying the works of his teacher, Yuzhogni also participated in surgical operations. He wrote works on medicine: «Medicine of the Kings», «The Purpose of Medicine», «Treasures of the Khorezm Shahs», «Memoirs in the Field of Medicine». The largest of these was the 12-volume «Treasures of the Khorezm Shahs»[335]. Although these treatises have not survived, it is known that they made a great contribution to the development of medical science in their time. Scholars were able to use them more widely thanks to the work of the teacher Allama Ibn Sina, who shortened and condensed the work of «Al-Qanun»[336].

---

[334] Sezgin F. Geaschichte des arabischen Schrifltums. - Leiden, 1974. - P. 326.
[335] Masharipova G. The influence of the natural science, socio-philosophical and spiritual heritage of scientists of the Khorezm Mamun Academy on the development of social thinking. Monography. – Tashkent: Navruz, 2019. – 157 p.
[336] Masharipova G. The influence of the natural science, socio-philosophical and spiritual heritage of scientists of the Khorezm Mamun Academy on the development of social thinking. Monography. – Tashkent: Navruz, 2019. – 158 p.

Mamun held scientific discussions with scholars in his palace. They expressed their opinions and argued about various issues in different fields. The winners of this scientific conference were rewarded with valuable gifts.

The scientists were led by Abu Rayhon Beruni, the prime minister of Khorezm, the patron of science, Abu Mansur al-Sakhri, who spared no effort to create a truly creative environment for scientists. Scientists studied in the rich library of Gurganch, deepened the knowledge of their students and broadened their thinking. The representatives of the Academy made a worthy contribution to the rise of science not only in Central Asia, but also in all countries of the East and West[337]. They served to further increase its influence in Movarunnahr and Khorasan.

Abu Raykhan Beruni, head of the Khorezm Mamun Academy, studied under the famous scientist of his time, Abu Nasr ibn Iraq. This teacher wrote several works on catastrophes, geometry and mathematics and dedicated 12 of them to Abu Raykhan Beruni. He introduced him to Euclid's geometry and Ptolemy's doctrine of the Apocalypse.

Abu Nasr Mansur ibn Iraq wrote in one of his scientific works that Abu Rayhon Beruni, although he was very young when he lived in Khorezm, made important observations of disasters in the city of Kot in 384-385 (994-995). AD). He himself invented the instruments for these observations. However, he was only able to determine the farthest, highest point of the ecliptic and the ecliptic without azimuth for the village south of Khorezm on the left bank of the Jeyhun (Amu Darya).

Abu Rayhon Beruni was educated by Abu Nasr ibn Iraq and became a mature scholar. At a young age he had a deep knowledge of mathematics, astrology and other sciences. First of all, it is remarkable that he knew many languages. Judging by the fact that all the scientist's works were written in Arabic, Arabic was the common scientific language in the countries where Islam was spreading at that time, and he

---

[337] Masharipova G. The influence of the natural science, socio-philosophical and spiritual heritage of scientists of the Khorezm Mamun Academy on the development of social thinking. Monography. – Tashkent: Navruz, 2019. – 157 p.

knew the grammar of this language deeply. His Mineralogy, India and other works show that he had an excellent knowledge of Arabic poetry and its meanings[338].

His works such as «Relics of Ancient Peoples», «Kanuni Masudi» and «Saydana» show that Abu Raikhan Beruni knew the Sogdian and Perso-Dari languages very well. According to Saidan, he studied Greek from an early age. He began to learn Sanskrit from Indian merchants in Khorezm at an early age[339].

The fact that Abu Rayhan Beruni was aware of the historical treatises written in these languages in his youth is reflected in his first major work (written between 1000 and 1003), «Relics from Ancient Nations».

His scientific, theoretical and experimental studies are of great scientific importance. In them, the «positions, movements and celestial processes» of the heavenly bodies are studied as follows 1) The fiery sphericity of the Sun and the stars[340], the movement of the stars[341], 2) The movement of the Earth's crust[342] (floating and returning)[343], 3) The rotation of the Earth around its axis[344], 4) The Earth[345], that the Sun and the stars have a spherical shape, 5) The movement of the Sun[346], 6) The rainbow[347], the obstacles[348], sunrise and sunset[349], 7) the solar corona[350], 8) the changing colour of the moon during an eclipse[351], 9) the

---

[338] Beruni Abu Rayhan. Selected works. T.3. Address delimitation to determine distances (between) residential buildings. [Geodesy] // Introduction, translation. and the author of the comments A. Akhmedov. – Tashkent: Science, 1982. – 24 p.

[339] Shamsi F. Abu al-Rayhan al-Bayruni. - P. 194-195; For more information about Beruni and philological iSSU,es, see pp. 41-52 of U.I. Karimov's study "Saidana".

[340] Eremeeva A.I., Tsitsin F.A. History of astronomy. - Moscow State University, 1976. - 114 p.

[341] Eremeeva A.I., Tsitsin F.A. History of astronomy. - Moscow State University, 1976. - 115 p.

[342] Bulgakov P.G. Life and works of Beruni. – Tashkent: Science, 1972. - 183 p.

[343] Beruni Abu Raihan. India. - Tashkent: Science, 1965. – 432 p.

[344] Beruni Abu Raihan. India. - P.255; Sadykov H.U. Beruni and his works on astronomy and mathematical geography. - Moscow: USSR Academy of Sciences, 1953. – 30 p.

[345] Bulgakov P.G. Life and works of Beruni. - Tashkent: Science, 1972. – 245 p.

[346] Sadykov Kh.U. Beruni and his works on astronomy and mathematical geography. - Moscow: USSR Academy of Sciences, 1953. – 29 p.

[347] Zikrillayev F. Beruni's works in the field of physics. - Tashkent: Science, 1973. - 6 p.

[348] Bulgakov P.G. Life and works of Beruni. – Tashkent: Science, 1972. – 120 p.

[349] Sadykov Kh.U. Beruni and his works on astronomy and mathematical geography. - Moscow: USSR Academy of Sciences, 1953. - P. 30, 118.

[350] Sadykov Kh.U. Beruni and his works on astronomy and mathematical geography. - Moscow: USSR Academy of Sciences, 1953. - P. 114, 116.

[351] Sadykov Kh.U. Beruni and his works on astronomy and mathematical geography. - Moscow: USSR Academy of Sciences, 1953. - P. 130.

phenomenon of gravity[352], 10) comets[353], meteors[354], their rain[355], 11) determining the position of the stars[356], 12) the inclination of the ecliptic to the equatorial plane[357], 13) the zodiac[358].

In the field of practical astronomy, Abu Rayhon Beruni expressed ideas on determining the latitude and longitude of places[359] and compiling calendars[360].

In his work «Cartography» he mentions two treatises: the first is «The Book on Compiling a Globe»[361], which is only mentioned in «Cartography», and the second is «The Book on Determining the Longitude and Latitude of the Earth». Places of the Earth»[362]. They are included in the list of scientific works of the encyclopaedist.

Abu Rayhon Beruni writes about lunar addresses in his book «Memorials of Ancient Nations»: «In those days when I was away from the High Court and deprived of the happiness of honourable service, I saw in the city of Ray a man who ranked among the scientists of science and astrology»[363]. The 'high academy' mentioned here is of course the palace of Khorezm's Abu Abdullah in Kot, and the 'honourable service' is his service to Khorezm. The deprivation of this by Abu Raikhan Beruni means the execution of Khorezm and his departure from Khorezm. After this incident, the scientist came to Ray in «Mineralogy» with the words «I had a friend of the Isfahan merchants in Ray, and sometimes I went to visit him as a guest», in «Geodesy» «But Abu Mahmud told me from his own mouth that his measurements... and that he was less pleased to determine the greatest deviation», is fully confirmed by his lines.

---

[352] Umarov G.Ya. Beruni, Copernicus and modern science. - Tashkent: Science, 1973. – 67 p.
[353] Sadykov Kh.U. Beruni and his works on astronomy and mathematical geography. – Moscow: USSR Academy of Sciences, 1953. – 29 p.
[354] Bulgakov P.G. Life and works of Beruni. – 148 pp.; Sadykov H.U. Beruni and his works on astronomy and mathematical geography. – 29 p.
[355] Beruni A.R. Collection of information for knowledge of jewelry (Mineralogy). - Moscow: Science, 1963. - 235 p.
[356] Ahmedov A. Khorazm Mamun Academy. - Tashkent: Science, 2005. – 59 p.
[357] Sadykov Kh.U. Beruni and his works on astronomy and mathematical geography. – 46 p.
[358] Bulgakov P.G. Life and works of Beruni. – 216 p.
[359] Sadykov Kh.U. Beruni and his works on astronomy and mathematical geography. - Moscow: USSR Academy of Sciences, 1953. – 77 p.
[360] Sirazhdinov S.Kh., Matviyevskaya G.P., Ahmedov A. Mathematics and astronomy in the works of Abu Raikhan Beruni. - Tashkent: Science, 1973. – 44 p.
[361] Beruni. Cartography. – 303 p.
[362] Beruni. Cartography. - 257 p.
[363] Abu Rayhan Beruni. Selected works. T. 1. MSSU,ments to past generations // Responsible editors I. Abdullayev, O. Faizullayev; Translation. A. Rasulov. - Tashkent: Science, 1968. - 399 p.

The scientist spent his entire life gathering information for Abu Rayhon Beruni's work 'Mineralogy'. During his childhood in Khorezm, and then during his stay in Iran, India and Afghanistan, he collected stories, tales and information about the properties of precious stones, the lands where they were mined and such minerals, and studied their physical and chemical properties. He describes the results of nearly 60 years of research in the field of mineralogy. For the first time in the history of science, he calculates the density and specific gravity of more than 50 substances with modern accuracy, and manufactures and describes special instruments for measuring the specific gravity of solids and liquids[364].

The scientist remained devoted to his love of science until the last moments of his life. Even on his deathbed he tried to study. During his lifetime, Abu Rayhon Beruni wrote 180 works on mathematics, astronomy, its instruments, geography, philosophy, mineralogy, pharmacognosy, history, ethnography, chronology and philology.

At the suggestion of Abu Rayhon Beruni, the Khorezm Shah, the patron of knowledge in Khorezm, began to gather many of the great scientists of the East in Gurganj. Among them were famous healers, philosophers, poets, mathematicians, astronomers, historians and linguists.

About one of them, Ahmad ibn Muhammad al-Sakhri, Abu Rayhon Beruni writes the following: «Sakhri worked with Mamunshah. He was a scholar and wrote poetry with a very beautiful and refined taste. The wide range of knowledge that interested the scholars of Khorezm at that time is surprising. They studied jurisprudence, geology, grammar, narrative, the theory of poetry, history, philosophy, logic, medicine, arithmetic, geometry, astronomy, music, mechanics, optics, chemistry, astrology, physiognomy, the interpretation of words, geodesy, topography, measures and weights, as well as the knowledge of measuring instruments, the

---

[364] Lemmlein G.G. Mineralogical information. - Moscow: USSR Academy of Sciences, 1992. - P. 292-402; Belenitsky A. Place of the mineralogical treatise. – Moscow, 1973. - P. 402-418; Akromkhozhayev O. Beruniy is one of the first researchers. - Tashkent: Science, 1976. - P. 32-63; Usmanov T. Beruni's place in the history of physics. - Tashkent: Science, 1977. - B. 179-197.

mixing of water and chemistry, the knowledge of magic, education, spirituality and witchcraft. All scientists were teachers and students of each other.

The scientists of the Mamun Academy were primarily creative minds in the exact sciences and medicine. Among them, the famous doctor, philosopher, astrologer, linguist, and ethicist Abu-l-Khair Hammar stood out for his productive activities.

Khorezmshah Mamun II, born in Baghdad, summoned Abu-l-Khair Hammar to Gurganj and appointed him as his personal physician and minister. Hammar served in the palace alongside Ibn Sina. Abu-l-Khair Hammar converted from Christianity to Islam.

He was interested in various sciences, becoming especially famous for his works on philosophy and medicine. He earned the title «Second Hippocrates» for his expertise. Well-versed in Greek medicine, he was known throughout the East for his scientific achievements in this field. Hammar actively participated in the academy's academic discussions and gained an excellent reputation. His time here was the most productive period of his scientific work.

After Mahmud Ghaznavi brought Khorezm under his control, he took Hammar with him to the capital. In the palace, Hammar served as the Sultan's personal physician, treating him for the rest of his life. The Sultan granted Hammar private land in a place called Hammar, and the place name became part of his own.

Abu-l-Khair Hammar was not only an author but also a translator. Some of his translated works that have survived include: «Kitab al-asor al-alwiyya» (كتاب الأثار العلوية) («The Book of Highest Impact») and «Kitab al-lubs fi-l-kutub al-arba'a fi-l-mantiq» (كتاب اللبس فى الكتب الأربعة فى المنطق) («The Book of Confusion in Four Books of Logic»).

Abu Ali Ibn Sina (980-1037) is one of the great figures who made a significant contribution to the development of world science. His scientific works, along with those of the Khorezm polymath Abu Rayhan Biruni, represent the pinnacle of scientific achievement during that era.

According to Ibn Sina, mathematical sciences include the following parts: number theory (علم العدد) ('ilm al-'adad), geometry (علم الغيامتريبة) ('ilm al-handasa), astronomy (علم الهيئة) ('ilm al- hay'a) and music (علم الموسيقي) ('ilm al-musiqi)[365].

The life and work of Abu Ali ibn Sina took place under extremely difficult conditions. Throughout his life he had to move from one city to another, from one country to another. In 999, the Samanid state was abolished; in 1002, Ibn Sina arrived in Khorezm from Bukhara[366]. In the manuscripts under number 9042 of the Institute of Oriental Studies named after Abu Rayhon Beruni of the Academy of Sciences of the Republic of Uzbekistan, there is a manuscript entitled «Ajaib at-tabakot». The author of this treatise is Muhammad Tahir ibn Abu-l-Qasim[367] and it consists of an introduction and seven sections (chapters). In the last part of the fourth chapter, information about him is given in red ink under the heading «Dhikri Sheikh Abu Ali ibn Sina»[368]. This manuscript is a geographical work[369]. On one of the pages devoted to Ibn Sina, concerning the length of his stay in Bukhara and Khorezm, the following lines are written

«Abu Ali ibn Abdullah ibn Sina, at the age of twenty-four, was knowledgeable in all intellectual, linguistic and mathematical sciences, and in Bukhara he argued with scientists and defeated them. Then he went to Khorezm and taught there for seven years. And from there he went to Jurjon»[370].

A similar opinion was expressed by Sharifjon Makhdoom Sadri Zia. In his work entitled «Tazkiray shuaroi mutakaddimin wa salatin», which is kept in the Manuscript Fund of the Republic of Uzbekistan named after Abu Raikhan Beruni, the following lines are written in this regard

---

[365] Matviyevskaya G.P. From the history of studying the physical and mathematical heritage of Ibn Sina // Mathematics and astronomy in the works of Ibn Sina, his contemporaries and followers. - Tashkent: Science, 1981. – 18 p.
[366] Collection of Eastern manuscripts, VIII. - Tashkent: 1967. - Pp. 72-73, inventory 5660.
[367] Collection of Eastern manuscripts, I, pp. 299-300; Descriptions 686-689.
[368] Fund of the Institute of Oriental Studies named after Abu Raikhan Beruni (hereinafter - AN RUZ. Institute of Oriental Studies) № 9042, l.174b.
[369] Collection of Eastern manuscripts, I. – Tashkent: Nauka, 1952. – 299 p.
[370] Muhammad Tahir ibn Abu-l-Qasim, Ajaib at-Tabakat, Manuscript Fund of Academy of Sciences of the Republic of Uzbekistan. Institute of Oriental Studies named after Abu Rayhan Beruniy, position № 9042, p. 175a. After this, it is said that Ibn Sina treated the sick in Jurjan; A. Irisov. Abu Ali ibn Sina. – Tashkent: Science, 1980. – 59 p.

«Abu Ali Sina debated with the scholars at the age of twelve and defeated them all. He was in the service of the Khorezm Shah for seven years»[371]. In both quotations the phrase 'seven years' is objectionable. For the year of Ibn Sina's departure from Khorezm is given by Yu.N. Zavadovsky as 401 AH/1011 AD[372]. Ibn Sina al-Masihi and they went to Jurjan and left through the Karakum desert.

There were many difficulties on the way, the guide got lost and Abu Sahl al-Masihi died on the way, unable to endure the hardships of the road and the lack of water. As a result, Ibn Sina and his guide, after many difficulties, reached Naso, which is about twenty miles from modern Ashgabat, and from there to Abivard. He visited several cities in Khorasan, but found no permanent refuge in any of them. The internal conflicts and upheavals in Khorasan haunted him.

According to the biography of Ibn Sina written by his disciple Abu Ubaid Jujani, who worked with him for a quarter of a century, he reached the maturity of science at the time when the Samani state reached a high level of political, economic and cultural development. He became famous as a scientist in the fields of medicine, logic, philosophy and natural sciences. Considering that there are sufficient grounds for a separate study of the natural sciences within the framework of scientific research, the opinions of Abu Ali ibn Sina, one of the scientists who worked at the Khorezm Mamun Academy, are of great importance.

Al-Bayhaqi (1105-1169), Ibn al-Qifti (1172-1227), Abu-l-Faraj Bar Ebrey (1226-1286), Ibn Khallikon (d. 1282) provide important information about the life and scientific activities of Abu Ali ibn Sina, which can be found in the writings of Ibn Abu Usaybia (12th century).

In the field of natural sciences, Ibn Sina read a number of treatises and wrote commentaries on Euclid's Foundations and Ptolemy's Almajisti. Important

---

[371] Sharifjon Makhdum Sadri Ziya, founder and director of Tazkiray Shuarai, Fund of Academy of Sciences of the Republic of Uzbekistan. Institute of Oriental Studies named after Abu Rayhan Beruniy, № 2193/X, p. 272a; Sakhobiddin Siddikov, Ibn Sina badi 900 sol (Ibn Sina after 900 years), gas. "Education and Culture". - Monday, February 28, 1980; A. Irisov. Same work, 59 p.
[372] Zavadovsky Yu.N. Materials for the biography of Abu Ali ibn Sina. - Taj.SSR: Izv. AN. Taj.SSR, dept. total science Vol. 2. 1958. – 11 p.

information on this can be found in all works on the history of medieval Eastern science[373].

Parts of this work relating to the natural sciences and metaphysics were lithographed in Teheran in 1887-88, and the logical part was printed in several volumes in Cairo from 1962. Only a few sections have been published in Persian, Hebrew, Latin, German, English, Russian, Syriac, French and Uzbek374. Besides the medical works of Abu Ali ibn Sina[375], the third part of «Al-Shifa» (the author calls it the third set, i.e. the series - G.M.) is devoted to mathematical sciences.

Ibn Sina's work Usul 'ilm al-Khandasa (أصول علم الهندسة) (Fundamentals of Geometry) consists of fifteen articles (we call the article a book because of its large size) containing 418 geometric figures.

During this period, Khorezm was one of the cultural centres of the East, where the conditions for creativity were somewhat better than in Bukhara. Abu Sahl Masihi, Abu Nasr ibn Iraq, Abu-l Khair Hammar, Abu Rayhon Beruni, Ibn Miskawaih and other famous scientists and poets lived here.

In the 10th century, Khorezm was somewhat peaceful after the Karakhanid invasion. Cultural and educational activities were well established. Mamun ibn Mamun gathered many scientists and virtuous people in the palace and created all the conditions for them to practise science.

According to Ibn Sina, Mamun's academy in Khorezm had a minister who was fond of science - Abu l-Hussein al-Sahli[376]. In his biography, Ibn Sina shows that

---

[373] Gartz J. De interpretibus et explanatoribus Euclidis arabicis. - Halae 1823; Klamroth M. Veber den arabischen Euklid. Zeitschr.d. Deutsch Morgenland. Ges.Bd 35. 1881. - P. 270-326; Steinsneider M. Euklid bei Arabern. Eine bibliographische Studie. «Zeitschr.fur Math. u. Phys». Bd 31. 1886. - P. 81-110; Steinschneider M. Die arabischen Ubersetzungen aus dem Griechischen. Zweiter Abschnitt. Mathematik // «Zeitschr. d. Deutsch. Morgenland. Ges.».Bd. 50. 1896. - P. 161-219; 337-417; Steinschneider M. Die arabischen Bearbeiter des Almagest//"Bibl. math.", F. 2, b. 6, 1892.

[375] Ibn Sina. Book I: Canon of Medical Sciences. - Tashkent: Science, 1954. - 458 p.; Ibn Sina. Book II: Canon of Medical Sciences. - Tashkent: Science, 1956. - 844 p.; Ibn Si№ Book IV: Canon of Medical Sciences. - Tashkent: Science, 1960. - 802 pp.; Ibn Sina. Book V: Canon of Medical Sciences. - Tashkent: Science, 1961. - 348 p.; Abu Ali ibn Sina. Canon of medical sciences. Selecting the third volume. Kh. Khikmatullaev, U. Karimov in collaboration. - Tashkent: Labor, 1993; Khikmatullaev H. Treatise of Abu Ali ibn Sina "Heart Medicines". - Tashkent: Science, 1966. - 181 p.; Karimov U.I. On the question of Ibn Sina's views on chemistry // Materials of the scientific session of the ANU UzSSR. dedicated to the 1000th anniversary of Ibn Sina. - Tashkent: Science, 1953. - P. 13-38.; Karimov U.I. Classification of sciences according to Ibn Sina // Materials of the First All-Union Scientific Conference of Orientalists in Tashkent, June 4-11, 1957. - Tashkent: Science, 1958. - pp. 986-990.

[376] Ibn Abi Usaybiya. Uyun al-anba fit-tabakat al-atibbo. - Cairo, 1882. - Volume II. - 4 p.

when Ali ibn Mamun (997-1009) was the emir of the country and went to Khorezm[377], Abu Ali ibn Sina entered the city dressed as a fiqh jurist. It seems that in those days those who wore such clothes were treated with respect and deference, and their strangeness was not so noticeable. This is how he reached the city of Gurganch, the capital of Khorezm. In his own words, the Khorezm Shah «appointed him a monthly salary sufficient for him»[378]. So Ibn Sina began to live peacefully in the land of Khorezm.

Conclusions under paragraph 2.1.

1. One of the factors motivating the development of science was the expansion of foreign relations. The exploration and settlement of new lands required the mastery of geography and ancient sciences. To improve the well-being of the people and to raise a healthy generation, it is necessary to study medicine and the spiritual heritage of our ancestors. It is clear that it is impossible to establish contacts with foreign countries without studying their life and culture. This situation makes it necessary to study the languages of other peoples. That is why the rulers tried to gather mature scientists in their country as much as possible and opened a wide way for translations.

2. The greatest philosophical work of Abu Ali ibn Sina is the «Kitab ash-shifa»; it can be called the scientific encyclopaedia of its time. It consists of four parts: 1) logical; 2) natural sciences (this section is devoted to minerals, plants, animals and human beings); 3) mathematical subjects are discussed (counting, geometry, philology and music); 4) metaphysics or astrology.

3. Abu Ali ibn Sina divided the philosophical sciences into two groups: theoretical (النظري) (ан-назари) and practical (العملي) (al-amali). He divides the theoretical sciences into physics (علم التبیعی) (`ilm al-tabi`i) and mathematics (علم الریاضی) (`ilm ar-riyadi).

4. At the Khorezm Mamun Academy, a scientific environment has been created for scientific research by world scientists, and scientific research is being carried out.

---

[377] Ibn Abi Usaybiya. Uyun al-anba fit-tabakat al-atibbo. - Cairo, 1882. - Volume II. - 4 p.
[378] Zavadovsky Yu.N. Materials for the bio-bibliography of Abu Ali ibn Sina. - News AN. Taj.SSR. dept. total science Vol. 2. – Tajikistan, 1958. – 58 p.

2.2. Development of natural science and historical and philosophical thought in the heritage of scientists of the Khorezm Mamun Academy

Muhammad ibn Musa al-Khwarizmi, Abu Ali ibn Sina, Abu Raikhan Beruni, Abu Nasr Farabi and other great scientists lived and worked in the 9th and 10th centuries. Because of the importance of the works they created, this period can be called the Renaissance in Central Asia. Characteristics of Renaissance science and culture are

1. Striving for the enlightenment of all people, using the heritage of the past and the scientific and cultural achievements of neighbouring countries, developing natural, philosophical and social sciences.

2. Study of nature, development of scientific knowledge, belief in the power of reason, focus on the knowledge of truth, recognition of truth as the basis of human knowledge.

3. Enhancement of the natural, artistic and spiritual qualities of man, glorification of humanity, observance of the highest moral laws in raising a perfect generation.

4. Universalism - interest in all problems of existence and social life, important aspects of the culture of this period.

The culture of this period served the development of universal human values. The development of trade, the expansion of economic relations, the exchange of cultural values between different provinces of the Caliphate and the strengthening of its relations with other countries, the study of natural and cultural resources, traditions, languages and histories of different peoples, the creation of the most correct way and methods of knowledge, the creation of the entire apparatus of the process of knowledge strengthened the need for improvement. The rapid development of such fields as optics, mathematics and astronomy created opportunities for in-depth study of nature and expansion of research methods. During the Middle Ages, Eastern philosophy developed not only at the heart of mythology and religion, but also at the heart of science. The achievements of Eastern scientists in the fields of mathematics, astronomy, geography, medicine, history and alchemy are well known. Eastern philosophers, who were usually healers, astrologers and travellers, relied more on natural science and experience than on abstract reasoning.

Apart from Abu Raikhan Beruni, there is no written information about the knowledge of the catastrophes of ancient Khorezm. According to him, the disaster was called «Akhtarvenik» in the language of the Khorezmians, who knew the position of the stars better than the pre-Islamic Arabs[379]. He continued: «The scientists of Khorezm who observed the movement of the moon and drew conclusions from it have passed away». From his words it is clear that before the Arab invasion there were many astrologers in Khorezm whose level of development was much higher than that of the pre-Islamic Arabs.

This is proved by information found during excavations in Koykyrylgan-kale. M.G. Vorobyova and M.M. Rozhanskaya stated that the monument of the Koykirian castle was built in such a way that it could also be used for monitoring disasters.

During excavations, clay discs and circles were found. Taken together, they resemble a reconstruction of a Greek astrolabe made by O. Schirmer, as described by the encyclopaedist[380].

Painting and sculpture were also well developed in ancient Khorezm. During the excavations of S.P. Tolstov in the city of Tuprokkala (3rd century BC), the researchers were surprised by the artistic monuments. They made a scientific discovery, because some of the paintings resemble Rome, the Egyptian «Faiyum paintings» and other ancient monuments of the Roman era[381]. Analysing the found objects, S.P. Tolstov evaluates them as follows: «The pictorial culture of Khorezm was created in ancient times. The sculpture, which amazes with the pride of its forms, the amazing plasticity of the clay figures and reliefs, the fine art of the Khorezm sculptors and, finally, the richness of the colours of the pictorial inscriptions, form a very original and complete

---

[379] Biruni Abu Raihan. Favorite works. T. 1. - Tashkent: Science, 1973. - 259 p.
[380] Rozhanskaya M.M. Mechanics in the Middle Ages East. - Moscow: Science. 1976. - P. 53-54; Vorobeva M.G., Rozhanskaya M.M. About some astronomical functions of Koi-kralgan-kala. - In the book: Koi-krylgan-kala - a cultural mSSU,ment of Ancient Khorezm of the 4th century. B.C. - IV century AD Proceedings of the Khorezm expedition. – Moscow, 1967. - P. 61, 251-258, 482.
[381] Stavisky B.Ya. Between the Pamirs and the Caspian: (Central Asia in ancient times). - Moscow: Science. 1966. – 243 p.

complex. This shows the independence of the creators of the ancient Khorezm civilisation, the strength of their thinking and artistic knowledge»[382].

The 9th century has its place in the history of the peoples of the countries of the Near and Middle East. It was a period of high development in medicine, mathematics, science and astrology. The introduction of the number system was a revolutionary event. The merits of Al-Khorezmi are great in this.

As a result of the development, some independent sciences separated from mathematics and astrology, e.g. algebra from mathematics, trigonometry from astronomy. A number of observatories also appeared. In the 9th century, in addition to the above sciences, history, philology and other social sciences developed.

In the course of 100 years, beginning in the 70s and 80s of the 8th century, a number of works were published by more than several hundred scientists, including Euclid, Archimedes, Aristotle, Apollonius, Hippocrates, Galen, Menelaus, Theodosius, Heron, Ptolemy, Vettius, were translated into Arabic.

In the 9th to 12th centuries, Movarunnahr was famous as the most scientifically and culturally developed country in the entire Muslim world, where along with philosophical sciences, natural sciences developed - astronomy, mathematics, medicine, chemistry, medicine, geography, ancient traditions, partly Indian, Persian religious and secular sciences based on the fusion of Arab and ancient Greek scientific and cultural traditions. Famous schools of hadith, Islamic jurisprudence and jurisprudence were established here, and important works of historiography were written.

In the «Monuments» of Abu Rayhon Beruni, first published by Zahau[383], the local historical tradition sheds light on the appearance of the history of Khorezm. He noted that the information he provided was not recorded in written sources, but was based on what the priests of Mug had said orally[384].

---

[382] Tolstov S.P. In the footsteps of the ancient Khorezmian civilization. - Moscow-Leningrad: USSR Academy of Sciences, 1948. - P. 189-190.
[383] Beruniy. "MSSU,ments" - 72 p.
[384] Ed.Sachauzur Geschichte and Chronologie von Khwarizm, SBWAW, PhHCL, B. 73, 1873.

According to the conclusions of scientists, brief information about Khorezm, found in various ancient literary monuments, indicates that it occupied an important place in the ancient history of the Middle East and Eastern Europe.

At the end of the 10th century, important events took place in the history of Khorezm. After the reign of Khorezm Shah Abu Ali Mamun I (995-997), full of bloody military events and complex political intrigues, his eldest son Abu-l-Hasan Ali ibn Mamun (997-1009) reigned. After this, the reign of Abu-l-Abbas Mamun ibn Mamun, one of Mamun I's sons, begins in the history of Khorezm.

Ancient Greek mathematicians were unable to solve three problems:

1) quadrature of a given circle; 2) division of an arbitrary angle or arc into three equal parts (trisection of an angle); 3) making a cube twice the size of a given cube (doubling of a cube).

The history of the problem of squaring the circle lasted four thousand years, it became a synonym for an unsolvable problem.

The views of the authors in the works of ancient geometry belong mainly to the school of philosophers, and the first definitions were explained philosophically.

The Pythagoreans approached the definition of the concept of 'geometry' from their own point of view. In particular, they looked at points, right angles, squares, triangles and other figures in terms of numbers and defined them as units and their combinations[385].

Democritus (460-370 BC) defined a point as an indivisible particle of space, an atom. In his interpretation, a chain of these particles, a geometric body, is a collection of particles in space[386].

Aristotle focuses on the definition of basic geometric concepts. According to him, every science has its roots. He describes these principles as «they cannot be proved, it is their existence». For example, if we accept a number, a line, a triangle, then one and the measure are accepted and the other is proven[387]. In the ideas of the

---

[385] Raik A.E. Essays on the history of mathematics in ancient times. – Saransk, 1967. - 370 p.
[386] Kuliyeva G.Z. Basic concepts of mathematics among Nasiriddin Tusi's predecessors: Abstract. diss....cand. physics and mathematics science – Baku, 1962. - 11 p.
[387] Aristotle. Essays. In 4 volumes - Moscow: Mysl, 1978. Vol.2. - 548 p.

ancient Greek scientists, the principles of Aristotle for Euclid acquired great importance.

Hajjaj ibn Yusuf translated Euclid's Principles into Arabic for the first and second time during the reign of the Caliph of Baghdad, Harun al-Rashid Caliph al-Mamun, and for the third time by Thabit ibn Qurra (830-901), a mathematician from Baghdad who translated it into Arabic and corrected errors in previous translations[388].

From the 6th century, the centre of mathematical research moved to India and China, and then to the countries of the Middle East and Central Asia. The Chinese developed a method of sequential elimination of the unknown to solve a system of linear equations and described a new method of approximate solution of higher order equations. Indian scientists used negative numbers by perfecting literal symbols. But as a special branch of mathematics, describing problems associated with solving algebraic equations, the works of scientists from the Middle East and Central Asia were formed. In the 9th century, the famous encyclopaedist Muhammad ibn Musa al-Khwarizmi (783-850) created the work «A Short Book on Algebra and Al-Muqabala». In this work he gave a general rule for solving linear equations, divided quadratic equations into classes and showed ways of solving them.

The development of arithmetic in the Middle Ages is associated with the East, India and the Arab Caliphate. Muhammad ibn Musa al-Khwarizmi has great merit in the creation of numbers. In his work On Indian Arithmetic, numbers, zero and the positional counting system spread from India to the Arab Caliphate and from there to Europe. Decimal fractions were introduced into accounting through the work of Ghiyaziddin Jamshid al-Qoshi, a scientist working at the Ulugbek Observatory in Samarkand.

Thanks to the development of trade and the influence of Eastern culture, from the 13th century onwards there was a growing interest in accounting in Europe. It is worth remembering the name of the Italian scientist Leonardo of Pisa (Fibonacci). From about the 16th century, the development of pure calculus problems was

---

[388] Yushkevich A.P. History of mathematics in the Middle Ages. - Moscow: publishing house; physical and mathematical, 1961. - 238 p.

combined with algebra. An important step in this field was the work of the French scientist F. Vieux, in which numbers began to be identified by letters. From then on, the basic rules of arithmetic began to be considered from a strictly algebraic point of view. The subject of number theory was the «higher» problems of calculation. Natural numbers, i.e. 1,2,3,4, etc., are obtained by counting certain objects. An important task of counting is to learn to understand the specific meaning of the names of the counting objects, to learn to ignore their shape, size and colour.

The great scientist Muhammad ibn Musa al-Khorezmi is one of the encyclopaedic scientists who made a great contribution to world science. He was one of the greatest scholars of the Al-Mamun Academy in Baghdad. He was commissioned by Caliph al-Mamun (c. 830) to write his treatise «Al-kitab al-mukhtasar, fi-hisab al-jabr wa-l-mukabala» («A Short Book on the Calculation of Additions and Contrasts»). The preface to the work states: «Imam al-Mamun's interest in science and his ability to help scientists in this field with difficulties arising in their work prompted me to write a short treatise on the calculation. In writing this work, I have endeavoured to be a guide for the readers that is understandable, simple, useful and will help to facilitate the work of calculation in problems between people, especially in the distribution of inheritance, the conclusion of transactions, commercial work, land surveying and other similar calculations»[389].

The mathematical ideas of Muhammad ibn Musa al-Khwarizmi were described by Abu Kamil (850-930), Abu-l-Wafa al-Bozhani (940-998), Abu Rayhon al-Abu Rayhon Beruni, Omar Khayyam in «Al-Jabr wal- muqabala», they wrote books about it, expanded and deepened it.

According to some researchers, one of the reasons for the practice of catastrophism in Baghdad was that the Baghdadis were aware of the knowledge of the Indians[390].

It is known that al-Mamun was Caliph Harun al-Rashid's deputy in Marwah from 809, became Caliph in 813 and moved to Baghdad in 819. Al-Mamun called al-

---

[389] Sal'e M. Muhammad al-Khwarizmi is a great scientist. - Tashkent: Science, 1954. – 15 p.
[390] Yushkevich A.P. Osha Asar, 171 b.; Brockelmann C. Geschichte der Arabischen Literatur, Bd I, Weimar, 1898. -R. 215-216; Brockelman C. Geschichte der Arabischen Litteratur, Erster Supplementband. Leiden, 1937. - R. 381-382.

Khwarizmi, who was in Marwah, to his palace. He headed the Beit al-Hikma library[391].

During the reign of Caliph al-Mamun, a group of great scholars from Central Asia and Khorasan, such as Muhammad ibn Musa al-Khwarizmi, Yahya ibn Abu Mansur, Ahmad al-Farghani, Habash al-Marwazi, Khalid ibn Abdumalik al-Marwarrudi, Abu-l-Abbas al-Jawhari and others.

In Baghdad, Khalifa al-Mamun improved the activities of the Bayt al-Hikma scientific centre founded by his father in every way possible, giving it the status of a major government institution and beginning translation activities on a large scale. Many books were brought from Byzantium and India, and the activities of the Bayt al-Hikma were expanded with the construction of two observatories: the first in 828 in the al-Shammosia area of Baghdad, and the second in 831 on Mount Qasiyoun near Damascus.

Among the most important translators who worked in this field of knowledge were Hajjaj ibn Yusuf ibn Matar, Abu Zakariya Yuhanno ibn al-Bitrik (9th century), Hunayn ibn Ishaq (9th century) and Cousteau ibn Luqa al-Baalbakki (9th century). . Among the Central Asian scientists who came to Baghdad, the famous astronomer Ahmad ibn Kathir al-Fargani should be mentioned. Yahya ibn Abu Mansur became the founder and director of the observatory in the al-Shammosiya area of Baghdad.

Al-Khwarizmi is the founder of algebra. «Algebra» is taken from his treatise «Al-kitab al-mukhtasar fi lisb al-jabr wa-l-mukabala». Another of his treatises on arithmetic was based on Indian numerals, which led to the spread of the decimal counting system and its operations that we use today in Europe. His works on geography provided the basis for the creation of dozens of geographical works in Arabic.

Al-Khwarizmi's calculus, the decimal number system he introduced, and algebraic mathematics marked the beginning of a new era in the history of mathematics - medieval mathematics, which had an incomparable influence on the development of science in the centuries that followed. They served as the basis for

---

[391] Ibn al-Qifti. Kitab akhbar al-ulama bi-akhbar al-hukama. - Cairo, 1326/1908. - R. 177-178.

many studies, which were examined by a number of authors and parts of which were included in other works. Centuries later, several generations would draw mathematical information from these works. In his mathematical works, the scientist collected the most necessary information for scientists and craftsmen, taking into account the requirements and needs of everyday life, and wrote concisely, concisely and in simple expressions.

In his work, Al-Khwarizmi referred to the operations of multiplication and division, two implementations. At the beginning of the treatise, after the praise, the great scientist says that he wants to explain the Indian method of counting with the help of nine letters, i.e. numbers, that any number can be easily expressed briefly with the help of «letters», and he wants to explain the operations on them. In the Latin manuscript, only the Indian numbers 1, 2, 3, 5 are written in circles instead of zero. Hindi numbers are not provided and are left blank. The examples use Roman numerals, which were common in Western Europe during the Middle Ages, and leave the corresponding Indian numerals blank. Al-Khwarizmi's treatise on accounting reflects ancient Greek philosophy rather than Indian accounting. In addition, it is clear that he used earlier works in mathematics in this work. Such thoughts are confirmed by his following words: «Consequently, one is a part of every number. This is also mentioned in another book. One is the root of every number. So it's beyond numbers. Therefore it is the root of any number and can be used to determine any number.

Therefore it is beyond numbers, it is determined by itself, that is, without any other number»[392].

Here «the one is contained in every number», «the root of every number» and its «outside numbers», i.e. the indivisible, belong on the one hand to the Pythagorean views[393], on the other hand to Aristotelianism[394].

---

[392] Translations 102a-p.
[393] Raik A.E. Essays on the history of mathematics in ancient times. - Saransk, 1967. - P. 150-151.
[394] Aristotle. Metaphysics. Translation and notes by E.V. Kubitsky. - Moscow-Leningrad: USSR Academy of Sciences, 1934 – 86 p.

After detailing the writing of numbers in the decimal system in Indian numerals and the use of a «small circle like 0», al-Khwarizmi teaches the reading and writing of large numbers using only the names of the units, tens, hundreds and thousands. As an example, al-Khwarizmi gives the reading of this number (not given in the manuscript) 1180 073 051 492 863, which must have been uncomfortable to read. This awkward reading of numbers persisted for a long time in both the East and the West, and only disappeared with the decisive triumph of the decimal system.

This book by Muhammad ibn Musa al-Khwarizmi gives many examples of wills.

In Western Europe, al-Jabr, founded by al-Khwarizmi, began to be studied in the 13th century. The treatise «Book of Accounts» (1202) by the Italian Leonardo of Pisa (Fibonacci) (1170-1228), a major scientist of the time, provides information from calculus and algebra to quadratic equations. The first major independent achievement of Western European scientists in the 16th century was the discovery of a formula for solving cubic equations. This is the merit of Italian scientists - S. Del Ferro, N. Tartaglia and G. Carda№ J. Cardano's student L. Ferrari solved a fourth degree equation. The study of problems connected with the roots of the cubic equation led the Italian R. Bombelli to the discovery of complex numbers.

The lack of a convenient and developed road system hampered the development of al-Jabr. At the end of the 16th century, the French scientist The French scientist F. Vieux introduced letter designations not only for unknowns but also for arbitrary invariants.

At the beginning of the 17th century, the French philosopher and mathematician R. Descartes brought these symbols into their present form and even introduced a notation for the exponent.

Many of Al-Khwarizmi's works were later used by Eastern scholars. One of these was Abu Rayhon al-Biruni.

There is evidence that he was one of al-Khwarizmi's successors in popularising the decimal positional counting system in his works. Hasan Ali ibn Ahmad al-Nasawi (d. 1030) of Nisa - one of al-Khwarizmi's successors. It is not known when he wrote his treatise «The Sufficiency of Indian Arithmetic», but it is known that Abu Rayhon Beruni wrote a special treatise on this problem «Notes on counting in Sindhi and Indian numerals». Unfortunately, it has not reached us. Abu Rayhon Beruni continued the great work started by al-Khwarizmi. In Gurganj he was far from knowledge of Sanskrit and the main sources of Hinduism. Therefore, only al-Khwarizmi's treatise on accountancy can be called his only support in this field.

We know that Abu Rayhon Beruni al-Khwarizmi was well acquainted with works on disasters, especially Zij. This treatise incorporated Indian, Iranian and Hellenistic traditions and was also popular in Abu Rayhon Beruni's time. In his works, he repeatedly referred to Indian scientists to resolve ideas about the earth, the height of the lights and the distances between them. He writes: «I did what any man in his field should do - accept with grace the efforts of previous scholars and correct their shortcomings». He opposed al-Khwarizmi's Zij and defended it against unfounded accusations, taking on the major task of reworking the theoretical foundations of al-Khwarizmi's scheme and correcting some of its superficial aspects.

According to our observations, in the second stage of his activity, that is, in 1005 and 1017, the encyclopaedist dedicated three major scientific works to «Zij» to al-Khwarizmi. Unfortunately, we have not reached: «Useful Questions and Correct Answers», according to the author: contains the theoretical basis of al-Khwarizmi's tables and refers to this book of 250 pages. In another of his works, he shows that he solved problems such as determining the positions and heights of the disc parts of the Sun and Moon using geometrical methods.

Another scientific treatise is entitled: «Proving the Correctness of the Practices in Zij al-Khwarizmi by Arguments»: it criticises the contradictory theoretical explanations of the al-Khwarizmi tables compiled by Dr. Talha. This book has 360 pages.

Abu Rayhon Beruni's third and largest work on the subject defends al-Khwarizmi's tables against the unfair criticism of the 9th century catastrophist Hasan al-Ahwarzi. Abu Rayhon Beruni called it «an intermediate book between the scientific views of al-Khwarizmi and al-Ahwarzi». The work is 600 pages long.

He congratulated al-Khwarizmi and carried out extensive activities to study, improve and disseminate his scientific legacy, while at the same time revealing some shortcomings in his tables. Al-Khwarizmi's «Book of Surat ul-arz», which was revised by Claudius Ptolemy into the book «Geography», has survived to this day. (كتاب صورة العرض) («Book of the Image of the Earth») The question of the attitude of Abu Rayhon Beruni is also important. If we compare it with Ptolemy's book, we can see that there are a number of innovations in al-Khwarizmi's work. The geographical section of Abu Rayhon Beruni's main philological work «Qanuni Masudi» allows us to shed light on the problems of both scientists in this area.

It is known that al-Khwarizmi's «Sura al-Arz» contains tables of latitudes and longitudes of settlements known to him. We see a similar table, but defined and updated many times, in the «Kanuni Masudi». If we compare them, Al-Khorezmi has the geographical coordinates of 539 cities and Abu Rayhon Beruni has 603[395].

A comparison of the geographical coordinates in the works of Abu Rayhon Beruni and al-Khwarizmi shows that Abu Rayhon Beruni did not include many cities of Western Europe (except Spain) in his tables, but extended his table to include the cities of Iran, Iraq, the Caucasus, Khorasan, Central Asia and India. The coordinates of the cities in these regions do not match in the books of Abu Rayhon Beruni and al-Khwarizmi, the reason being the difference of 200 years in the time of their lives, and Abu Rayhon Beruni had more accurate information about these cities and contributed to the exact knowledge of their coordinates.

As for the coordinates of the cities of North and East Africa, the Arabian Peninsula, Iraq and Byzantium, the situation is somewhat different. Abu Rayhon Beruni never visited these countries, he did not receive scientific knowledge, he did not study their geography, therefore he had the opportunity to examine, compare and identify the works of the scientists who lived before him. For these regions, we observe that the coordinates of many cities in the tables of al-Khwarizmi and al-Abu Rayhon Beruni coincide. These include the length and width of 26 residential areas.

---

[395] Beruni. Selected works. V., Book 1. - B. 400-428; Muhammad al-Khwarizmi. Selected works. - Tashkent: Science, 1983. - 304 p.

These include Kairuwan, Aswan, Kulzum, Hadhramaut, Al-Yaman, Jarmi, Siraf, Gaza, Al-Ramla, Arsuf, Saida, Beirut, Jubail, Antioch, Tarsus, Wasit, Kufa, Basra, Jannaba, Mahruban, Ahwazia, Shamshat , The cities of Constantinople, Nicomedia, Chalcedon, Heraclea are included.

Conclusions under paragraph 2.2:

1. Since Abu Rayhon Beruni did not have the opportunity to directly determine the coordinates of the cities, he received information about them from al-Khorezmi and was within the limits of his creative influence.

2. Main aspects of the scientific legacy of Muhammad ibn Musa al-Khwarizmi and Abu Rayhon Beruni:

Muhammad ibn Musa al-Khwarizmi	Abu Rayhon Beruni
1. The creation of number theory is a necessity	1. Calculate the radius of the earth.
2. The coordinates of many towns: the longitude and latitude of 26 settlements coincide. Among them are Kairuwan, Aswan, Kulzum, Hadhramaut, Al-Yaman, Jarmi, Siraf, Gaza, Al-Ramla, Arsuf, Saida, Beirut, Jubail, Antioch, Tarsus, Wasit, Kufa, Basra, Jannaba, Mahruban, Ahwazia, Shamshat. included the cities of Constantinople, Nicomedia, Chalcedon, Heraclea.	
3. The latitude, longitude and geographical coordinates of 539 settlements in Central Asia, Khorasan, India and Western Europe are given.	3. The latitude, longitude and geographical coordinates of 603 settlements in Central Asia, Khorasan, India and Western Europe are given.
4. 6 canonical equations were created.	4. Lunar movements and eclipses were observed.

Based on the above, it is clear that the scientists of the Khorezm Mamun Academy developed the development of science by

1. Since ancient times, painting and sculpture have been highly developed in Khorezm.

2. Muhammad ibn Musa al-Khwarizmi developed a counting system based on the treatises of Indian scientists.

3. Some independent disciplines separated from the science of astrology, e.g. algebra from mathematics, trigonometry from catastrophes. But each specific science is explained on the basis of a philosophical approach.

4. The positional system of zero and counting that he created spread among the Indians and from there to Europe. Later, in the work of Ghiaziddin Jamshid al-Koshi, a scientist working at the Ulugbek Observatory in Samarkand, decimal fractions were included in the calculation, and from the 13th century, interest in this science grew in Western Europe. A method for solving cubic equations was discovered in Western Europe in the 16th century.

5. Scientists from Khorezm observed the movement of the moon and conducted scientific research.

6. Based on the information of Abu Rayhon Beruni, the Greek Asturloba created by O. Schirmer was reconstructed.

7. The latitude, longitude and geographical coordinates of the cities of Central Asia, Khorasan, India and Western Europe were determined.

8. The development of productive forces in Khorezm, free from war and other dangers, created excellent conditions for a certain improvement of the economic situation in the country. As a result, the situation in the field of culture and education became much better, which was the reason for the opening of the Mamun Academy. The «Mamun Academy» was not an accidental and temporary organisation; its creation personified the social life, economic and cultural progress and political status that was emerging in Khorezm.

2.3. Social and philosophical views in the natural science thinking of scientists of the Khorezm Mamun Academy

Social and philosophical views occupy an important place in the scientific thought of the scientists of the Khorezm Mamun Academy. Moreover, Abu Rayhon Beruni's life in Ghazn in 1017-1048 was extremely difficult, but it was also the most productive period for his scientific work. A scientist living abroad and free from interference in government affairs, he spent his free time on scientific research. During this period, his works «Famous People of Khorezm» and «Tahdid nihayot al-amokin li tashih masofat al-masokin» were published هايات الأماكن لتصحيح مسافات (المساكن) («Determination of address boundaries for determining distances [between] places of residence»)[396].

As can be seen from the title of the work, it is devoted to special problems of disaster and geodesy. They are solved by mathematical, more precisely trigonometric methods.

He used simple and easy methods to solve such problems. One of the most important problems he solved in geodesy was the measurement of the Earth's radius. This work was carried out at Nandna Fort during one of Mahmud Ghazni's campaigns in India in 1020. In Figure 1, the viewing angle FKE=h, the distance from the centre of the Earth K to the top of the mountain E, is equal to EK=L+R according to the definition of the cosine of a right triangle FKE, Cosh = sinh/sinh+L or $Cosh = \frac{R}{R+l}$.

Using this rule, he calculated with great accuracy the geographical latitudes of Khorezm, Movarunnahr, Khorasan and all the major cities of Afghanistan.

The manuscript of one of Abu Rayhon Beruni's most important treatises, «Basic Concepts of the Art of Astrology» (التفهيم) («Tafhim»), is kept in the Institute of Oriental Studies named after Abu Rayhon Beruni of the Academy of Sciences of the Republic. Uzbekistan. It was also written in Ghazna in 1029. The work is in Arabic and Persian. In 1975 B.A. Rosenfeld and A. Akhmedov published its fully annotated Russian translation[397].

---

[396] The complete Arabic copy of this work was published in 1962 by P.G. Bulgakov in the 8th iSSU,e of the journal "Institute of Arabic Manuscripts", published in Cairo. In the same year, an Arabic version was published in Ankara by Muhammad al-Tanji. The Russian translation of this work was also published by P. G. Bulgakov (Abu Reykhan Biruni. Selected Works, III, Geodesy. - Tashkent: Science, 1966). An Uzbek translation with a full scientific explanation was published by A. Akhmedov in 1982, see: Beruniy Abu Raikhan. Selected works, volume III, "Determination of address boundaries for determining distances [between] populated areas" [Geodesy]. The author of the introduction, translation and comments is Ashraf Akhmedov. - Tashkent: Science, 1982.

[397] Beruni Abu Raihan. Selected Works, vol. VI, "The Book of Understanding the Elements of the Science of the Stars" ["Tafhim"]. Introductory article, translation and notes by B.A. Rosenfeld and A. Akhmedov with the participation of M.M. Rozhanskaya, A.A. Abdurakhmanov and N.D. Sergeeva. - Tashkent: Science, 1975.

In 2005 the Uzbek translation of this work was published by A. Akhmedov[398]. In 2022, before the 1050th anniversary of the birth of Abu Rayhon Beruni, this work was republished[399].

This work of Abu Rayhon Beruni is a self-contained textbook dedicated to providing information on various disciplines that astrologers and astrologers need to know. Thus, in addition to catastrophes and astrology, it contains information on mathematics, geography, chronology and the rules for using astrolabes. The work is written in the form of 530 questions and short and concise answers to them.

It is not divided into chapters. However, Romsey Wright, who published the English translation along with the Arabic text, divided it into eight chapters according to the topic[400].

Although the basic concepts of geometry, planimetry, the theory of proportions, stereometry and spherical geometry are presented in simple terms, the Tafhim contains deep semantic considerations. For example, in the first question at the beginning of the book, geometry is defined as follows: «It is the study of the forms and properties of bodies in terms of quantities and their relative quantities [to each other]. It transforms the science of numbers from the particular to the general, and the science of catastrophes from hypotheses and assumptions to reality»[401]. The first part of this two-part definition reveals the nature of geometry as a science, and the second part reveals its relation to number theory. Abu Rayhon Beruni contrasts the «general» science of numbers with the classical science of numbers, natural numbers, and says that geometry «transforms the science of numbers from the particular to the general». This shows that the object of science is not only natural numbers, but also geometric quantities. So, at the same time, he puts forward the idea of extending the concept of «number» to the concept of «positive real numbers». He thinks a little more about this in Article III of the Kanuni Masudi. He writes: «Of the things represented by numbers, not one is real in itself. An example of this is the fact that geometers

---

[398] Ahmedov A. Tafhim. - Tashkent: Science, 2005.
[399] Akhmedov A. Beruni Abu Raikhan. Tavhim//Selected Works Volume VI. - Tashkent: NMIU "Uzbekistan", 2022.
[400] Abu'l-Rayhan al-Biruni.The Book of instruction in the elements of the art of astrology. Ed. And tronsl.By R.Wright. - London, 1934.
[401] Beruni. Book of understanding. - Tashkent: Science, 1973. – 21 p.

consider the circumference of a circle to be three hundred and sixty parts. There is a ratio of the circumference of a circle to its diameter, as well as a ratio of the number of circles to the number of diameters, although this ratio is unknown (irrational)»[402].

In the above definition it is said that geometry «brings the science of catastrophes from assumptions and suppositions to reality», it is clear that Abu Rayhon Beruni recognised the science that explains the movement of the heavenly bodies on the basis of geometry as a real catastrophe.

It seems that the author followed a deep logical principle in explaining each chapter of Tafhim. In the first chapter, after defining geometry, concepts such as solids, dimensions of space, sides, faces, lines and points are given. This is followed by the definition of surface, plane and line. Their order is different from that of Euclid's principles. Abu Rayhon Beruni defines the body first, then the surface, the line and the point. He explains the body as a self-existent thing perceived by the senses, the surface is the boundary of the body, the line is the boundary of the surface, the point is the end of the line, i.e. the end. From this it is clear that he had two aims: the first is profoundly scientific and logical, and the second is educational and pedagogical, and they are closely related. According to the first of these aims, the direction should be from the simplest abstraction to the most complex. In fact, the concept of a «mathematical body» is formed as a result of abstraction from its natural properties. At the next stage, an understanding of the surface is formed, ignoring one dimension of the body, namely its depth. Then the concept of 'line' is formed by ignoring one dimension of the surface, for example its width. Continuing in this way, the concept of «point» is formed regardless of the length of the line. This rule also corresponds to the pedagogical objective set by the scientist. This point of view in the description of geometry belongs to Aristotle and was first propagated in the East by Abu Nasr Farabi and then by Abu Rayhon Beruni. In his opinion, if education is meant when describing geometry, then it is necessary to start with something close to

---

[402] Beruniy Abu Rayhon. Selected works, V. 1 book. Kanoni Masudi (I-V articles). - Tashkent: Science, 1973. – 239 p.

the feeling of intuition. «The closest thing to feeling is the body, then the surface, then the line, and the most distant point of all,» he says[403].

It is clear from the above that the logical structure of his treatise is combined with the method of mathematical seriousness. At the same time, the author maintains a scientific approach to the description of the work.

In the stereometric section of Tafhim, the cube is defined as a cube, a prism, a straight and an oblong cylinder, a cone, its sections, a sphere, figures drawn inside it, five regular polygons, a large and a small circle on a sphere, a pole and an axis. Scientists call the cube, icosahedron, octahedron, tetrahedron and dodecahedron «earth», «water», «air», «grass» and «sky» respectively. They were named by Plato because he believed that the atoms of fire (grass) have the shape of a tetrahedron, the earth - a cube, the air - an octahedron, the water - an icosahedron and the water atoms - an icosahedron. the whole universe is a dodecahedron.

Abu Rayhon Beruni, in his books «Geodesy» and «Kanuni Masudi», explains in detail previous attempts to measure the size of the Earth, and he excellently dwells on a new method: «On the Measurements of the Earth» by Abu Rayhon Beruni. writes: «Only Romanian and Indian experts tell us». In each of them the number of sizes [units] was different. The Indians measured the circumference of the earth by the distance between our one and eight miles. In different dimensions their opinion changed, in each of the five «siddihants» the circumference of the earth was described differently from the others. The Romans measured it by size and called it «stadion». Galen says that Eratosthenes made his measurements in the cities of Aswan and Alexandria, which were on the same meridian. Again, according to Galen's Proofs, Ptolemy's Introduction to Spherical Art and Geography, the quantities differ. Such disagreements led Mamun ibn al-Rashid, with the help of local leaders in the Sinjar desert in Mosul, to refocus [the problem].

One of the greatest treatises of the great scientist, 'Tafhim' is a kind of textbook dedicated to explaining information about various sciences that astrologers and

---

[403] Al-Farabi Abu Nasr. Commentaries on the introductions to the first and fifth books of Euclid. Translation by M.F. Beckstein. Mathematical treatises. - Alma-Ata, 1972. - P. 238-239.

astrologers should know. Therefore, it also contains information on mathematics, geography, chronology and rules for the use of astrolabes. The work is written in the form of 530 questions and short answers to them.

Thus, Tafhim is a work based on a profound scientific and methodological principle, written by Abu Rayhon Beruni as an encyclopaedia of various sciences of his time in the form of a unified logical system.

Abu Rayhon Beruni used the results of the treatises and observations of many ancient Greek, Iranian, Indian and Muslim scholars in writing «Qanuni Masudi». Ptolemy's «Almagist» is the most important one. From him he received a lot of information about ancient observations. In addition, Meton (5th century B.C.), Euctemon (5th century B.C.), Hippocrates (460-377 B.C.), Aristarchus (4th century B.C.), Aristotle (4th century B.C., IV century), Galen (IV century B.C.), Archimedes. (287-212 BC), Timocharis (III century BC), Aristyllus (III century BC), Aratus (3rd century BC), Hipparchus (2nd century BC), Agricpa (1st century BC), Menelaus (1st century BC), Serenus (4th century BC). works, used the results of his scientific views and observations.

Among the scientists of Muslim countries who influenced the «Qanuni Masudi» with their researches and treatises, the author of the Arabic «Sindhinda» Abu Ishaq Ibrahim ibn Habib al-Fazari (VIII century), Yaqub ibn Tariq (VIII century), the great scientist Muhammad ibn Musa al-Khwarizmi can be recalled. After them come the names of scientists who lived and worked in the 9th century. Among them are Abu Ja'far Muhammad ibn Musa (d. 872), known as Banu Musa, and Ahmad ibn Musa (9th century), al-Hasan ibn Musa (9th century), Habash al-Khasib al-Marwazi (c. 770 - c. 870), Hamid ibn Abdulmalik al-Marwarrudi (first half of the 9th century), Suleiman ibn Ismat al-Samarkandi (9th century), Yahya ibn Abu Mansur (d. 830), Muhammad ibn Ali al-Makki (9th century), Yaqub ibn Ishaq al-Kindi (d. about 873), Ali ibn Isa al-Karrani (9th century), Sanad ibn Ali (9th century), Thabit ibn Qurra (9th century) and others.

Besides them, Abu-l-Abbas an-Nairizi (d. 922), Abu-l-Hussein al-Sufi (903-998), Muhammad ibn Jabir al-Battani (10th century), Abu Jafar al-Khozin (d. 961 or between 971), Abul Fazl al-Hirawi, Abu Mahmud al-Khojandi (d. 1000), Abu-l-Wafa Bozhani (940-998), Abu Sahl al-Kohi (10th century), Nazif ibn Yaman (10th century), Abu Hamid al-Saghani (d. 990), Abul Hasan al-Samiri (IX-X century), Muhammad ibn Ishaq al-Sarakhsi (IX-X century) and others.

Abu Rayhon Beruni also used in Qanuni Masudi the works of authors whose names are rarely mentioned in other sources, or information received from them. Among them are Abul Abbas al-Iranshahri (8th century), Moshula ibn Asari al-Basri (8th-9th century), known in the West as Messehalla in the Middle Ages, Muhammad ibn Kunasa al-Asadi (8th century), Abul Hasan al-Qasi (8th century), Omar ibn Farrukh al-Tabari (8th century) and his son Abu Bakr Muhammad ibn Umar al-Farruhan, Abu Sahr Abdulaziz ibn Uthman ibn Ali al-Kabisi (8th century), known in Europe as alkabicins, are scientists.

He also mentions the names of scientists who are not mentioned in other sources - Qatrab (9th century) and an-Nasr ibn Shamil (9th century).

In «Kanuni Masudi» he collected all the achievements of his predecessors and contemporaries in the field of astronomy and mathematics. He critically examined them and added the results of his own observations and research. In his work, the encyclopaedist focused on all the problems of astronomy and mathematics that were relevant to his time. Thus, we can say that «Kanuni Masudi» is an encyclopaedia of medieval oriental philology and mathematics.

In Movarunnahr, Khorasan and Khorezm, unprecedented achievements were made in the field of exact sciences. The information given by Abu Rayhon Beruni gives us a clear idea of this. According to him, there were observatories in some cities of Central Asia as early as the 9th century, where catastrophes were continuously observed. For example, Muhammad ibn Ishaq al-Sarakhsi[404], Abu Mashar al-

---

[404] Abu Rayhan Beruni. Selected works. 5-t. Book 2. Lo Masudi. Articles 6–11 // Transl. A. Rasulov; The author of the preface and indicators is A. A. Akhmedov; A. Akhmedov and B. Rosenfeld made comments. - Tashkent: Science, 1976. - 57 p.

Balkhi[405] and Sulayman ibn Ismat al-Samarkandi in Balkh[406] and Mansur ibn Talha in Marwah conducted disaster observations based on the same system.

The number of such cities increased in the 10th and 11th centuries. During this period, Muhammad ibn Ali al-Makki in Nishapur, Abu l-Fazl al-Hirawi, Abu Jafar al-Khozin and Abu Mahmud al-Khojandi in Raya, Abu Nasr ibn Iraq, Abu Rayhon Beruni in Kot and Gurganch. Ibn Sina and Abu Rayhon Beruni made observations in Gurganch.

The process of the powerful cultural upsurge that took place in the 9th and 10th centuries is based on information collected over the centuries. That is why the following words of N. I. Conrad are remarkable. Conrad are noteworthy: «The first states in Central Asia were Khorezm and Bactria. They were founded in the 7th-6th centuries. Thus, like the Italians and the Greeks, the peoples of this part of the world had their own common antiquity»[407].

First of all, it should be said that the culture of higher mathematics and astronomy in Central Asia in the 9th-15th centuries was undoubtedly based on local scientific traditions formed in Khorezm, Sogd, Margion, Bactria and other countries that have a special place on this earth[408]. Thus, the majority of scientists at the Baghdad and Gurganj academies came from Central Asia. According to Y. Ruska, almost all the mathematicians and astronomers in the list compiled by H. Suter came from Khorasan, Movarunnahr, Bactria and Fergana. If there was no ancient scientific base in Central Asia and neighbouring countries, such a situation could not have happened.

Information about the catastrophes of ancient Khorezm and Sogd has been preserved in the works of Abu Raikhan Beruni[409]. Speaking about the stars belonging to the constellations, he says: «The inhabitants of Khorezm knew the constellations

---

[405] Abu Rayhan Beruni. Selected works. 5-t. Book 2. Lo Masudi. Articles 6–11 // Transl. A. Rasulov; The author of the preface and indicators is A. A. Akhmedov; A. Akhmedov and B. Rosenfeld made comments. - Tashkent: Science, 1976. - 46, 73, 144 p.

[406] Abu Rayhan Beruni. Selected works. 5-t. Book 2. Lo Masudi. Articles 6–11 // Transl. A. Rasulov; The author of the preface and indicators is A. A. Akhmedov; A. Akhmedov and B. Rosenfeld made comments. - Tashkent: Science, 1976. - 281 p., 96 p.

[407] Konrad N.I. About the Renaissance. - Moscow: Nauka, 1966. – 238 p.

[408] Rozhanskaya M.M. Mechanics. - Moscow: Science, 1976. - 53 p.

[409] Tolstov S.P. Biruni and the problem. – Moscow, 1948. - P. 125-130.

better than the Arabs»[410], and in some of them he proves with examples that the stars of the Arabs are wrong, while those of the peoples are correct. Khorezm, and he gives the names of the constellations in Khorezm.

Abu Raikhan Beruni, commenting on the Khorezmian and Sogdian calendars, wrote: «The beginnings of the year and months in Khorezm correspond to those of the Sogdians and are opposite to those of the Iranians. The paintings of the Khorezmians are similar to those of the Sogdians, and for them the beginning of summer is the beginning of winter»[411]. This information alone is clear evidence of the existence of mathematical traditions in pre-Islamic Khorezm and Sogd[412].

Mathematicians and astrologers in the Near and Middle East paid great attention to the theory of the astrolabe, as this simple instrument was very useful in determining the coordinates of luminaries, distances to fixed objects, and solving other problems of practical astrophysics and geodesy.

Abu Rayhon Beruni in Khorezm and Abu-l-Wafa Muhammad ibn Muhammad al-Bojani in Baghdad agreed to observe the eclipse at the same time. As a result of this observation, Abu Rayhon Beruni invented his rule for determining the longitude of cities by lunar eclipses.

Abu Ali ibn Sina was a great thinker in the fields of medicine and philosophy, and one of the most mature scholars in the field of mathematics of his time. He was able to solve very subtle and complex problems, especially in the field of arithmetic and number theory.

Treatises on geometry by Abu Ali ibn Sina include «Donishnama»[413], «Commentaries on Euclid»[414], «Usul 'ilm al-Khandasa» («Fundamentals of Geometry»). In 1957 A.M.Bogouddinov translated the philosophical, logical and physical parts of «Donishnom» into Russian with commentaries.

---

[410] Beruni. MSSU,ments to past generations. – Tashkent: Science, 1973. – 282 p.
[411] Beruni. MSSU,ments to past generations. – Tashkent: Science, 1973. – 280 p.
[412] Livshits V.A. Khorezm calendar. - Moscow: Science, 1970. - P. 161-169; Henning W.B. The choresmian documents. P. 158-168; Weinberg B.I. Specific minting. - Moscow: Nauka, 1977. - P. 114-115; Weinberg B.I. Coins of ancient Khorezm. - Moscow: Science, 1977. - P. 77-80; Livshits V.A. Khorezmian calendar and eras. - Moscow: Science, 1970. - P. 5-16.
[413] Ibn Sina. Danish-name - "Book of Knowledge." - Dushanbe: Tajik State Publishing House.. 1967. - 180 p..
[414] Ibn Sina Abu Ali. Edited by Uklidis. Microfilm of the manuscript of the work from the library of Ayo Sofia № 2720.

In the Middle Ages, four mathematical subjects were taught together: geometry, arithmetic, calculus and music. Ibn Sina interpreted Euclid's principles on the basis of the «quadrivium». The great scientist's «Usul ilm al-Khandasa» was published in Cairo in 1976 under the title «Negizlar». According to it, he called the axioms «General Concepts». All the information presented in this chapter has been translated from Arabic into Uzbek by the author.

In Ibn Sina's time, the laws of arithmetic were called axioms, some of which have been proven to this day. They are based on the definitions of Leibniz. Currently, the definition of a sector in a secondary school geometry textbook is: «A sector is a part inside the inner central corner of a circle». It can be seen that Ibn Sina's definition of sector is used in modern geometry textbooks.

The fifth book of V is very short, consisting of only five sentences. These sentences are the same both in the work and in the manuscript of the work «Fundamentals of Geometry» published in Cairo. But the forms are different.

The manuscript № 2720, taken from the library of the Ayo Sophia Cathedral, stored in the manuscript collection of the Abu Rayhon Beruni Institute of Oriental Studies of the Academy of Sciences of the Republic of Uzbekistan, was selected from pages 1ab-89ab and presented 15 articles. The sentences and forms in the manuscript are not ordered. There are 462 sentences and 424 tables. Therefore, they are different from each other.

As for the views on the theory of parallels, they were first set out in Euclid's «Principles». Also at the end of the 17th century. J.Wallis (lectures 1651-1663, published 1693)[415], G. Saccheri (1733)[416] and A.M.Legendre (published several times 1794-1823)[417], I.G.Lambert (published 1766, 1786)[418]. Geometry textbooks contain important information on the theory of parallels.

In the countries of the Near and Middle East with the theory of parallel lines, al-Jawhari, Thabit ibn Qurra, Hatim an-Nayrizi, Ibn al-Haytham, Abu Ali ibn Sina, Abu

---

[415] Wallis J. De postulato quinto et definitione quinta lib. 6 Euclidis; disceptatio geometrica. - Opera mathematica. Oxoniae, 1693, t. 2.- P. 665-678.
[416] Saccheri G. Euclides ab omni naevo vindicanus/Ed. and transl. G.B.Halsted/ Chicago. - London, 1920.
[418] Legendre A.M. Elements de geometrie/1eme ed. P. 3eme ed. P.1800.^{12eme} ed. - P., 1823.

Raihan Beruni, Omar Khayyam, Nasiriddin al- - Tusi, al -Maghribi (XIII-2 half centuries), Shamsiddin as-Samarkandi (XII-XIV centuries) and others. They tried to prove postulate V in their works written in Arabic, and there is earlier evidence from the Byzantine Aganis and Simplicus who lived in the 5th-6th centuries.

Abu Rayhon Beruni did not openly state his theory of parallels in Tafhim. But he did write a special work in which he explained his views in detail. Its title: «A work on the infinite division of quantities, analogous to the case of two mutually converging lines which do not intersect at any length». It is mentioned in the list of works of the great scientist[419]. Only part of this treatise has survived, and it contains three prefaces. The first introduction shows that sets can be infinite[420]. According to him, this introduction belongs to the famous scientist Abu Yusuf Yaqub ibn Ishaq al-Kindi, who lived in the 9th century. On this basis, two other introductions are presented. The first states that if two straight lines are drawn parallel to each other, they will never intersect. If at each position of the two parallel lines such points are chosen as lie on the same line, then it is shown that two lines approaching from the same side will not meet[421]. In the next introduction it will be shown that if monotonically decreasing perpendicular segments are placed on a straight line and the second ends of these segments lie on the same straight line, then both straight lines converge on the decreasing side of the segments. According to the first entry, they do not meet in this direction[422].

It is known that these two cases are relevant in the geometry of N.I.Lobachevsky.

The theory of parallels of Abu Rayhon Beruni was fundamentally different from the theory of Euclid, and N.I.Lobachevsky was an important step in the creation of non-euclidean geometry.

---

[420] Bulgakov P.G., Akhmedov A. Theory of parallel Beruniy al-Kindi // Society. science in Uzbekistan. – Tashkent, 1977.№ 8. - P. 30-36..

[421] Bulgakov P.G., Akhmedov A. Theory of parallel Beruniy al-Kindi // Society. science in Uzbekistan. – Tashkent, 1977. № 8. - P. 30-36..

[422] Bulgakov P.G., Akhmedov A. Theory of parallel Beruniy al-Kindi // Society. science in Uzbekistan. – Tashkent, 1977. № 8. - P. 30-36..

Abu Ali ibn Sina tried to prove Euclid's postulate V, as did the scientists of medieval Islamic countries. To do this, he quoted special propositions in the works 'Donishnama' and 'Usul ilm al-Khandasa'. Ibn Sina tried to prove the postulate of parallel lines, but these theorems have not been fully proven because they have many shortcomings. But this desire of the scientist greatly influenced the scientific activities of his followers.

In the mathematical section of The Enlightenment, Abu Ali ibn Sina stated that an understanding of astronomy was necessary for him. Therefore, he presents his arguments and proofs in simple language and short sentences. The purpose and method of explaining Ibn Sina's geometry in this work is to explain the foundations of this science. Ibn Sina's work on the theory of parallel lines and his doctrine of complex proportions also had a great influence on the work of Omar Khayyam. He wrote a special treatise on this problem. Omar Khayyam had a certain influence on his work. Unlike Aristotle and Euclid, Omar Khayyam continued and deepened the theory of Ibn Sina, who made extensive use of motion in mathematics.

He also made extensive use of motion in the definitions and proofs of some theorems in the Donishnama, Usul ilm al-Khandasa. This was a major innovation and a step into the future of medieval mathematics.

From the above, it is clear that Ibn Sina's treatises «Enlightenment» and «Kitab al-Shifa» were important scientific works not only in the field of philosophy but also in the field of mathematics and geometry. The scientist was respectfully called «Hakim» because he was not only a sage, doctor and philosopher, but also a mathematician.

Due to wars and natural disasters in the past, only a part of the rich scientific heritage of many of our scientists has been preserved. Little is known of their lives. One of our most famous scientists is Abu Abdullah al-Khwarizmi. In literature, the scientist's full name is written as Abu Abdullah Muhammad ibn Ahmad Yusuf Katib al-Khwarizmi. He lived and worked in the 10th century and studied mathematics, astronomy and geography.

According to sources, he worked in Nishapur in 975-991 and was secretary to the minister al-Utbi. He wrote a work called Mafatih al-Ulum (Keys of Knowledge). There are four copies of the manuscript[423]. Three are in the British Museum under the numbers 7528, 23429 and 2524, and the fourth is in the Berlin Library under the number 1051. The English scholar K. Bosworth found out in the 60s of the 20th century that there were six other copies of this work in Turkish libraries. They are kept in the libraries of Istanbul.

This work by Abu Abdullah al-Khwarizmi attracted the attention of many scholars as a rare source on the history of the development of science in the Middle Ages. The Dutch orientalist Van Vloten was the first to study this source and published it in 1895. See also V. Bartold, K. Brockelman, I. Krachkovsky, E. Wiedemann, G. Sarton, M. Khairullayev, U. Karimov, G. Matviyevskaya, Kh. Hasanov, A. Sharipov, R. Bakhadirov and J. Ibodov, who studied the work from different angles.

Abu Abdullah Khorezmi distinguishes the following classification of sciences[424]:

I. Sharia and the sciences of the «Arabs».

1. Fiqh, i.e. Muslim jurisprudence.

2. The Word, i.e. the foundations of religion.

3. Grammar.

4. Economics.

5. Poetic presentation.

6. History.

II. The «non-Arab» sciences (Greek and other peoples).

1. Theoretical philosophy:

a) natural sciences - medicine, celestial phenomena - meteorology, mineralogy, alchemy, mechanics - astronomy, music;

---

[423] Stars of Spirituality. – Tashkent: Science, 2000. – 80 p.
[424] Bahodirov R. Abu Abdullah al-Khorazmiy va illmlar tasnifi tarihidan. - Tashkent: Uzbekiston, 1995. - 24 points; Ibodov Zh.Kh. Physics and mathematics chapters of the encyclopedia "Keys of Sciences" ("Mafotih al-ulum") by Abu Abdullah al-Khorezmi (10th century) - Tashkent: Science, 2005. - 54 p.

b) Divine, i.e. metaphysics;

c) Logic.

2. Practical philosophy:

a) morality - ethics (human management);

b) housekeeping (management of the home);

c) Politics (government of a city, country).

The book «Mafatih al-Uloom» consists of two parts, the first part consists of 5 sections and the second part consists of 9 sections.

The first part includes the following sections

Grammar, Speaking, Writing, Poetry and Poetry Writing, Short Stories.

The second part consists of the following sections:

Philosophy, Logic, Medicine, Arithmetic, Geometry, Astronomy, Music, Mechanics, Chemistry.

Abu Abdullah Khorezmi studies the book in the book of accounts and divides it into five sections. According to him, arithmetic is the science of numbers. It is divided into even and odd numbers. Odd numbers are those that are not divisible by two, while even numbers are divisible by two. When an even number is added to an odd number, the result is divided by two again until the quotient is one.

The second part of the book is interesting for naturalists and mathematicians with the work of Abu Abdullah al-Khwarizmi[425] «Mafatih al-ulum» (مفاتيح العلوم). Chapter 8 is devoted to mechanics, in which the movements of solid, liquid and gaseous bodies and their masses were studied by the ancient scientists of the East.

The geometrical part of the work includes problems on concepts, lines, surfaces and bodies. Abu Abdullah al-Khwarizmi writes: «The ancient Greeks called this art «geometry», a word that means «measurement of the earth». He said that the word «geometry» is an Arabised word. In Persian this word is called model or size. After this, evidence comes from the writing of Euclid's Principles, its dissemination in the

---

[425] Ibodov J.H. Physics and mathematics chapters of the encyclopedia "Keys of Sciences" ("Mafotih al-ulum") by Abu Abdullah al-Khorezmi (10th century) - Tashkent: Science, 2005. - 54 p.

East, among Muslims in general, as well as the interpretation of Euclid's geometry by some scientists.

Abu Abdullah al-Khwarizmi divides solids into nine types:

1. Tetrahedron. It is bounded by a regular quadrilateral or four equilateral triangles. It has four faces, four ends and six ribs.

2. The cube is bounded by six squares with equal sides and angles. It has six sides, twelve ribs and eight vertices.

3. The octahedron is a regular octahedron. It is bounded by eight equilateral and equiangular triangles. It has eight sides, six triangles and twelve edges.

4. Icosahedron - bounded by twenty equilateral and equiangular triangles. It has twenty faces, twelve triangles and thirty edges.

5. Dodecahedron - bounded by twelve regular pentagons with equal sides. It has twelve sides, twenty-three and thirty edges.

6. A cylinder is a body that begins with a circle and ends with an equal circle. It is restricted to the surface.

7. A cone is a body that starts from a point and ends in a circle. It is bounded first by a circle and then by the surface of a cone.

8. A sphere is a body such that all points on its surface are equidistant from a point inside. This is called the centre of the sphere. Any straight line from the centre of a sphere to its surface is its radius. The straight line passing through its centre and joining its two poles is called the axis of the sphere.

9. A ring is a body surrounded by a circular surface. Other shapes are sickle and onion.

Chapter summaries:

By the end of the 10th century, the Samanid dynasty had been abolished. At the suggestion of Ibn Iraq and Abu Rayhon Beruni, scientists from Nishapur, Balkh, Bukhara and Iraq came to Gurganj in 1004, as Khorezmshah Mamun created houses and conditions for scientists and allocated plots of land. Salaries were also fixed according to the work done. According to Abu Rayhon Beruni, translation work from Greek and Syriac was carried out in this academy.

2. Abu Abdullah al-Biyan an-Naysaburi (d. 1004), Abu Sahl Isa ibn Yahya al-Jurjani al-Masihi (977-1011), Abu Rayhon Beruni, Abu Abdullah Ilaqi (d. 1068) Ahmad at the Khorezm Mamun Academy Ibn Muhammad al-Sakhri al-Khwarizmi (d. 1015), Ma'mun ibn Ma'mun (d. 1017), Zainuddin ibn Ma'mun (d. 1017). 1017), Zainuddin Jurjani (IX-X century), Abu Nasr ibn Iraq, Abu Said ibn Ahmad ibn Muhammad ibn Miskawaih (d. 1030), Abu Ali ibn Sina, Abu l-Khair Hammar, Abu Mansur al-Salibi (961-1038), Abulkarim Zirgali (9th century), Abu Muhammad ibn Khidr al-Khojandi and other scholars. They studied various fields of science such as mathematics, physics, astronomy, linguistics, psychology, education, medicine, philosophy, history, literature, music, geography, topography, mechanics, geodesy, logic, alchemy, chemistry.

3. From many years of research in the history of mathematics, it is known that the proof of the theorem of sines for plane and three-dimensional triangles was first made by the Khorezmian scientist Abu Nasr ibn Iraq.

One of the important problems solved by Abu Rayhon Beruni in his «Geodesy» is the measurement of the Earth's radius. This is the radius of the earth R.

$R = \frac{l \cosh}{1 - \cosh}$ is calculated with great accuracy using the formula where: $h \neq 0$, h - angle, l - length, cos h - cosine of the angle.

4. Abu Ali ibn Sina divided the philosophical sciences into two groups: theoretical (an-nazari) and practical (al-amali). He divided the theoretical sciences into physics (ilm at-tabiy) and mathematics (ilm al-riyadi). According to him, the mathematical sciences include: number theory (ilm al-adad), geometry (ilm al-handasa), astronomy (ilm al-hay`a) and music (ilm al-musik).

5. Considering that mathematical sciences occupy an important place in the scientific heritage of Khorezm scientists, fundamentally important discoveries were made in the field of calculus, algebra and trigonometry: 1) improvement of the hexadecimal position system for arithmetic and combinations; 2) recognition of decimal places; 3) development of methods for extracting roots of numbers; 4) use of «Newton's binomial formula» for any natural indicator; 5) extension of the concept of

a real positive number; 6) the application of digital algebra to geometry and trigonometry and the discovery of the method of integration; 7) the creation of a geometric theory for solving cubic equations; 8) the creation of a system of plane and spatial trigonometry; 9) the calculation of extremely accurate and perfect trigonometric tables, etc.

6. The «Chronology» of Abu Rayhon Beruni is important because it is written about geometric projections. He opened a cylindrical projection and, for the first time in the history of physics and mineralogy, accurately measured the specific gravity. As a result of his observations, he was the first to determine complex problems of astronomy, geography and geodesy, including the longitude and latitude of the city, the equinoxes and solstices, the maximum and minimum altitudes, the angle of deviation of the ecliptic from the celestial equator. and the local time of the city. A number of our scholars wrote commentaries on the mathematical treatises of Muhammad ibn Musa al-Khwarizmi and Abu Rayhon Beruni.

7. Abu Abdullah Khorezmi used the concept of «figurative numbers» in science. They are expressed in the form of a triangle, rectangle, pentagon, hexagon, heptagon and other geometric shapes. He also defined 9 complex solids - tetrahedron, cube, octahedron, icosahedron, dodecahedron, cylinder, cone, sphere and rings.

8. Scientists of the Khorezm Mamun Academy gave their opinion on the theory of parallels. According to the definition of Abu Rayhon Beruni, if two parallel straight lines are given, then it is written that if they are drawn directly towards each other, they will never overlap. It has been shown that two lines converging on one side will not meet if we choose points where both parallel lines are drawn so that they lie on the same line. Also, if monotonically decreasing perpendicular sections are placed on a line and their second ends lie on the same line, then both lines converge on the side of the decreasing sections, and by the first definition it is shown that they do not meet in this direction. Abu Ali ibn Sina also makes extensive use of motion in his works «Donishnama», «Usul ilm al-Khandasa», in the proofs of some theorems. This is good news for the Middle Ages.

9. It can be said that Abu Ali ibn Sina's rule for checking the square of any

number in a series of natural numbers using 9 is as rigorous as the problem of comparing two numbers modulo a known number in modern number theory. This practice has become important in everyday life and in the development of entrepreneurship.

10. Such works of Abu Rayhon Beruni as «Famous People of Khorezm», «Treatise on the Mukanna Uprising», «Memorials», «India», «Useful Questions and Correct Answers», «On Differences in Determining Years», «Cleansing History» . from unnecessary words - science applied to practice. Moreover, Abu Rayhon Beruni told history truthfully and treated all peoples with equal respect.

CHAPTER III. SOCIAL RELATIONS AND SOCIAL LIFE IN THE HISTORICAL AND PHILOSOPHICAL HERITAGE OF THE SCHOLARS OF THE MAMUN ACADEMY OF KHOREZM

This chapter presents an analysis of the historical and philosophical heritage of the scientists of the Khorezm Academy of Mamun, including their views on social relations, science, education, lifestyle, and social life. It also examines the dialectics of the natural scientific paradigm and ontological views of Abu Nasr ibn Iraq and Abu Rayhon Beruni, as well as the neoplatonic elements in the ontological teaching of Abu Ali ibn Sina. The classification of sciences and the humanistic essence of moral views are also discussed, along with their influence on the development of historical and philosophical thinking, based on scientific study of sources. The influence of a universal system of norms that regulate social relations, human activity, and behavior can help explain the diversity of civilizations. The characteristics of civilizations are influenced by their prevailing religious and ideological goals, their place in the political, social, and cultural process, their level of technical and economic development, and the pace of economic and social processes. Each civilization type has specific political system characteristics and legal norms. Civilizations differ in the way they encode, store, and transmit information from generation to generation[426].

The influence of a universal system of norms regulating social relations, human activity, and behavior helps explain the diversity of civilizations. The characteristics of civilizations are influenced by their prevailing religious and ideological goals, their place in the political, social, and cultural process, their level of technical and economic development, and the pace of economic and social processes. Each civilization type has specific political system characteristics and legal norms. Civilisations differ in the way they encode, store and transmit information from generation to generation.

---

[426] Shermukhamedova N. Philosophy. – Tashkent: University, 2015. – P. 541-542.

Abu Raikhan Beruni, an Eastern philosopher, was the first to study the relationship between humans, nature, and the universe from a scientific perspective. He argued that differences in human constitution, including colour, appearance, character, and morals, are not solely due to ancestry, but also to differences in soil, water, air, and geographical location[427]. The diversity of languages arises from the need of different groups of people to express their unique desires. Abu Raikhan Beruni, an Eastern thinker, was the first to study the relationship between humans, nature, and the universe from a global perspective. He stated: The variations in human constitution, including colour, appearance, character, and morals, are not solely due to differences in ancestry, but also to variations in soil, water, air, and geographical location. The diversity of languages arises from the separation of people into distinct groups, each requiring words to express their unique desires.

3.1. Views on social relations, science, education, lifestyle, and social life in the historical and philosophical heritage of scientists of the Khorezm Academy Mamun

According to Abu Rayhon Beruni, the natural environment has a direct impact on a person's character, spiritual views, image, and behavior. He believed that geographical conditions play a significant role in the formation of peoples and nations. Beruni also observed that the human body is a complex system, with opposing parts that are united by the force of subordination. Beruni also observed that the human body is a complex system, with opposing parts that are united by the force of subordination[428]. Beruni stated that all people have both similarities and differences. Phrases grew larger over time, were remembered, and eventually organized into content through repetition[429].

---

[427] Beruniy A. Selected works. Volume 1 - Tashkent: Science, 1968. - P. 16-17.
[428] See: Irisov A. The Wisdom of Abu Raikhan Beruni. -Tashkent: Young Guard, 1973. - B.40-43.
[429] See: Irisov A. The Wisdom of Abu Raikhan Beruni. -Tashkent: Young Guard, 1973. - B.40-43.

Abu Ali ibn Sina noted that humans differ from other animals in their speech, language, and thinking. He believed that studying various sciences enriches the human mind[430].

Therefore, it is essential to organize, strengthen, and improve their life with the help of others. This is a fundamental truth that no one can achieve alone. Abu Nasr Farabi believed that individuals can only satisfy their needs and reach a higher spiritual level in society[431] by being the architect and creator of their life, cultivating virtues and talents.

As members of various social groups, including family, production teams, and nations, individuals are in constant contact with others. All human activities occur within the social framework of a given society, including political, legal, economic, moral, and other relations. The development of certain qualities in people and society primarily depends on material production, rather than the geographical environment. To discuss how natural conditions influence social processes, it is necessary to analyze the historically changeable nature of human production. Using precise subject-specific vocabulary when necessary, it is important to maintain a clear and objective language, avoiding biased or emotional language.Man plays an active role in the interaction between nature and society, and it is the social environment that determines the natural environment, not the other way around. The text should also adhere to conventional academic structure and formatting, with clear and concise sentences and a logical flow of information. Man plays an active role in the interaction between nature and society, and it is the social environment that determines the natural environment, not the other way around. Individuals regulate their metabolism in harmony with nature, maintaining a level of control and preventing the unpredictable forces of nature from overpowering them[432].

The development of moral thinking in the medieval Muslim East was greatly influenced by the famous pannomas. These were artistic and didactic works that

---

[430] Ibn Sina. Danishname. - Dushanbe: 1957. – 59 p.
[431] Farabi Abu Nasr. City of virtuous people. -Tashkent: People's Heritage Publishing House named after Abdulla Kadyri, 1993. - 69 p.
[432] Shermukhamedova N. Philosophy. -Tashkent: University, 2014. – 252 p.

explained the essence of morality and promoted moral values. They were widely distributed among the people and had a common feature of transmitting moral norms, principles, and factors of moral culture through understandable and colourful forms. Ethics is the science that studies moral phenomena in unity and relativity. It is an ancient science with roots dating back to the distant past, known under various names such as 'Etiquette', 'Science of Ethics', 'Science of Morals'. The science of ethics examines people's behaviour, lifestyle, and moral relations with each other in society. Morality is a set of stable and specific norms and rules that govern historical behaviour, conduct, social and personal life, as well as relationships with society. The term 'ethics' has two different meanings: the object of scientific study and the embodiment of human character and behaviour. It is widely accepted that morality is a property of human nature and is behaviour that manifests itself without any necessity or mental effort. For this reason, human morality is to some extent innate and can only be refined through protection from negative influences. Positive behaviours and attitudes are considered moral, while negative ones are deemed immoral.

Etiquette is founded on moral principles, norms, education levels, and aesthetic ideals. It encompasses beautiful patterns of behaviour based on national traditions that create a pleasant impression on individuals, but are not of great importance to society and humanity. Etiquette refers to a set of rules governing how individuals should behave in public, including how to treat others, organize their lives, and spend their free time. Manners are typically developed within the family environment, as well as through education, social work, and practical experience.

Morals are positive characteristics that can serve as examples throughout human history and society. Although social consciousness is one of the oldest forms of consciousness, it changes over time, develops, and improves, becoming one of the manifestations of spiritual culture.

The emergence of Sufism facilitated the introduction of Islam into Central Asia and developed the ideas of classical ethics from the ancient world. This solved the problems posed by the classical ethics and created important theoretical and artistic-ethical works relevant for that period and subsequent years. These works were mainly produced in the Muslim East.

It is important to note that cognition is always influenced by social relations and the cultural world. Social order is shaped by the important needs of society, which are only knowable within the conditions of the present time. These conditions also influence the cognitive process to varying degrees. Social order is shaped by the important needs of society, which are only knowable within the conditions of the present time. In Islam, the Holy Quran and Hadith regulate religious, educational, scientific, cultural, and socio-political life. The hadiths describe the rules and requirements of the Islamic religion, morality, and high human qualities.

Medieval encyclopedic scientists such as Abu Ali ibn Sina, Abu Nasr Farabi, Mahmud al-Zamakhshari, and Abu Raikhan Beruni worked in the theoretical and practical fields of moral science. Abu Nasr Farabi divides philosophy into two categories: theoretical and practical philosophy, with ethical issues falling under the latter. Ethical issues were raised in works such as 'The Book of the Path to Happiness', 'On Finding Happiness', 'The Wisdom of a Statesman', and 'The City of Virtuous People'. These works highlight human happiness as the main problem. Abu Nasr Farabi also discusses the problem of life and death in detail. According to him, a person must be mature to perform good deeds in life. Compliance with the norm in human behavior determines virtue and maturity of behavior. The author defines morality as a social phenomenon that benefits the wealthy and disadvantages the poor. The text is grammatically correct and free from errors. Morality reflects the needs and interests of society and is expressed through demands and assessments that are supported by public opinion, accepted social models, customs, and mores. The language used is clear, objective, and value-neutral, with a formal register and precise word choice. The text adheres to conventional structure and formatting features, with consistent citation and footnote style. The author avoids biased language and employs passive tone and impersonal construction. No changes in content have been made[433].

---

[433] Philosophy: Encyclopedic Dictionary. – Tashkent: Shark, 2004. – 41 p.

From the late 8th to early 9th centuries, the spirituality of Central Asian peoples matured and developed into a unified Islamic culture that lasted from the 9th to the 15th centuries[434]. During this historical period, several notable figures made significant contributions to the development of world science. These figures include Abu Raikhan Beruni, Amir Temur, Ahmed Fargani, Muhammad Khorezmi, Abu Ali ibn Sina, Alisher Navai, Zahiriddin Muhammad Babur, Imam Bukhari, and Mirza Ulugbek.

Among them, Abu Rayhon Beruni stands out as a mature thinker and great genius of his time. Beruni was well-versed in various sciences of his time, including theology, physics, mineralogy, pharmacology, mathematics, and catastrophism[435]. His contributions to the development of these sciences have earned him a prominent place in the world of science. According to[436], Beruni was known for his impartial and truthful approach to scientific matters, as well as his assessments of historical events and his contemporaries.

In terms of his philosophical views, Beruni was closely aligned with deism. The author recognises that God is the creator and grants nature the right to preserve and develop its divine original force. The author posits that existence is both ancient and eternal, and that the elements of fire, air, and earth are derived from water. He disagreed with Aristotle's objection to this idea and[437], like Democritus and Epicurus, believed in the existence of many worlds with the same natural properties. The scientist expressed his philosophical views on the existence of multiple worlds. Additionally, he contemplated the eternity of the material world and how time is measured, ultimately concluding that it is measured by the movement of the planets.

Beruni posits that nothing exists separately from God and primordial matter. He raises the question of how time is measured, suggesting that a second may have been considered a long time in the past. However, Beruni's logic leads to the conclusion

---

[434] Masharipova G.K. The influence of the natural science, socio-philosophical and spiritual heritage of scientists of the Khorezm Mamun Academy on the development of social thinking. Monography. – Tashkent: Navruz, 2019. – 161 p.
[435] Masharipova G.K. The role of the scientific, philosophical and spiritual heritage of Abu Ali ibn Sina in the life of society. Monograph. – Tashkent: Navruz, 2020. – 76 p.
[436] Karimov I.A. High spirituality is an invincible force. - Tashkent: Spirituality, 2008. - 42 p.
[437] About the scientific heritage of our ancestors and youth. – Tashkent, 2008. – 18 p.

that time is immeasurable and eternal, and that the world was created outside of time. In his reflection on the relationship between matter and form, he states that motion belongs to matter by its general nature and causes the soul to take on various forms.

Therefore, matter is active, and everything connected with it contributes to its movement. External matter consists of concreteness and manifests itself in various forms. Existence is always in a state of change and development, driven by natural forces.

Philosophers rely on experience and logic as important means of knowledge and criteria of truth. Beruni argues that the beginning of knowledge stems from feelings and that feelings play a significant role in the process of acquiring knowledge. He asserts that external perception is a characteristic shared by animals and humans, and that perception is linked to consciousness through the organs of hearing and vision. Beruni also posits that reason, which represents the highest level of knowledge, is bestowed by God. The task at hand is to comprehend the world and utilise it for the betterment of humanity while maintaining harmony with nature.

The scientific significance of Abu Rayhon Beruni's works lies in the historical information he provides about the high development of national and religious tolerance in the territory of our Motherland, located on the Great Silk Road. His opinions offer valuable insights into the character of our people[438]. It is important to note that his evaluations are objective and free from bias. Beruniy mentioned in his works that thousands of years ago in the city of Urgench there were Jewish quarters, Christian churches, and people from Arab, Indian, Chinese, and Slavic backgrounds. According to Beruniy, people form societies to help each other, create everything necessary for life, avoid disasters, and live without danger. The main reason for the creation of human communities is mutual assistance, sympathy, and support. Alternatively, Beruni, as a humanist thinker, explains that this state and order were subsequently disrupted by various robberies and military actions. For instance, in Mineralogy, Beruni states that «Man's needs are so diverse that he alone cannot satisfy them. One assistant is not enough to satisfy them. The needs are varied and

---

[438] Abu Raikhon Beruni. Tafhim. - Tashkent, 2005. – 58 p.

numerous. Only a team of several people can satisfy them. And for this, people need to build cities»[439]. He further elaborates on this idea in Geodesy: Due to the abundance of human needs and the lack of means for self-defense, as well as the abundance of enemies, humans were able to unite with their brothers in a society where members engage in work that satisfies their own needs and those of others[440], while also being in a relationship of mutual assistance. This article provides a scientific analysis of Abu Rayhon Beruni's views in the religious sphere. Researchers A.B.Kholidov and B.T.Erman express the opinion that, based on the views of that time, Beruni gave religion a broad meaning and understood it as the entire complex of spiritual life, including many areas of human practical life[441].

According to A. Irisov, a major researcher of the philosophical views of Abu Raykhan Beruni who wrote the preface to the work 'India', Beruni's definition of religion was all-encompassing. Perhaps the authors wanted to highlight Beruni's rationalistic approach to religion with their definitions. Beruni concludes that these rights are absolute, at least in this sense[442].

If we consider the idea that many figures in Central Asia possessed both a religious worldview and encyclopedic knowledge, then the conclusions of the aforementioned researchers are partially justified. Beruni was a scientist, encyclopedist and thinker who sought to find the scientific and historical basis of social events and relations that occur in society. He may have believed that religion, including Islam, encompasses all areas of spiritual life. Beruni condemned enmity, strife and bloody wars based on religious fanaticism and intolerance. The author advocates for an objective evaluation of religious beliefs and instructions based on reason. They also call for an unbiased assessment of other religions, including their purpose and spiritual essence[443]. One medieval scholar, Abul Abbas Iranshahri[444], is praised for their ability to tell accurate stories without deviation or hypocrisy. The

---

[439] Abu Rayhan Beruniy. Collection of information for the knowledge of jewelry (Mineralogy) - Moscow, 1963. – 11 p.
[440] Abu Rayhan Beruniy. Determining the boundaries of places to clarify the distance between populated areas. Geodesy T. III. - Tashkent: Science, 1966. – 83 p.
[441] Kholidov A.B, Erman B.T. Preface to Beruni's "India" // India. T. II. -Moscow, 1963. -.47 p.
[442] From the history of progressive thinking of the peoples of Central Asia. – Tashkent, 1990. – 96 p.
[443] Beruni Abu Rayhan. MSSU,ments of past generations. - Tashkent: Science, 1968. - 188 p.
[444] Information about Abul Abbas Iranshahi. Western India, Volume II. - Tashkent: Science, 1965. - 477 p.

author of the book did not express support or opposition towards any religion. Instead, he may have developed his own approach to writing about religions and encouraged others to do the same. The author provided a clear explanation of the religions of Jews and Christians as presented in the Torah and the Bible[445].

In the early Middle Ages, Abu Rayhon Beruni wrote about the immoral behaviour that had become a habit among the Nestorians, a sect of the Christian religion. He also wrote about the commendable Christian way of life of the people in general, which includes refraining from insults. Christians who exhibit humility, righteousness, and compassion towards all can be seen as a high example of respect for those who practice other religions. He explained that this was a call to promote interfaith reconciliation, spiritual growth, and trust.

Beruni believed that the purpose of life is to achieve happiness through knowledge and learning. His worldview, philosophical and moral views on existence, society, and humanity are a striking example of medieval humanism.

The approach towards nature is fundamentally positive. It originated in the middle of the 1st millennium and underwent significant changes with the introduction of theoretical thinking. This was the primary objective of philosophy. This type of thinking became an essential component of philosophy, which emerged as a distinct historical form of worldview. The earliest philosophers attempted to study nature to discover the composition of the world, which they referred to as the cosmos.

During the 7th-9th centuries in the Middle East, Aristotle's works were translated into Arabic and commentaries were written on them, leading to widespread acceptance of his ideas. Even during the Renaissance, Aristotle remained a prominent figure in discussions of important scientific and philosophical issues in the East. By this point, familiarity with the works of Aristotle and knowledge of his ideas had become essential to the study of philosophy and the acquisition of worldly knowledge. This led to the formation and development of Eastern Aristotelianism (Peripatetism). The concept of 'Eastern Aristotelianism' encompasses not only Aristotle's philosophical system but also rationalism, which is closely linked to

---

[445] Beruni, India Volume II. - Toshken, 1965. - 27 p.

natural philosophy and medieval rationalistic philosophy. It is worth noting that the question of the spread of Greek philosophical heritage in Central Asia remains unanswered, and there are still aspects that require clarification. There is no clear answer to the question of how the culture of antiquity first spread in the East and not in the West. The countries that were part of the Baghdad Caliphate became the heirs of the ancient culture under these conditions[446].

The conditions that led to the development of secular knowledge must be explained by the continuous struggle against Islam by peoples who were oppressed by the Arabs. This struggle resulted in the widespread dissemination of the achievements of Indian, Central Asian, Iranian, and especially Greek scientific thought, which made the development of secular sciences possible[447]. The language used is clear, objective, and value-neutral, and the sentence structure is simple and logical. It should be noted that although there were attempts to establish a unique scientific and cultural centre with a large library and an astronomical observatory during the reign of Caliph Harun al-Rashid[448], the construction of the 'House of the Sages' ('Bayt ul-Hikma') during the reign of the renowned Caliph Mamun, its peak period (813-832), corresponds to later periods.

Beruni objected to Aristotle's question regarding the book 'Heaven and the Universe'. Ibn Sina argued that fire is a substance and an element with a natural place, and that it does not arise from the movement of the sky. The text contains technical terms such as 'substance', 'element', and 'natural place', which are explained in context. The language is clear, concise, and objective, with a formal register and no filler words. The text is grammatically correct and free from spelling and punctuation errors. No changes in content were made. Ibn Sina argued that fire is a substance and an element with a natural place, and that it does not arise from the movement of the sky. For instance, Thales referred to this element as water, while Phoclitus

---

[446] Sharipov A. Humanistic views of Beruni // Important stages in the history of socio-ethical and humanistic thought in Uzbekistan. - Tashkent: Philosophy and Law, 2007. - pp. 44-45.
[447] Bulatov M.S. Ulugbek Observatory in Samarkand // Historical and astronomical studies. Vol. XVIII. - Moscow: 1986. – 111 p.
[448] Abdukhalimov B. "Bayt al-hikma" and the scientific activity of Central Asian scientists in Baghdad (exact and natural sciences in the 9th-11th centuries). - Tashkent: "Tashkent Islamic University". - 2004. – 236 p.

(Heraclitus) referred to it as fire. Devion (Diogenes) called it the substance between air and water, and Anikisidiris (Anaximander) referred to it as air. The word 'this' in the last sentence is ambiguous and should be replaced with it[449]. According to Ibn Sina, it is important to understand that Aristotle's assertion that the Universe has no beginning does not imply that the Universe lacks a creator. Rather, it means that the creator of the Universe is devoid of any work, i.e. creation[450].

The disputes between Buruni and Ibn Sina were not accidental. Aristotle's works, including 'Metaphysics', 'Physics', 'On the Heavens', 'On Appearance and Disappearance', and 'Meteorology', contain historical sources about correspondence from both Eastern thinkers and his compatriots. The early Renaissance period is considered an important time in the history of Central Asia. The unique characteristics of this period, including strong socio-political and ideological processes, are reflected in the social environment of Khorezm, Samarkand, and Bukhara, as well as in spiritual life and the development of science. The Khorezm Mamun Academy, created during this time, is a testament to the rich scientific and cultural traditions that have been developed over centuries by peoples throughout Central Asia, the Near East, and the Middle East. The peoples of Central Asia have created flourishing oases, built magnificent cities, developed crafts, and expanded international trade relations through caravans, river and sea routes. Economic, political and cultural ties between the countries of East and West have been revived. The development of scientific thinking was facilitated by the centuries-old religious and social-philosophical traditions that emerged in ancient and early Middle Ages oases, where various social groups settled and exchanged ideas. The rapid development of relationships between nomadic steppe people, science, and culture provided a necessary historical background.

During their debates, Beruni and Ibn Sina employed the dialectical method, which is a scientific knowledge method. Beruni questioned Ibn Sina's cosmological

---

[449] Ten questions of Beruni on Aristotle's book "Heaven and the Universe" and Ibn Sina's answers to them // From the history of advanced social and philosophical thought in Uzbekistan. - Tashkent: Science, 1959. - P. 140-141.
[450] Ten questions of Beruni on Aristotle's book "Heaven and the Universe" and Ibn Sina's answers to them // From the history of advanced social and philosophical thought in Uzbekistan. - Tashkent: Science, 1959. - P. 139.

theory, specifically regarding the heaviness and lightness of the celestial sphere, the absence of rectilinear motion, the movement of matter, and the theory of gravity of bodies. In Ibn Sina's scientific views of the Universe, circular motion is recognised as an alternative form of rectilinear motion. According to Ibn Sina, the movement of a body in a straight line is forced, caused by some external force, and therefore contrary to natural movement. Ibn Sina distinguishes between motion and matter, considering matter to be a phenomenon in a static state. According to Ibn Sina, movement is a constant and gradual change in the state of the body. This change is directed towards an object-controlled thing and can be adapted to it in a neutral, rather than active, state. Aristotle's cosmological theory associates the rectilinear movement of things with the movement of the Earth and the Universe towards or away from the center. The essence of this movement is one. According to Aristotle's 'Physics and the Heavens', if a body moves upward, it consists of the elements of fire or air. Conversely, if it moves downward, it is considered to consist of water and earth or their elements.

Aristotle also posits that circular motion is the perfection of motion, formed from the perfect nature of a circular form, while rectilinear movement is an imperfect and incomplete form of movement. A segment can be added to a straight line since it has neither an end nor a beginning. The movement of the celestial sphere is a highly developed and perfect phenomenon of circular motion. Objects moving in a circle are not heavy or light as they do not move up or down[451].

Ibn Sina supports Aristotle's theory that heavy bodies and their elements move towards the center of the Earth, while light bodies move away from it. Beruni suggests that all bodies and their elements move towards the center, while Ibn Sina does not address this specifically. Beruni and Ibn Sina approach the issue of natural movement differently. Beruni questions Ibn Sina about Aristotle's recognition of the fallacy of the doctrine of the 'indivisibility of the atom' and his doctrine of the 'infinite

---

[451] Toychiev B. Scientific and philosophical correspondence between Beruni and Ibn Sina. – Tashkent: "Ijod-print", 2020. – 18 p.

division of bodies.' According to Aristotle, space is an infinite number of indivisible points, and the movement of a body in space means passing through infinite points.

Based on Beruni's inquiries, it appears that he had doubts about Aristotle's belief in the round shape of celestial bodies. G. Jalolov, a renowned astronomer who extensively researched this topic, stated that Beruni's perspective was only validated several centuries later[452].

It is worth noting that this supports Beruni's assertion that celestial bodies are spherical in shape. Beruni discusses Aristotle's theory on the origin of fire, specifically the notion that fire is produced through the interaction and friction of celestial bodies when they collide with air. Ibn Sina counters this argument by stating that Aristotle's view is supported by most philosophers. Fire is a unique form of matter that does not manifest itself in any recognizable way and has a distinct nature. Ibn Sina observes that Beruni's perspective on fire was also shared by ancient Greek philosophers such as Mileticus (7th century BC), Heraclitus (5th century BC), and Anaximenes (6-7th centuries BC). It is known from the history of philosophy that Aristotle strongly criticised their views. This is because fire, air, water, and other elements are considered the fundamental basis of existence and universal elements, and cannot gradually arise from one another. According to Beruni, this question raises inquiries about the nature of things and events, their determinants, and the transition of things from one qualitative state to another on essential grounds. Beruni's opinion is based on the separation of small particles. Ibn Sina rejects Beruni's opinion and instead supports Aristotle's view that the substance, or primary matter, of any object or body undergoes a change in form, leading to a change in the fundamental quality of things and events. In other words, the transition from one formal state to another is the primary cause of qualitative changes in things. This reflects Aristotle's philosophy of form and substance, which is also evident in his other works.

Ways and methods of understanding the world are developed in philosophy, which is expressed in methodology (the study of methods). Social philosophy

---

[452] Zhalolov G. Beruniy and astronomical science. - Tashkent: Science, 1950. – P. 122-134.

discusses ways and methods of studying man and society[453]. Abu Rayhon Beruni emphasizes that one of the ideas formed as a result of the evolutionary process is worldview. "This supports the idea that the source governing the universe is the contradiction of 'structure and destruction"[454]. At the same time, Beruni says that the force that leads the world to social development is not contradictions and conflicts, but compromise and consensus. "How can you believe in something that clearly contradicts?"[455]. Observation also plays an important role in Beruni's research[456]. Observation also plays an important role in Beruni's research[456]. In the scientific study of nature, observation is interconnected with other forms of knowledge. According to Beruni, the observer perceives the observed phenomenon in the place where it occurs[457]. Consequently, observation records this or that event in its specific form[458]. Old observational data can greatly distort the true characteristics of an object. Beruni notes that the experiment conducted by the researcher and its result are practically reliable. He writes that "there is no program of priority other than testing, no program leading to success except the test of experience"[459].

Abu Ali Ahmad ibn Muhammad ibn Yaqub ibn Miskawaih - an enlightened and famous scientist, a scientist who explored Muslim countries, summarized his educational and moral views in the works "Jovidoni Khurd" and "The Book of Experiences of the People".

In the course of our research work, we paid special attention to the study of the works of scientists of the Khorezm Mamun Academy, stored in the manuscript collection of the Institute of Oriental Studies named after Abu Rayhon Beruni of the Academy of Sciences of the Republic of Uzbekistan, and as a result of research we found the following works by Abu Ali ibn Muhammad ibn Yaqub ibn Miskawaikh:

---

[453] Karimov I., Valieva S., Tulenova K. Social philosophy (methodological manual). - Tashkent: Science, 200. - 5 p.
[454] Abu Rayhan Beruni. Selected works. T.1. – Tashkent: Science, 1968. – 26 p.
[455] Abu Rayhan Beruni. MSSU,ments of past generations // Selected works. T.1. - Tashkent: Science, 1957. – 99 p.
[456] Masharipova G.K. The influence of the natural science heritage of scientists of the Khorezm Mamun Academy on the development of social and philosophical thinking. (Monography). – Tashkent: Navruz, 2019. – 241 p.
[456] Masharipova G.K. The influence of the natural science heritage of scientists of the Khorezm Mamun Academy on the development of social and philosophical thinking. (Monography). – Tashkent: Navruz, 2019. – 241 p.
[457] Abu Rayhon Beruni. Selected works. At 6 o'clock T. 3. - Tashkent: Science, 1963. – 57 p.
[458] Abu Rayhon Beruni. Selected works. At 6 o'clock T. 3. - Tashkent: Science, 1963. – 260 p.
[459] Abu Rayhon Beruni. Selected works. At 6 o'clock T. 3. - Tashkent: Science, 1963. – 340 p.

"Jovidoni Khurd" № 2213/11 pp. 29a-64b, rewritten in 1344, in Arabic. An excerpt from the work ("Eternal Thought") translated from Pahlavi into Arabic. Consists of 6 parts on a moral topic:

1. Wise thoughts and advice from the Persians.
2. Hindu instructions.
3. Wise thoughts of the Arabs.
4. Wise thoughts and advice of the Greeks.
5. Advice from modern philosophers to the author.

The moral part of this work was translated by Ghaibullah al-Salam and Hamidjan Hamidi.

6. «Tajarib al-umam» (تجاريب الأمم) («Book of the Experience of Nations»), parts III and VI, rewritten in 1199 (p. 227) and 1111-1112 (p. 122), respectively.

The treatise is dedicated to the history of Muslim peoples (from ancient times to the 10th century) and is written with a love for the land of the Persians, dear to the author. He describes the rise of the Sassanids. The work also contains valuable information about the history, treasury, and tax system of the falling Abbasid dynasty. In this case, official documents are widely used.

Handwritten copies of the book were discovered in Amsterdam, Oxford, Paris, and Istanbul. They were studied by I.Krachkovsky, V.Ivanov, and A.Schmidt. In 1906, Professor H.Horowitz found a six-volume copy of this work in the library of Hagia Sophia in Istanbul.

Ibn Miskawaih believes that the science of history embodies human thinking and teaches us to understand what is happening and find the right path in various situations. The task of the historian is to tell the story of how people behaved in certain situations, assuming that history consists of a system of events, each process of which is repeated. Therefore, he calls on young people to have a perfect knowledge of history, which has incomparable significance in everyday life and big politics[460].

---

[460] Arabic anonymous 11th century. - Moscow: Eastern literature, 1960. – 22 p.

Later, in the worldviews of Christianity and Islam, this approach, which implied a connection with nature, was replaced by a special attitude towards it. As a result, nature was interpreted as created, and therefore transient and changeable. Thus, God, with an immortal soul, was placed above transitory nature. This prioritization, although not decreasing people's dependence on natural forces, created a distinction between the material and spiritual realms within the structure of humans (spiritual beings) and the soulless natural world. Religious beliefs are considered eternal, with the spiritual basis (God) taking precedence over the soul at the highest level. This situation was especially pronounced in medieval philosophy, where theological beliefs were placed above philosophical teachings and formed the basis of most people's worldviews.

Abdumalik ibn Muhammad ibn Ismail al-Saalibi an-Naysaburi is another great scientist and poet who worked in this field. Abu Mansur al-Saalibi was born in Nishapur in 961, where he received his primary education. From a young age, he enjoyed the conversations of many of the city's scholars and poets, who were patrons of Allomaamir and the poet Abu-l-Fadl al-Mikoli. He was also involved in professional trading, which gave him the opportunity to visit many countries. For example, Saolibi came to Bukhara in 992-993. In this city, he joined the circle of scientists, made many friends, and participated in public meetings. After some time, he went to the palace of Allama Khorezmshah. Saolibi writes about the reasons for his visit to the palace and his work there: «After finishing the first three chapters of the book (Yatimat ad-dar), times changed, and my life faced various obstacles and misfortunes. The stay at the court of Khorezmshah Abu-l-Abbas had a positive influence on the author (Saalibi). He was inspired by the actions of the emir and made the manuscript worthy of his library[461].

Abu Muzaffar Nasr ibn Sabuktegin, brother of Sultan Mahmud, also patronized al-Saalibi. The scholar died in Nishapur in 1038.

Brochures written by al-Saalibi:

---

[461] Abdullayev I. Poetry in Arabic in Central Asia and Khorasan of the 10th century. - beginning of the 11th century. - Tashkent: Science, 1984. – 36 p.

1. "Kitab al-jaz wa'al-a'jaz" ("Book of Wonderful and Permissible Points") № 1848/1, pp. 1b-25a, rewritten in 1227. The work consists of poetic and prose instructions from rulers and statesmen.

2. "Kuntz al-kuttab" ("Treasure of Books") № 1848/II, pp. 26b-118b and "Kitab al-muhadara" ("Book of Lectures") № 1848/III, pp. 119b-193b, rewritten in 1727. The work is dedicated to secretaries. To facilitate fulfilling the strict requirements placed on them, al-Saalibi systematized excerpts from the works of various poets that could be used in official documents. It was rewritten in 1727.

Abu Sahl Isa ibn Yahya al-Masihi al-Jurjani (970-1011) was born in Jurjan. A doctor, he studied in Baghdad and was the teacher of Ibn Sina. His most famous work is Commentaries Written for the Library of Mamun ibn Mamun. This scholar also authored works such as "One Hundred Questions on Medicine," "Treatise on the Soul," "Collection of Christian Treatises," and "Book of Nature".

Abu Sahl is a great scholar who occupies a unique place, as well as leaving an educational and moral legacy, in the Christian Mamun Academy. There is no doubt that his wisdom will be a close companion to our youth in their honorable task of building a happy future and will be of great importance in achieving their goals.

Conclusions under paragraph 3.1:

1. In the 10th century, religious beliefs were an extremely sensitive issue in Khorezm. This led to disagreements and conflicts between different rulers and great statesmen. However, the peculiarity of the Mamun Academy was that, in addition to Muslims, representatives of other religions also worked there. This openness indicates that an atmosphere of internationalism and friendship prevailed at the university.

2. Fundamental research is being carried out to study the scientific and philosophical heritage of Abu Rayhan Biruni and Abu Ali Ibn Sina. Their connection with theoretical issues of philosophy, geometry, astronomy, physics, and other sciences is a source of significant scientific and practical value, even in the modern era. This connection holds importance in the history of science of New Uzbekistan.

3. The legacy of the scientists of the Khorezm Mamun Academy lies with those who defended the idea that it is necessary to try to understand the general laws of nature, not to resist them and obey them.

4. In philosophy, ways and methods of understanding the world have been developed, which is expressed in methodology (the doctrine of methods). Social philosophy discusses ways and methods of studying human beings and society. Abu Rayhan Biruni supports the idea that one of the ideas formed as a result of the evolutionary process is the conflict of «structure and destruction» - the worldview is the source that governs the Universe. However, Biruni argues that the force that leads the world to social development is not contradictions and conflicts, but compromise and consensus.

3.2. Dialectics of the aesthetic paradigm and ontological views of Abu Nasra ibn Iraka and Abu Raykhana Beruni

One of the talented scientists of the Khorezm Shah Academy is Abu Nasr Mansur ibn Iraq. With his achievements in the field of exact sciences, he was far ahead of his time. His manuscripts on mathematics and astronomy are a valuable source of information on the state of scientific understanding and thinking in the Middle Ages. Due to the fact that the scientist's biography has not reached us, we will gather information about his activities from various sources. He became well-known for his discoveries in the fields of mathematics and astronomy. According to sources, Abu Abdullah Muhammad ibn Ahmad ibn Iraq, who ruled Kotda during the late 10th century, is the uncle of the Khorezm Shah, and Ali ibn Iraq is the father of Abu Nasr Mansur ibn Ali ibn Iraq.

Abu Nasr ibn Iraq received his primary education in Khorezm. From a young age he developed an interest in the natural sciences, especially mathematics and astronomy. He became well acquainted with the works of the ancient Greek scientists Euclid, Ptolemy, Menelaus, Theodosius, and Archimedes. From many years of research in the history of mathematics, it is known that Abu Nasr ibn Iraq developed a proof of the theorem of sines for plane and spherical triangles. Abu Rayhon Beruni and Nasiriddin Tusi also confirmed this. Abu Nasr is considered the founder of plane and spherical trigonometry.

Abu Nasr Mansur ibn Ali ibn Iraq is one of the mathematicians who lived in the 10th century. There is no doubt that his life was spent in Khorezm. The fact that Abu Rayhon Beruni respects him as a «Teacher» in his work is proof enough. There was a warm relationship between them. European historians have acknowledged that Abu Nasr ibn Iraq translated «Makala fi islax shakl Menelay fi kuriyyat» (Article on the Improvement of the Spherical Application of Menelaus) by Menelaus of Alexandria in the 1st century into Arabic[462].

Some Europeans, especially Weinrich [Weinrich], suspect that this is the same person as Abu Nasr Farabi. Abu Nasr ibn Iraq likely came from Khwarezm.

Abu Nasr ibn Iraq remained in Khwarezm for a long time and gained the favor of Abu-l-Abbas Ali ibn Mamun, the last of the Khwarezm shahs. After the execution of this ruler in 407 AH/1018 CE, Sultan Mahmud of Ghazna took all the scientists of Khwarezm to Ghazna, along with Abu Rayhan Biruni.

Abu Rayhan Biruni wrote in 427 AH/1035-36 CE in his famous work, «Risalat al-Fihrist» («Treatise of the Fihrist»), that Abu Nasr ibn Iraq's most important treatise, «Al-Majisti al-Shahi» (المجيسطي الشاهي) («King of the King»), was dedicated to Khwarezm shah Abu-l-Abbas Ali ibn Ma'mun.

Abu Nasr ibn Iraq made significant contributions to the development of mathematical sciences at the Khwarezm Mamun Academy. According to Abu Rayhan Biruni, Abu Nasr ibn Iraq was the first to introduce a concept related to spherical triangles.

Abu Nasr ibn Iraq wrote several treatises on astronomy, geometry, and mathematics, dedicating 12 of them to Abu Rayhan Biruni. These works are as follows[463]:

---

[462] Zaki Salih. Osor al-bakiya, 1 volume. Istanbul Printing Science. 1329. Institute of Oriental Studies named after Abu Raikhan Beruni of the Academy of Sciences of the Republic of Uzbekistan. № 18464.
[463] Zaki Salih. Osor al-bakiya, 1 volume. Istanbul Printing Science. 1329. Institute of Oriental Studies named after Abu Raikhan Beruni of the Academy of Sciences of the Republic of Uzbekistan. № 18464.

1. Kitab as-Sumut (كتاب السموت)(«Book of Azimuths»).

2. Kitab fi'illati Tansif at-Ta'dil'inda Ashhab as-Sind (كتاب في علة تنصيف التعديل عند أصحاب السند) (A Book on the Reason for Dividing an Equation into Equal Halves According to Sindhi Authors)

3. Kitab fi Tashihi Kitab Ibrahim ibn Sinan fi Tashihi Ikhtilaf al-Kawakib al-Ulwiya (كتاب في تصحيح كتاب ابراهيم ابن سنان في تصحيح اختلاف الكواكب العلوية) (A Book on Correcting the Book of Ibrahim ibn Sinan «On Correcting the Differences in the Movement of the Heavenly Bodies»)

4. Risala fi-l-Barakhin ala Amal Habash bi Jadwal at-Taqwim (رسالة في البراهين على عمل حبش بجدول التقويم) (Treatise on the Evidence of the Abyssinian Method of Compiling a Calendar Table)

5. Risala fi Tashihi ma Wakaa li-Abu Jafar al-Khozin min al-Sahwi fi Zij al-Safa'ih (رسالة في تصحيح ما وقع لأبي جعفر الخازن من السهو في زيج السفائح) (Treatise on Correcting an Error in the Zij-al-Safa'ih by Abu Jafar Khazin)

6. Risala fi Majazaat Dawa'ir as-Sumut fi-l-Asturlab (رساة في مجازات دوائر السموت في الاسترلاب) (Treatise on the Intersection of Azimuth Circles in the Astrolabe)

7. «Risala fi table ad-dakaiq» (رسالة في جدول الدقائق)(«Treatise on the Table of Minutes»).

8. Risala fi-l-Barakini 'ala Amali Muhammad ibn as-Sabbah fi Imtihan ash-Shams (رسالة فى البراهين على عمل محمد بن السباح في امتحان الشمس) (Treatise on the Evidence for the Method of Muhammad ibn al-Sabbah for Studying the Sun)

9. Risala fi-d-Dawa'ir allati Tahuddu as-Sa'at az-Zamaniyya (رسالة في الدوائر التى تحد السعات الزمانية) (Treatise on Circles Indicating the Limits of the Clock of Time)

10. Risala fi-l-Burhan 'ala Amali Habash fi Matali' as-Sumt fi Zijihi (رسالة في البرهان على عمل حبش في مطالع السمت في زيجه) (Treatise on the Evidence Adduced for the Practice of Abyssinia in the Work of Azimuth Motels in His Own City)

11. Risala fi Ma'rifat al-Qasi al-Falakiyya bi-Tarikin Ghair Tarikin Nisbat al-Mu'allafa (رسالة في معرفة القسي الفلكية بطريق غير طريق سبة المألفة) (Treatise on the

Determination of Two Arcs of a Sphere by a Method Other Than the Method of Complex Relations)

12. Risala fi Hall Shubha Arāda Lahu fi-l-Maqalat ath-Thalathatha 'Ashara min Kitab Uqlidis «al-Usul» (رسالة في حل الشبهة أراد له في المقالات الثلاثة عشر من كتاب) (Treatise on the Resolution of Doubt in the Thirteenth [Chapter] of Euclid's «Elements»)

According to the famous European historians of mathematics K. Zahar (1845-1930) and M. Krause (1909-1944), the work of Abu Nasr ibn Iraq, «Al-Majisti al-Shahi» (المجسطي الشاهي) (King of the King), is dedicated to the Khwarezm shah Abu-l-Abbas Ali ibn Ma'mun. This book was likely written between 997-1010 CE at the Mamun Academy. Additionally, the book about Menelaus' «Spherics» was written in 1007-10.

In 1017, Abu Nasr went to Ghazna along with Abu Rayhan Beruni and all the scholars of the Mamun Academy. Although little is known about his life during this period, Abu Nasr is credited with the following mathematical and astronomical works:

1. "Risala fi hall shubha waraqa lahu fi al-maqalat al-thalatha 'ashara min kitab al-Usul" (رسالة في حل الشبهة أراد له في المقالات الثلاثة عشر من كتاب الأصول) ("Euclid's Treatise on the Resolution of the Doubt that Arose in the Thirteenth [Chapter] of the Book of Elements").

2. "Islah kitab Manalaus fi al-kuriyya" (اصلاح كتاب منالاى في الكرية) ("Commentary on Menelaus' Spherica").

3. "Kitab fi kuriyyat al-sama" (كتاب في كرية السما) ("Treatise on the Celestial Sphere"). The manuscript of this work is kept in the Patna Library under number 2468/22.

4. "Tahdhib al-ta'lim" (تهذيب التعاليم) ("Mathematical Education").

5. "Risala fi jawab masa'il al-handasa" (رسالة في جواب مسائل الهندسة) ("Treatise on Answers to Certain Questions of Geometry"). The manuscript of this treatise is preserved in Patna under number 2468/19.

6. "Risala fi sanat al-asturlab bi-al-tariq al-sina'i ila Abu 'Abdallah Muhammad ibn 'Ali al-Ma'muni" (رساة في صنعة الاسترلاب بالطريق الصناعة الى أبي عبد الله محمد بن على

المأموى ("A Treatise on His Proposals to Abu Abdullah Muhammad ibn Ali al-Mamun on the Construction of the Astrolabe by Artistic Method") and similar works in Patna are stored under nos. 2468/9, 2468/10, 2468/11, 2468/12, 2468/13, 2468/14, 2468/15, 2468/16, 2468/17, 2468/18, 2468/19, 2468/20, 2468/21, and 2468/22.

Omar Khayyam evaluates the works of Abu Nasr in the field of mathematics and astronomy as follows: «The greatest of the scientists involved in mathematical science is Abu Nasr ibn Iraq[464].

Mustafa ibn Abdullah Katib Celebi, also known as Haji Khalifa (1609-1657), in his work Kashf al-Zunun 'an Asami al-Kutub wa-l-Funun (Exposure of the Doubts Concerning the Names of Books and Arts) provides the following information about Abu Nasr's Bearbeitung [German for Bearbeitung meaning Bearbeitung, Bearbeitung, Bearbeitung of] of Menelaus of Alexandria (1st-2nd centuries) under the title «Spherical»:

«The scientist who first worked on this work of Menelaus was Muhammad ibn Isa Abu Abdullah al-Makhani (9th century). For the second time, Abu Fazl Ahmad ibn Abu Said Hirawi, a famous mathematician of his time, took up this problem. The work he started remained unfinished. Amir Abu Nasr Mansur ibn Iraq was the scholar who completed the work of correcting the Book of Menelaus. His commentary on the Spherics of Menelaus consists of three parts, and there are 31 geometric names in the treatise.

Among scholars of the later period, there were slightly different opinions about the number of propositions in Abu Nasr's treatise. Some scholars say there are 25 or 39 propositions in Abu Nasr's work, while others confirm there are 24. Another group of scholars determined the number of propositions in Abu Nasr ibn Iraq's work to be 85. This last opinion is confirmed by Nasir al-Din al-Tusi (1201-1274). Nasir al-Din al-Tusi once again compared all the copies of the works of the scientists who revised this work of Menelaus. Since the scholars' opinions did not coincide, preference was given to Abu Nasr's conclusion among these findings. Nasir al-Din al-Tusi wrote his treatise on this issue in Sha'ban 663 AH (August 1265).

---

[464] Omar Khayyam. Treatises. – Moscow: State Literature, 1961. – 313 p..

According to Abu Nasr ibn Iraq, these [referring back to the scientists mentioned earlier] played an important role in public administration[465].

According to the researchers, «Biruni can reasonably be considered one of the creators of the empirical method in medieval science. He conducted a number of experiments to determine the properties and specific gravity of metals and minerals»[466]. Experienced knowledge is interpreted by the thinker as reliable knowledge according to certain standards. Among these standards, we can note the observability of objects, the reproducibility of experiments, and the verifiability of observations. These considerations suggest that experience as a method of acquiring knowledge and testing its reliability was quite widespread back in the medieval period. Importantly, the idea is developed that the acquisition of reliable knowledge is associated with experience, and the reliability of the knowledge is verified by experience.

Observation plays an important role in Biruni's work. In the scientific study of nature, observation is interconnected with other forms of knowledge.

According to Biruni, the observer perceives the observed phenomenon in the place where it occurs[467]. Consequently, observations record this or that phenomenon in its specific form[468]. Old observational data can greatly distort the true characteristics of an object.

Beruni notes that the experiment conducted by the researcher and its result are practically reliable. He writes that "there is no other priority program than testing, no program leading to success except the test of experience"[469].

With the help of astronomical observations, Beruni endeavored to solve complex problems such as eclipses of the Moon and Sun, their impact on life on Earth, climate, natural and artificial selection, conservation, and developmental

---

[465] Abu Rayhon al-Biruni. Selected works in 6 volumes -T. 3. -Tashkent: Science, 1963. – 44 p.
[466] Khairullayev M. Philosophical heritage of the peoples of Central Asia and the struggle of ideas. - Fergana, 1988. - 39 p.
[467] Abu Rayhon Beruni. Selected works. At 6 o'clock T. 3. – Tashkent: Science, 1963. – 57 p.
[468] Abu Rayhon Beruni. Selected works. At 6 o'clock T. 3. – Tashkent: Science, 1963. – 260 p.
[469] Abu Rayhon Beruni. Selected works. At 6 o'clock T. 3. – Tashkent: Science, 1963. – 340 p.

anomalies. He employed new progressive methods and theoretical principles in his investigations.

Beruni also holds a leading place in the history of technological development for creating astronomical observation instruments in the East. He focused on improving existing instruments used in scientific research at that time and even devised new ones. The scientist was particularly interested in the possibility of creating observation devices with exceptional accuracy and precision.

Therefore, one of Beruni's greatest contributions can be considered his awareness of the importance of understanding celestial bodies not only through instruments but also through the inherent nature of the objects themselves. This methodological approach played a crucial role in his search for new methods and means of scientific exploration, despite the limitations inherent to scientific research during his time

The historian of science, George Sarton, referred to the first half of the 11th century as the «Beruni period»[470]. After all, scientists around the world recognized the breadth and depth of Abu Rayhon Beruni's scientific interests, scientific and theoretical analysis, and the genius of his teaching. This fact is why he is called the second Erosthenes, the second Ptolemy, and the second Leonardo da Vinci.

Abu Rayhon Beruni is considered one of the greatest thinkers not only of Central Asia, but also of the East as a whole, in the history of world science and culture. His works, «India», «Historical Monuments of Ancient Peoples,» and «Mineralogy,» study issues such as people's lifestyles, social life, and social relations. The preface to the work «Mineralogy» reflects valuable thoughts about the social status of man, nobility, public life, duty on earth, and social justice.

Abu Rayhon Beruni was a politician and statesman of his time. In his work, «Historical Lies of Ancient Peoples,» he left necessary and interesting information about various peoples: Greeks, Persians, Manichaean Christians, Jews and pagans, Christians, pagan Arabs, Sabians, Turks, Muslim Arabs, and others.

---

[470] Sarton G. Introduction to the histori of science, vol. I-III, Baltimore, 1927-1948. - vol.I. - P.707.

In his work «India,» he gave reliable opinions about Indian society, customs, internal structure, family relationships, year, month and historical dates, rituals, and marriage issues.

Abu Rayhon Beruni put forward and proved important scientific and philosophical ideas about nature, natural phenomena, and the processes that occur within it. He explores the fundamental nature of change in the world, investigating the structure and specific reasons for the appearance and disappearance of disturbances. His work incorporates both natural scientific and sociological considerations.

Abu Rayhan Beruni recalls his youth in the work «Saidana» and writes: «Since childhood, I have longed to learn as much as possible, depending on my age and circumstances. As proof of this, consider the following: a Greek moved to the place where we lived. I used to bring him all kinds of grains, seeds, fruits, and so on»[471].

From his youth, Abu Rayhon Beruni endeavored to master many languages, especially Arabic, the lingua franca of science in the Muslim world at that time. «Every nation,» he writes in Saidan, «loves the language it has learned for its needs, the language in which it communicates with its own kind.» He reflects further: «No matter how surprised they would be to see a camel on the Kaaba or a giraffe among Arabian horses, they would be equally amused if I wrote a scientific work in my native language.» Thus, he began writing in Arabic and Farsi, but since neither was his mother tongue, he found it difficult to fully express his thoughts.

Abu Rayhon Beruni's rich cultural heritage extended beyond his scientific and literary works. The polymath also held an interest in political and legal matters. One of his political ideas concerns the origins of the state. He proposes that people are driven to unite in an organized way to combat enemies and fulfill basic needs. Therefore, the fundamental rules governing their coexistence should be based on principles like mutual aid, peaceful cohabitation, and pursuit of common interests. Work constitutes a primary human obligation, as achievement stems from diligent

---

[471] Shamsi F. Abu al-Rayhan al-Bayruni. - P. 194-195; For more information about Beruni and philological iSSU,es, see pp. 41-52 of U.I. Karimov's study in Saidan.

effort. Property inequality, exemplified by the concepts of rich and poor, is considered the main reason for the societal division between oppressors and the oppressed. Labor and barter contracts established between citizens are categorized into two types: first, legal or fair contracts, where wages are commensurate with the work performed; and second, illegal or unfair contracts, which involve elements of fraud, coercion, or unfairness, and serve only one party's interests[472].

Abu Rayhon Beruni was an encyclopaedist who was also interested in political and legal issues and was literally one of the most knowledgeable people of his time in matters of state and administration. Like Abu Nasr Farabi, he looked for questions about the state, the emergence of law and its duties from natural needs. His ideas have a sense of opposition to despotism, and people unite in a state based on an agreement to establish a system of social justice, says Abu Raihan. - Although enlightened kings are glorified, he believes that society should not serve the king, but the king should serve society. «The essence of administration and management is to protect the rights of those who have suffered at the hands of oppressors, to lose their own peace for the sake of the peace of others. It consists in exhausting the body to protect and defend its family, its life and its property. According to his political views, the head of state must have the natural ability to rule. The head of state must have the natural ability to govern, be firm in his opinions and decisions, and follow the laws of the sages in solving important issues of the state. He explains this by the example of Aristotle's advice to Alexander and the account of Alexander's adherence to it: «The duty of a just ruler is to establish equality and justice between the higher and lower classes, the strong and the weak»[473]. To do this, the head of state should follow the laws of the sages in resolving important issues of the state. Abu Rayhon Beruni gives the example of Aristotle's advice to Alexander, which Alexander followed. According to Abu Rayhon Beruni, «the task of a just ruler is to establish equality and justice between the upper and lower classes, the strong and the weak».

---

[472] Masharipova G.K. The influence of the natural science, socio-philosophical and spiritual heritage of scientists of the Khorezm Mamun Academy on the development of social thinking. Monography. – Tashkent: Navruz, 2019. – pp. 171-172.
[473] Abu Rayhan Beruni. Selected works. MSSU,ments of past peoples // Translation from Arabic by A. Rasulov. Notes I. Abdullaev, A. Rasulova. T. I. Tashkent, 1968. – 73 p.

Abu Rayhon Beruni, seeing that rule has become an inheritance, rejects the transfer of the law of the state from one generation to another, and the position of a person in society is determined by the antiquity of the generation, the merits of the ancestors. On this occasion he says: «Whoever says that he will receive a position (royal or gubernatorial) through his deceased relatives and ancestors, he himself is dead, such descendants are alive». In his opinion, the leadership of the state depends on the abilities of a person; he puts forward the idea that the ability of a particular statesman to manage power does not depend on the abilities of his descendants. Nowadays, the colour, language and appearance of people differ not only from generation to generation, but also from the environment, air and water in which they live. In his opinion, the existence of different states and the existence of different rulers depend on the above[474].

The political views of Abu Rayhon Beruni put forward the idea that the governor elected by the people to rule the state must be fair and humane[475]. This idea is illustrated by the example of a story in the work «Mineralogy»: «There, the representatives of the land administration and the landowners took turns, and whoever got the turn ruled for those three months. At the end of his term, he would give alms as a sign of gratitude and return to his people, rejoicing with them as if he had been freed from bondage, and go about his business. This is because it is said that governing is a deprivation of pleasure. In this case, he means that he will make the oppressors fair to the oppressed. And this is the torture of a lifetime to prepare a military event to protect your subordinates and yourself...»[476].

Abu Rayhon Beruni, in his studies on spirituality and enlightenment, says that thinking determines intelligence, education, work, human life and economic essence. He proved that such important factors as joint activities based on mutual assistance, socio-economic, spiritual and educational ties and relationships played a role in the development of society even in the Middle Ages. The emergence and development of

---

[474] Abu-r-Rayhan Muhammad ibn Ahmed al-Biruni. Collection of information for the knowledge of jewelry (Mineralogy) // Transl. A. M. Belenitsky. Leningrad, 1963. – 235 p.
[475] Abu-r-Rayhan Muhammad ibn Ahmed al-Biruni. Collection of information for the knowledge of jewelry (Mineralogy) // Transl. A. M. Belenitsky. Leningrad, 1963. – 237 p.
[476] Beruni A.R. Collection of information for knowledge of jewelry (Mineralogy). - Moscow, 1963. - 237 p.

society, the concept of the spiritual and moral character of man are the result of the creation of people in joint work, this is often mentioned in the teachings of Abu Rayhon Beruni.

The need to carry out certain tasks together lies at the heart of the existence of human activity. «The dignity and the most important task of man is to realise his own interests at an excellent level, so in this place work is valued, thanks to his work a man can reach high positions», writes Abu Rayhon Beruni in Geodesy[477].

Work is the basis for the spiritual and moral improvement of a person. It is through work that man gets what he wants, he explains, and it is through the lack of work that there is no joy in life. This idea becomes the main theme in the socio-political and philosophical teachings of Abu Rayhon Beruni, especially in his views on spirituality and enlightenment. In the teachings of Abu Rayhon Beruni, those related to spiritual and educational views, morality, work, profession, education and knowledge are analysed and interpreted in a dialectical unity. No wonder he wrote that no field of practical human activity can be realised without their interdependence. Honesty, fairness, justice - these are the signs of Beruni's excellent manners and high spirituality. He teaches that even at one's own expense, not to turn away from the truth, to speak the truth, to approach everything fairly and impartially, he himself becomes an example of lifelong loyalty to these ideas and teachings.

The teachings of Abu Rayhon Beruni on spirituality and enlightenment, universal ideas such as science, brotherhood, culture, sincerity, justice, equality, humanity, goodness, correctness, serve as the moral, ethical, spiritual and philosophical basis for the formation of a new national education of thought.

On the one hand, Abu Rayhon Beruni's thought creatively developed the advanced traditions of Central Asia; on the other hand, Beruni's maturity testifies to the breadth of his thought. It is noteworthy that he raised the question of the «cause of causes» of man and the emergence of human society. «The oldest and most famous of

---

[477] Bulgakov P.G. Beruni and his "Geodesy". - In the book: Abu Reyhan Biruni. Favorite works: T.3. Determining the boundaries of places to clarify the distances between populated areas ["Geodesy"]. Note translation and notes by P.G. Bulgakov. - Tashkent: Science, 1966. – 132 p.

the ancient stories is the beginning of mankind»[478]. At this point we see that Beruni takes a rationalist position on the emergence of individual society. When Beruni spoke of the existence of tawafut between people, he was thinking only of external differences. But the internal structure and organisation of human beings is, in his opinion, the same for everyone.

He notes that there are similarities between humans and apes. Analysing the differences between Muslim and Hindu customs in his work 'India', he put forward the idea that they depend on geographical conditions; further analysing the role of the geographical factor, he believed that even the diversity of languages depends on geographical conditions. conditions. «The reason why languages vary is because people divide into groups and stay away from each other».

Abu Rayhon Beruni recognises that social life is built on the basis of a special «contract»: «Man begins to realise his needs and the need to live with people like himself. Therefore, they begin to draw up a «contract» of mutual agreement. The cohabitation of people does not lead man to real power, to the satisfaction of his needs; for that, too, one must work». Continuing this thought, he wrote: «The dignity of man consists in fulfilling his duty with excellence: therefore, the most important duty and place of a person is determined by work, a person achieves his desire through work».

Abu Rayhon Beruni was one of the founders of true science; in its various fields, he put forward ideas and scientific hypotheses that were astounding for his time, and which were confirmed by European science several centuries later. Beruni was one of the pioneers of precise scientific thinking based on real experience, observation and experimentation in the Middle Ages. He also worked in the field of philology, studying the structure of Indian poetry and translating classical Arabic poetry and examples of Iranian folklore into Arabic. Beruni understood that the development of the country was inseparable from the development of science[479].

---

[478] Abu Rayhan Beruni. Selected works. MSSU,ments of past generations // Translation from Arabic by A. Rasulov. Notes I. Abdullaev, A. Rasulova. T.I. – Tashkent, 1968. – 50 p.
[479] Targ S.M. Inertial force // Physical encyclopedia: [in 5 volumes] Ch. editor A.M. Prokhorov. – Moscow, 1994. – P. 126-138.

«Every scientist must base his reasoning on practice, work continuously in his research, be precise, look for and correct all kinds of fabrications for the sake of truth in science, and fight superficiality,» he said. He fought for the unity of peoples and strongly condemned wars that destroy humanity and the science and culture it has created. In his work «India», he wrote with regret that «there is much friction and strife between the peoples». His extensive research in India focused on issues of friendship and the strengthening of mutual cooperation and cultural ties between peoples. It is clear that Beruni attached great importance to the widespread dissemination of cultural knowledge and cooperation.

Beruni places particular emphasis on emotional cognition. He writes: «As the fields of knowledge develop more and more, they will increase as the intellect of the people joins them, and a sign of this is the desire of the people for science, respect for it, respect for scientists». Regarding the knowledge of the unknown principles of reality, he says: «All phenomena that need to be known have a way by which knowledge can be obtained.

Abu Rayhon Beruni's encyclopaedic book entitled «Relics of Ancient Peoples»[480] can be considered a classic encyclopaedic work devoted to the analysis and synthesis of the events of the last 5,000 years of human history. In this book, the great thinker spoke about the methods he used in the process of writing the work and wrote about his scientific and philosophical research: «While writing this work, I became convinced that it is impossible to obtain real information by citing evidence from intellectual things and comparing them with observable things. This is determined by following only the «people of the book» and various religious figures, people of various professions and beliefs who follow these (beliefs) and their concepts are always justified. Then you can find out by comparing words and beliefs»[481].

Ways and methods of knowing the world have been developed in philosophy, and this is expressed in methodology (doctrine of methods). Abu Rayhan Beruni's

---

[480] Abu Rayhan Beruni. Selected works. Volume 1. - Tashkent: Science, 1968.
[481] Abu Rayhan Beruni. Selected works. Volume 1. – Tashkent: Science, 1968. – 406 p.

social philosophy is based on the debate about ways and methods of studying man and society[482]. Abu Rayhan Beruni states that the landscape of the world was formed as a result of the evolutionary process. «He supports the idea that the source governing the universe is a conflict consisting of «structure and destruction»[483].

At the same time, Beruni says that the force that leads the world to social development is not conflict and contradiction, but reconciliation and harmony at different social levels. «How can you believe in something whose contradictions are clear and obvious?»[484]. The thinker points out that there is a growing need to change contradictory processes. Throughout his creative career, the scientist was interested in questions of social life and expressed his philosophical views in the works «India» and «Relics of Ancient Nations».

Abu Rayhon Beruni developed the philosophical ideas of the thinkers of Central Asia and the East. In particular, in his work «Memorials of Ancient Peoples», he tried to solve the problem of human life on a scientific basis. He showed the importance of the geographical factor in the life of society and people, its influence on social events. He attributed differences in Muslim and Hindu traditions to geographical conditions and even attributed differences in languages to geographical factors. According to him, the way to philosophy is through the natural sciences, which allow us to understand existence in depth. In general, Beruni agrees with the definition of philosophy as a science that recognises the nature of existence. He also agreed with Abu Mashar al-Balkhi's view that «nature is the strongest»[485]. Scientists of the East and the West have made a significant contribution to the creation and development of world socio-philosophical doctrine. During certain periods of social development, the countries of the East took a leading position. Theoretically, it is wrong to exaggerate or underestimate the role of the peoples of Asia and Europe in the development of world philosophy. Every science is universal by nature. Every nation on earth, regardless of its size, contributes to its development.

---

[482] Karimov I., Valieva S., Tulenova K. Social philosophy (methodological guide). – Tashkent: Science, 2008. – 5 p.
[483] Abu Rayhan Beruni. Selected works. Volume 1. – Tashkent: Science, 1968. – 26 p.
[484] Abu Rayhan Beruni. Selected works. Volume 1. – Tashkent: Science, 1968. – 44 p.
[485] Abu Rayhan Beruni. MSSU,ments of past generations // Selected works. - Tashkent: Science, 1957. - Volume 1. – 99 p.

As the spirituality of mankind grew, the views of society also improved; more complex and reliable scientific and philosophical views of society emerged in comparison with very simple religious and mythological views of society. Great scholars such as Farobi, Abu Rayhon Beruni and Ibn Sina made significant contributions to the development of consistent scientific and philosophical views of society. For many centuries, their progressive views were important in improving social relations and forming a perfect human personality, and are still relevant today.

Abu Rayhon Beruni founded real scientific natural science in the conditions of the Middle Eastern Renaissance; he put forward scientific and hypothetical ideas in various fields of natural science which were astonishing for his time and which were proven in European science several centuries later. It should be noted that Beruni's works express deep socio-scientific and philosophical considerations and generalisations related to his scientific views. Based on the scientific and philosophical teachings of Farabi, he believes that Allah is the root cause of everything. He understands that God is recognised as the creator of all things. But Beruni gives nature the right to develop and change everything that comes from the root cause. According to his teachings, everything in nature is created on the basis of natural laws, nature has its own natural force, and under the influence of this force, processes of continuous movement, change, growth, development, emergence, decay and destruction occur in nature. We can conclude that Beruni was close to deism in his scientific and philosophical views. He speaks of the literature of the material world[486].

Abu Rayhon Beruni's socio-political views are imbued with humanitarian ideas. He declares man to be the most noble creature. He emphasises that people should not live for themselves alone, but should help each other. He believes that the differences between people are more external and that they have something in common in terms of internal structure and organisation.

---

[486] Masharipova G.K. The influence of the natural science, socio-philosophical and spiritual heritage of scientists of the Khorezm Mamun Academy on the development of social thinking. Monography. – Tashkent: Navruz, 2019. – 177 p.

Beruni knows that the development of the country and the well-being of the nation are inextricably linked to the development of science. He wrote: «Every scientist must be practical in his reasoning, have a clear goal in his research, work tirelessly, find and correct errors, fight all kinds of fabrication and superficiality for the sake of truth». He vehemently condemned wars, which destroy humanity, and called for peace, fighting for the peoples of the land to live in friendship, harmony and unity.

When Islam gained a strong position in Mowarunnahr, on the one hand, various religious teachings appeared, especially the schools of Kalam, in the 9th-12th centuries in Central Asia, the main attention was paid to the sciences of tafsir, hadith and jurisprudence; on the other hand, the development of Islamic sciences led to the emergence of Sufism in this area and served as the main factor for its widespread spread. The teachings of Sufism, which penetrated deeply into the social and spiritual life of the countries of the Muslim East, had a great positive influence on the development of science, culture and literature. Since the 11th century, almost all the influential poets and writers, thinkers and scientists of the East have been nourished by Sufism and inspired by its ideas of humanity and justice. In this sense, the famous scholar E.E.Bertels remarked: «It is impossible to have an idea of the cultural life of the medieval Muslim East without studying Sufi literature, and it is difficult to understand the East itself without realising this»[487].

The misconception that prevents scientific knowledge of the external world also affects the objective and subjective reasons for narratives. They are indicated as follows:

1. A person should not refer directly to the source he studies;

2. Mixing scientific knowledge (science) with religious views;

3. The inability to get rid of false information;

4. Ignorance of people. Ignorance leads to imitation rather than scientific reasoning. This takes away the joy of creative exploration.

---

[487] Bertels E.E. Sufism and Sufi literature - Moscow: Nauka, 1995. – 54 p.

5. The underdevelopment of one of the senses also leads to errors in scientific knowledge, because a person whose intuition is dead does not understand or comprehend anything.

Beruni shows the source and causes of false knowledge and relates them to the social life of the human world. They manifest themselves in conflicts of interest, deep-rooted bad habits, cowardice, conflicts, power struggles, etc.

The scientist urged researchers to be consistent and not to kneel before superstition. Beruni always encourages scientists to be disciplined and observant in the search for scientific truth. Academician I. Mominov appreciates the scientist's opinion about the need to observe the outside world and learn through experience.

It is clear as a mirror that the accuracy or inaccuracy of our knowledge in modern science depends on the unity and harmony of the means of knowledge used by the observer. Beruni was also able to show the internal contradictions of the above-mentioned unity of components. This demonstrates the sharp mind of the great scientist and his thoroughness in scientific fundamentals.

Beruni recommended repeated observations to resolve these conflicts. Thus he realised that in the process of knowledge there must be harmony between the observer, the source and the means of observation. But it is necessary to generalise, compare and draw conclusions, not limited to the process of knowledge and experience.

Beruni's ideas about the methods of scientific research and some necessary conditions for a scientist are of great importance today.

Conclusion 3.2 paragraphs

1. In the mid-nineteenth century, major discoveries in the natural sciences (the theory of evolution, the theory of the cell, the law of conservation and transformation of energy) gave rise to a change in philosophical worldview and the emergence of scientific theories about society. Society is a very complex and multifaceted phenomenon, characterised by constant change and development. Since ancient times, the great thinkers of humanity have tried to understand the nature of society and to determine man's place and role in it. In different historical periods,

mythological, religious, scientific and philosophical views have provided certain knowledge and ideas about the origin and development of society.

2. One of the most important ways of acquiring knowledge begins with becoming a friend to everyone and knowing how to do good. Knowledge cannot be acquired alone, but together with members of the community. Since science is a product of human society, one person cannot create the necessary knowledge for himself. Young people of the 21st century are very interested in knowing what they do not know and cannot know.

3. Beruni believed that scientific truth should be a certain criterion. He knew that the complex and difficult problem of proving the unfoundedness of false, unexamined, heartrending, intrusive myths and unsubstantiated claims could be solved by experience and practice. At the same time, we have every right to say that he is a great scientist who understood the importance of logical conclusions and taught us to see the concepts of «intuitive knowledge» and «mental knowledge» together.

4. The study of the scientific heritage of Abu Rayhon Beruni makes it clear that the scientist recognises observation as the first stage of scientific knowledge, and also raises observation to the level of conducting active experiments, which he used extensively in his scientific and creative activities.

5. The scientific heritage of Abu Raikhan Beruni, the problems raised by specific sciences, play an important role in the creation of a general picture of the world, that is, in the formation of a philosophical world view. In his astronomical table, Beruni presented the heliocentric hypothesis, according to which the centre of the universe is not the Earth but the Sun, and all the planets, including the Earth, revolve around the Sun. The scientist's scientific conclusion was confirmed 500 years later in the heliocentric system of the great astronomer Copernicus. In a discussion with Abu Ali ibn Sina, Beruni concluded that the planets in the universe, including the Earth, were mutually attractive. His scientific assumption was confirmed by the law of universal gravitation, discovered by the English scientist Newton at the beginning of the 18th century. With his socio-political views, Abu Rayhon Beruni

developed the advanced traditions not only of Central Asian, but also of ancient Indian, Greek and Iranian thinkers, and became known to the world as a historical sociologist.

3.3. Neoplatonic elements in the ontological doctrine of Abu Ali ibn Sina, the classification of sciences, the humanistic nature of moral views and their influence on the development of historical and philosophical thought.

An analysis of the legacy of Abu Ali ibn Sina shows that his scientific interests were very broad and that he was the possessor of encyclopaedic knowledge. Ibn Sina proposed a classification based on the division of sciences according to the objects of their study.

One of the Central Asian scientists is Abu Ali ibn Sina. Ibn Sina, who continued the traditions of Abu Nasr Farabi in philosophy, emphasised the need for social sciences in his work «Donishnama»: «In every science there are things to be studied. These things are of two kinds: one is things whose existence depends on our action, and the other is things whose existence does not depend on our action. The first is an example of our actions, and the second is an example of the earth, the sky, animals and plants[488]. Ibn Sina tries to determine the place of moral science in practical philosophy. In his opinion, since philosophy is divided into practical and theoretical parts, practical philosophy cannot be identified with ethics. Therefore, it is more correct to call it the science of ethics.

Abu Ali ibn Sina wrote many works on Sufi philosophy and ethics. His famous «Ishq Risola» is noteworthy in this regard. The main problem in this treatise is the problem of the ideal human being. When the Naqshbandi sect was founded, «Ishq Risola» served as the theoretical basis and the first theoretical foundation of Sufi philosophy and ethics. It is well known that Sharia is the external legal form of Islam and Tariqa is its internal moral form. Ultimately, Sufism functions as a philosophy of Islamic ethics.

---

[488] Abu Ali ibn Sina. Danish-name - "Book of Knowledge." - Dushanbe: Tajik State Publishing House, 1967. – 76 p.

In the works of Abu Ali ibn Sina, a special place is given to the consideration of the structure of science, the determination of the order of sciences and their classification. And in this matter, the scientist Farobi tries to develop the issue of classification of sciences. In the works of Ibn Sina, which represent a philosophical system («Kitab ush-shifa», «Kitab un-najot», «Wisdom»), philosophical knowledge is presented in the order: logic, physics, mathematics, metaphysics. Among them, logic is interpreted as a method of knowledge, a scientific method for studying existence and thinking about it. «Logic,» writes Ibn Sina, «gives a man such a rule that with the help of this rule he is protected from mistakes. With the help of logic, a person separates true knowledge from lies and learns the unknown. He paid great attention to the study of logic and devoted special treatises to it. In particular, he made a great contribution to the study of logical methods of definition, judgement, inference, and proof, and developed the science of logic as the correct method of knowledge after Farabi. In his work «Aqsam ul-ulum ul-aqliya» («Classification of Intellectual Knowledge»), Ibn Sina lists and defines all other sciences, except logic, as sciences of nature and social phenomena[489].

Abu Ali ibn Sina divides the philosophical sciences into two: theoretical and practical sciences. If the theoretical sciences correctly understood the truth, then the applied sciences served as a programme for economic activity.

All three types of sciences included in the philosophical and theoretical sciences are divided into main and subsidiary parts; natural sciences include seven different branches such as astrology, medicine and chemistry. Mathematics is divided into 4 sections: arithmetic, geometry, astronomy, music. The work mentions 29 branches of science.

Abu Ali ibn Sina's world view is based on the pantheistic principle: God and existence are not contradictory, mutually exclusive things; on the contrary, they form a single existence. Eternity belongs to God. God and nature are connected by certain steps. At one end of the long and complete chain is the Creator God, a necessary

---

[489] Masharipova G. The influence of the natural science, socio-philosophical and spiritual heritage of scientists of the Khorezm Mamun Academy on the development of social thinking. Monographyy. – Tashkent: Navruz, 2019. – P. 158-159.

being, and at the other end is nature. According to Ibn Sina, true moral qualities and an ideal community can be achieved in this existing world, where people should live on the basis of mutual help. He insists that society should be governed by just laws made by mutual consent of the people. All members of society must obey these laws, and violations and injustices must be punished, provided that if the king himself allows injustice, then the people's rebellion against him must be just and supported by society.

Ibn Sina played an important role in the development of world culture with his fruitful work and rich legacy. Thanks to his creativity and scientific activities, Ibn Sina was able to embody the spiritual achievements of a high cultural upsurge and cultural «awakening» in the countries of Central Asia, the Near and Middle East, and thus had a great influence on the development of education and culture throughout the East and Europe. He once received the greatest titles in the East and Europe, such as «Sheikh Ur-Rais», «Chief Scientist», «King of Doctors». As a famous teacher, Abu Ali ibn Sina educated such students as Abu Ubayd Jurjani, Omar Isfahani, Muhammad Sherazi, Ahmed Masuri, the famous Azerbaijani thinker Bahmanyar ibn Marzban, Yusuf Ilaki, the outstanding scientist and poet Omar Khayyam. In Renaissance miniatures and paintings, Ibn Sina is depicted alongside the famous ancient Greek scientists Aristotle, Galen, Hippocrates, Ptolemy and Euclid. The naturalist Carl Linnaeus, who created the first scientific classification of plants, named the evergreen plant «Avicenia» in honour of Ibn Sina. Ibn Sina's works were translated into Latin in Europe from the 12th century. The work «Laws of Medicine» itself was published in Latin more than 30 times. Many sections of the «Kitab ush-shifo», Logic, Music, Structure of the Earth, Geological Processes, Metaphysics were also published in Latin. Recent scholarly research shows that Ibn Sina influenced the literature of the East and gave impetus to the development of the rubaiyat genre and philosophical stories expressing deep philosophical content[490].

---

[490] Masharipova G.K. The role of the scientific, philosophical and spiritual heritage of Abu Ali ibn Sina in the life of society. Monographyy. – Tashkent: Navruz, 2020. – 91 p.

The scientific legacy of Abu Ali ibn Sina can be divided into 4 parts: philosophical, natural, literary and medical. If we look at the quantitative ratio of his works, we can see that the scientist's interest and attention is largely focused on philosophy and medicine. Although it was his medical legacy that made him famous in the West as «Avicenna», especially his «Laws of Medicine», the name «Shaykhur-Rais» is primarily a reference to his great philosophy.

The greatest and most important work of the philosopher is «Kitab ash-shifa». It consists of 4 parts: 1) Logic is divided into 9 parts: al-madkhal - (المدخل) introduction to logic; al-makulot (المقولات) - categories; al-ibarat (العبارات) - interpretation; al-qiyas (القياس) - syllogism; al-burhan (البرهان) - proof, evidence; al-jadal (الجدل) - argument, dialectic; as-safsata (السفسطة) - sophistry; al-hitaba (الخطابة) - rhetoric; ash-sheer (الشعر) - poetics (the art of poetry); 2) nature (here minerals, plants, fauna and humans are considered in separate sections; 3) mathematics is divided into 4 subjects: Counting (arithmetic), Geometry, Astronomy, Music; 4) Metaphysics or Theology. Parts of this work have been published in Latin, Syriac, Hebrew, German, English, French, Russian, Persian and Uzbek.

«Kitab al-Najat» (كتاب النجات) by Abu Ali ibn Sina is a shortened form of «Kitab al-Shifa» (كتاب الشفا), which has also been partially translated into several languages of the world. The philosophical views of the scientist are also «Al-Isharat wat-tanbihat» (الاشارات والتنبيهات) («Hints and Tanbihs»), «Hikmat al-mashrikiyin» (حكمة المشرقيين) («Philosophy of the Oriental Dov»), «Kitab al-Isharat». fil-mantiq wal -hikmat» كتاب) اشارات في المنطق والحكمة) («Advice of Logic and Philosophy»), written in Persian «Danishnama» (دا شنامة) («Book of Knowledge») and other philosophical treatises of various lengths, and also such as «The Tale of Taira», «Salomon and Ibsol», «Hay ibn Yaqzan», «The Tale of Yusuf» and was reflected in artistic stories of philosophical content.

The world view of Abu Ali ibn Sina was formed under the influence of the teachings of Aristotle and the works of Farabi. According to him, the task of philosophy is to comprehensively study existence, i.e. all existing things, their origin, order, interaction, and transition into each other, based on the factors of necessity, possibility, reality, and causality. All things in the universe are divided into two parts: necessary existence (wujudi wajib) and possible existence (wujudi possible). The necessary being is the all-willful, all-powerful and all-wise God. Everything else exists as possibility and comes from God. The connection between Necessary Existence and Possible Existence is cause and effect. In this process, everything in the universe is gradually realised in the form of emanation, that is, in the form of light emanating from the sun. In this order, mind, soul, body, existing in the form of potentiality, and the celestial spheres associated with them arise. All these are substances (jauhar) and there are accidents in existence - colour, size, signs, types of things. The body is made of matter and form. God is eternal, and matter, which is His consequence, is also eternal. He himself is the basis of other finite bodies. The material basis of things never disappears. The simplest indivisible form of matter consists of 4 elements: water, air, fire, earth. As a result of their various interactions, complex material objects are formed. Complex things can change shape, but the 4 elements that make up their material basis are eternally preserved and do not disappear[491].

According to Abu Ali ibn Sina, stones arose first, then plants, animals and, as a result of evolution, man, who differed from other creatures in his mind, ability to think and language. Deep knowledge of phenomena and science is unique to man. Human knowledge comes from cognition. Cognition consists of sensory perception and conceptual thinking. When the senses know some external signs and individual aspects of phenomena, the mind can know their essence and internal aspects through abstraction and generalisation. People become rich and develop through the study of different sciences. According to Abu Ali ibn Sina, one can know God through the deep study of knowledge. He understands that only a person who has acquired existing knowledge can become a true Muslim. For him, logic is a scientific method of knowledge and the study of existence. «Logic,» writes Abu Ali ibn Sina, «gives such a rule to a person that with the help of this rule a person is protected from

---

[491] Masharipova G.K. The role of the scientific, philosophical and spiritual heritage of Abu Ali ibn Sina in the life of society. Monographyy. – Tashkent: Navruz, 2020. – 95 p.

making mistakes. He studied logical methods, definitions, judgments, conclusions and proofs in depth and developed the science of logic after Farobi as the correct method of knowledge.

Abu Ali ibn Sina is a scientist who once made a great contribution to the development of natural sciences. His scientific views are presented in the science section of the Kitab al-Shifa. The scientist's comments on some geological processes are very close to modern scientific theories. According to him, volcanoes are actually related to mountain building and earthquakes. The formation of the mountain itself occurs in 2 ways: 1) by the rise of the earth's crust during a strong earthquake; 2) as a result of the gradual action of water and air, deep canyons are formed, and a hill is formed beside them. There are several reasons for earthquakes. One of them is gaseous or flammable vapour. This steam moves the earth. Earthquakes are also caused by water seeping underground, the edge of the flat earth collapsing and sometimes the violent collapse of mountain peaks. According to the scientist, a certain part of the Earth's surface was once the seabed, and over time the geological process has changed the location of the reservoirs. Fossils of marine animals are preserved in areas that were once seas but are now dry land. Among such areas, he includes the lands of Kufa, Egypt and Khorezm.

The scientist also did important work in the field of mineralogy. He proposed an original classification of minerals. According to this, all minerals are divided into 4 groups: stones, soluble bodies (metals), combustible sulphur compounds and salts. This classification remained almost unchanged until the 19th century. Ibn Sina's thoughts on geology and mineralogy can also be found in his work Al-af'ol wa-linfiolot (Influence and Influence).

Abu Ali ibn Sina was interested in astronomy from an early age and this interest continued until the end of his life. He devoted 8 independent treatises and separate chapters in the mathematical parts of Kitab ash-shifa and Donishnoma to astronomy. He revised Ptolemy's Almagest and used it as a guide to practical astronomy. He determined the geographical extent of the city of Jurjon by observing the highest point of the moon - a completely new method for his time. Beruni, in his work

«Geodesy», speaks of the correctness of this method and associates it only with the name of Ibn Sina. This method was rediscovered in Europe 500 years later (1514) by the astronomer Werner.

In the field of mathematics, Abu Ali ibn Sina revised Euclid's book «Principles», added commentaries and additions to it, applied arithmetic terminology to geometric measurements, and expanded the scope of the concept of «number» far beyond «natural number». We touched on this in chapter two.

Abu Ali ibn Sina also left a significant mark in the field of poetry. He wrote some of his medical works («Urjuza») in Rajaz poetry. He also wrote several philosophical tales, which later had a profound influence on Persian-Tajik literature. The scientist has written several ghazals and poems in Persian, more than 40 rubai. Some of his poetic legacy has been published in Russian and Uzbek.

Abu Ali ibn Sina is a great theorist who continued Farabi's scientific direction in the field of music. The work on music «Javame' ilm ul-musiki» («Collection on the Science of Music») is part of the «Kitab ash-shifa» and consists of 6 sections with several chapters in each. In «An-najot», «Donishnoma», «Medical Laws», «Risalai Ishq» and other works there are small sections on music; he reflected on some problems of music. He described all the problems of music of his time: nagma, bod (interval), cadence systems, iiko, melody, musical instruments, etc. In Europe, he was the first to establish a musical structure which was later called «pure ridge (tovushkator)».

Abu Ali ibn Sina presented a perfect doctrine of musical beauty and considered music to be the most perfect form of harmony. Aruz, like other theorists of Eastern music, considers questions of rhythm in the context of the artistic system. As a physician, he saw music as an important medical tool. The theory that music arose from the development of human speech sounds is consistent with modern music theories. He included music as one of the main instruments in his idea of educating a fully developed human being.

Abu Ali Ibn Sina's work in medicine made his name closely associated with this field of science for several centuries. The great merit of the scientist in the development of medicine is that he sorted out the information collected in the field of medical science by various people who came before him, arranged it in a certain order, enriched it with his own experience and generalised it on the basis of certain theories and laws. His «Laws of Medicine», as well as the place and fame of this work in the history of world medical science, are clear confirmation of this.

The work of the scientist in the field of medicine advanced the medicine of the time by several centuries and in some areas even brought it closer to modern medicine. During his life, the priority in this field was the teaching of the ancient scientists, especially Hippocrates, Galen, Dioscorides and others. In his medical work he also relied on their theoretical views and practical instructions, but developed and enriched them on the basis of his experience and knowledge of scientists from India, China, Central Asia and the East. One of the main reasons for his fame as a brilliant doctor is his excellent knowledge of medical theory, especially anatomy - the structure of the human body. Following Galen, he correctly thought about the structure of the skull and the structure of the teeth. His writings on the anatomy of the eye, the process of vision and the role of the pupil, and the position of the eye muscles are close to modern ophthalmology. His work on the structure and function of nerves, blood vessels and muscles demonstrates the relevance of anatomy to practice. It is on this basis that the Russian scientist N.I. Pirogov, recognised as the founder of practical anatomy, is described as a follower of Abu Ali ibn Sina[492].

Abu Ali ibn Sina was an excellent diagnostician. Some of his diagnostic methods are still relevant today. He used percussion (diagnosis by striking an organ), in particular to distinguish between ascites and flatulence, and to detect contractions (by tapping the abdomen). This method was rediscovered 600 years later by the Viennese doctor Leopold Auenbrugger (1722-1809) and put into practice 50 years later. The scientist studied in detail cases of haemoptysis and types of breathing and used them in diagnosis. Abu Ali ibn Sina pays great attention to the signs obtained from the pulse, urine and faeces in the differential diagnosis of various diseases and

---

[492] Masharipova G.K. The role of the scientific, philosophical and spiritual heritage of Abu Ali ibn Sina in the life of society. Monography. – Tashkent: Navruz, 2020. – 96 p.

in determining the general condition of the body. For example, he diagnosed diabetes (sugar) from the condition of the urine and the presence of a sweet substance in it. In 1775, the English scientist Dobson discovered that sugar was present in the urine of diabetics. Abu Ali ibn Sina was the first in the history of medicine to distinguish between plague and bubonic plague, emphasised that patients with infectious diseases should be kept separate from others, and described the symptoms and course of diseases such as meningitis, stomach ulcers, jaundice and pleurisy, leprosy, ulcers, measles, chickenpox and anthrax. Correctly described. The manifestations of rabies and its infectious nature very accurately determined the condition of the patient with this disease. In 1804, the European scientist Sinquet confirmed that the saliva of rabid animals was contagious. The scientist made many innovations in the description and treatment of mental disorders. In the treatment of these diseases, he focused on the influence of the environment, climate, diet and exercise, as well as measures to improve the patient's mood.

When treating patients, the scientist says, it is necessary to pay attention to 3 things - order (diet), treatment with drugs and the use of various medical measures (taking blood, putting it in a jar, applying leeches, etc.). He considered diet to be one of the most important factors in the treatment of diseases, and for each disease he gave his own diet. For example, he prescribes more raisins, figs and pomegranate juice for liver disease. This method is an ancient version of the current methods of treating such diseases with glucose and insulin. The merits of Abu Ali ibn Sina in the development of surgery are also great. In his medical writings, he describes some of the methods used in modern surgery. These include cauterising pus-filled lesions or opening them with a knife, suturing haemorrhoids, stopping bleeding with tampons, sharp objects or sutures, cutting the throat and inserting a tube (tracheotomy). The method of treating humeral dislocation with simple pressure is still called the «Avicenna method». The curvature of the spine was corrected by Abu Ali ibn Sina using a wooden device of his own invention. This method was rediscovered by the French doctor Calot in the 15th century. The method of casting bones was also widely used by Abu Ali ibn Sina, but was later forgotten and brought back into practice as a new invention by European doctors in 1852. Abu Ali ibn Sina was aware of almost all the methods used in eye surgery today. Bad cancerous tumours, removal of bladder stones, haemorrhoid surgery, skull surgery, etc. are some of the treatments used by Abu Ali ibn Sina. Abu Ali ibn Sina also paid attention to anaesthesia during surgery. He used opium, milk, hemp and drugs with similar narcotic effects. Abu Ali ibn Sina emphasised the importance of personal hygiene, sleep and exercise in the treatment of disease. His method of curing one disease by causing another is remarkable. For example, he believed that four days of fever was useful in treating convulsions. The Austrian psychiatrist J. Wagner-Jaureg (1857-1940) was awarded the Nobel Prize in 1927 for the use of this method and the treatment of wound disease by infection with malaria.

Abu Ali ibn Sina carried out extensive research in the field of medicine. He completed the formation of a new pharmacy that appeared in the Muslim East based on the pharmacy of the ancient scientists. The use of medicines such as sano, camphor, rovoch, tamr hindi (Indian persimmon) in medicine and the preparation of many medicines based on sugar instead of honey is also the merit of Abu Ali ibn Sina. His methods of collecting, storing and processing medicinal plants are very close to the methods of modern medicine. In addition to natural medicines, Abu Ali ibn Sina was one of the first to use chemically prepared medicines. Depending on the nature of the disease, it was treated first with simple and then with complex medicines. Most importantly, he attached great importance to the healing effects of food and began treatment with such foods (fruits, vegetables, milk, meat, etc.). He emphasised the need to consider the patient's client (hot, cold, wet, dry), age and climatic conditions when prescribing the drug. Abu Ali ibn Sina's pharmacy was based on a sophisticated method of pharmacological research, far superior to medieval European pharmacy and approaching modern pharmacology. Some of the drugs used by the scientists have an important place in existing pharmacopoeias.

Ibn Sina argued that nature was eternal, that its laws did not change by themselves, that man was capable of understanding them, that the soul was determined by the activities of the body and that its individual eternity was impossible. At that time there was no science that he did not study. In addition to medicine, he actively studied philosophy, especially the theory of knowledge.

Ibn Sina considers the objects of the material world as the source of sensations and illuminates their objective nature as a reflection of the external material world. He also recognises sensation as one of the properties of matter. Alloma associates feelings with higher forms of matter. Ibn Sina, classifying existing things, states that feelings are characteristic of bodies called animals[493].

The considers the Neoplatonic doctrine that the soul perceives sensible things without any part of the body to be unfounded. «In ancient times, some scientists (Neoplatonists) hypothesised that the soul perceives things directly, without any organs. As for the environment, the medium of vision is the air, and as for the organs, the organ of vision is the eye. But they are far from the truth, because if sensory perception were to occur in the soul without these organs, then these organs would have been created in vain and there would be no benefit from them,» he writes, emphasising that the views of Neoplatonists are unfounded and the truth is that feelings need body parts[494].

When Ibn Sina talks about sensations and sense organs, he is trying to explain scientifically the mechanism by which a particular sensation occurs. According to him, no body can have sound by itself. Sound is created by the vibration of the air and the movement of two bodies colliding. These waves travel very fast. When they reach the ear, the vibrating air touches the auditory nerves, which communicate with the soul[495]. Although this description is rather simplistic, it corresponds to the current understanding. It also shows that Ibn Sina did not yet perceive sensations as a subjective image of the objective world. By explaining sensations as the movement of external influences in the body, Ibn Sina interprets them mechanically.

---

[493] See Ibn Sina. Treatise on the division of existing things. - Tashkent: Shark, 1983. - 128 p.
[494] Ibn Sina. Book of healing. - Tashkent: Science, 1967. – P. 265-266.
[495] Ibn Sina. Canon of medical science. Book 1. - Tashkent: Science, 1996. - pp. 260-261.

Ibn Sina developed the doctrine of vision. By explaining the process of vision, he shows the inconsistency of Plato's teaching about vision. Ibn Sina mentions light as the main means of vision[496].

The scientist studied all forms of sensations and feelings and tried to explain their physiological basis, i.e. the location of sensory centres in the structure of the brain. Interpreting the brain as the main apparatus of reflective activity, he associated the form of emotional cognition with the brain and recognised it as the basis of perception and cognition[497].

According to Ibn Sina, perception does not depend on the reflective system alone. The sensory centre is located in the front part of the brain, the imaginative centre in the middle part of the brain and the ability to remember in the back part of the brain. In his work «Kitab un-najot», Ibn Sina, who explores the physiological basis of each sensation, states that the nerves play an important role in the process of emotional cognition. According to him, the brain transmits sensations and actions to other human organs through nerves. Nerves serve as conductors for the brain[498]. It is generally accepted that nerves originate from the brain and their branches end at the surface of the skin[499]. As we have seen, Ibn Sina attempts to explain scientifically the physical and physiological basis of emotional perception.

Ibn Sina, like other Central Asian thinkers, classifies imagination as an internal sense. A comparative study of his philosophical legacy shows that he relied on a unified approach to understanding the nature and epistemological function of the imagination. He states that the power of his imagination is that everything that is accessible to common sense reaches our senses[500].

According to the sage, the epistemological function of the imagination is that it embodies images of external things and retains them in memory even after sensory perception has disappeared.

---

[496] Ibn Sina. Book of Salvation. - Tashkent: Sharq, 1986. – 224 p.
[497] Ibn Sina. Canon of medical science. Book 1. -Tashkent: Science, 1986. – 38 p.
[498] Ibn Sina. Canon of medical science. Book 1. -Tashkent: Science, 1986. – 41 p.
[499] Ibn Sina. Canon of medical science. Book 1. -Tashkent: Science, 1986. – 99 p.
[500] See Ibn Sina. Donishnoma. – Tashkent: Science, 1976. – 264 p.

According to Ibn Sina, the essence manifests itself in three ways. First, things are reflected in the senses in the process of observing them. What is meant here is that things are directly reflected in the senses. Ibn Sina raises the question of the levels of cognition, pointing to the concept of perception as a process of cognition. It is well known that this aim was developed in modern philosophy and found its gradual completion in classical German philosophy.

Secondly, objective existence is understood as the essence of that which does not actually exist[501]. Here it is a matter of understanding the essence of idealised objects that acquire formal meaning and are not associated with material existence. This essence reveals the creative capacities of the human mind.

Thirdly, the image of an object can, under certain conditions, be clearly reflected in the mind of the knower. This principle refers to the power of abstraction, which allows us to abstract things from their sensory connections. In this case, the image of an object can be reflected despite the absence of its substrate. On this basis, Ibn Sina states that abstraction plays an important role in rational knowledge. «Cognition is a process that consists of several interrelated stages of abstraction of the image of an object, as a result of which a concept is created in the mind of the knower that represents the essence and characteristics of the object. There are four stages of such abstraction»[502].

Ibn Sina includes «general intuition» among the inner intuitions. According to him, the general sense is a power located in the front part of the brain, which independently perceives all the forms reflected by the five senses and the power they convey[503]. Therefore, in his opinion, the sensations received by the senses are combined by means of the common sense and create an emotional image of the object.

By image, a scientist understands the totality of external features and properties of a thing, the accidental aspects of matter. For example, speaking of a person and his

---

[501] See Ibn Sina. Selected philosophical works. -Moscow: Nauka, 1980. - 30 p.
[502] Ibn Sina. Book of Salvation. -Tashkent: Shark, 1986. - 31 p.
[503] See Ibn Sina. Donishnoma. – Tashkent: Science, 1976. – 266 p.

image, he writes: «His image is his length, width, quality, quantity and condition, that is, everything that relates to a person»[504].

The above-mentioned ideas of Ibn Sina were developed and enriched with new results in later periods of the formation of scientific thought.

In the philosophical teachings of Abu Ali ibn Sina, the scientific explanation of the problems of spirituality, enlightenment and ethics occupies an important place. In his works «Treatise on Morals», «Treatise on the Covenant», «Treatise on the Purification of the Soul», «Book of the Management of the Body», «Bird Treatise», he understands the science of ethics as a science that regulates human behaviour, character and conduct. Ibn Sina, in his book «Wisdom», divides the sciences known in his time into two: practical and theoretical sciences. «The first,» he wrote, «makes us aware of our actions... Its utility is that it teaches us how to act in order to manage our affairs in this world... And the second is that our soul takes its form and is happy in this world». tells us about the state of existence of objects.

Chapter summaries:

1. The philosophical views of Abu Rayhon Beruni study the national and religious views of the Central Asian region.

2. In Beruni's philosophical views, along with religious knowledge, his views on the worldly knowledge of natural science were confirmed in European science.

3. Beruni emphasises that the force leading to social development is not conflict and contradiction, but compromise and agreement at different social levels.

4. Abu Rayhon Beruny saw the development of the country and the well-being of the people as inseparable from the development of science. He stressed that it is necessary for every student to be practical in his discussions, to have a fringe cell in his research, to work constantly, not to work and to be correct, to struggle with superficiality for the sake of truth and science. chtoby jit v soyuze, narody drujat, reshitelno osujdayut voyny, nesushchie razrushenie chelovechestvu, prizyvayut lyudey k miru. Practical experience and creative analysis are also highly valued as observation and scientific knowledge.

---

[504] Ibn Sina. Donishnoma. – Tashkent: Science, 1976. – 267 p.

5. In his philosophical teachings, Abu Ali ibn Sina discussed pleasure and pain, good and evil, chastity, shame and dishonour, justice and injustice, generosity and avarice, wisdom and ignorance, humility and arrogance, love and hate, purity and impurity, and faithfulness. He paid special attention to issues related to manners, such as infidelity, arrogance and boasting. He tried to explain that, in his opinion, all good and bad behaviour comes from habit and the influence of government officials on whether people are good or bad.

Abu Ali ibn Sina emphasised that a person should refrain from bad behaviour and morals such as revenge, deceit, envy, slander, hatred, and should not engage in absurd ways.

6. One of the socio-political and legal views of Abu Ali ibn Sina is the need for all members of society to engage in useful work, and he emphasised that an enlightened king should be at the head of the state. Ibn Sina divides the structure of an ideal state into three groups:

1. Those engaged in administrative work.

2. The producers.

3. The military.

7. The social and political views of Abu Ali ibn Sina were strongly influenced by the teachings of Abu Nasr Farabi. According to Ibn Sina, «there can be no injustice in a country where common laws are established for its members». A member of an unjust society must be punished. If the ruler himself is unjust, rebellion against him must be approved and supported by society. If each man were to manage everything himself, he would be faced with a very difficult and impossible task. Therefore, an agreement between people, justice and established rules of law are necessary, and a lawyer must acquire a duty by virtue of the fact that he possesses such legal characteristics. Likewise, those who do good deeds and those who do evil deeds must be rewarded by Him who knows all things and can do all things. Therefore it is necessary to recognise the supremacy of the Judge and the Lawgiver.

8. The second part of Abu Ali ibn Sina's «Donishnom» was called «Metaphysics», which is considered one of the main parts of medieval philosophy,

and philosophical knowledge was divided into two types. One is 'practical knowledge', which informs us about our actions, and the other is 'theoretical knowledge', which informs us about the existence of things. And this was divided into three: first, knowledge of things outside nature; second, mathematical knowledge; third, knowledge of nature. So each of these two kinds of knowledge is in turn divided into three parts. The first is the knowledge that studies the issues necessary to manage a family, to provide for its needs, tasks and activities. This knowledge was also divided into two parts: 1) religious Shari'a; 2) political - it studied issues of government and governance, ensuring relations between the government and citizens, as well as between states. The second studies the fairness of relations between citizens of the state, spouses and children, masters and servants. Finally, the third is the knowledge of human behaviour.

9. The teachings of Abu Ali ibn Sina on spirituality, enlightenment and ethics have made a great contribution to the development of world science, culture and spirituality. The ultimate goal of the cognitive process is the complex process of realising the essence of objects. Central Asian thinkers of the Middle Ages believed that knowledge is the perception of a known object. The human sense organs are the direct link in this process, i.e. the source of knowledge is the objective world that can be perceived through the senses.

Conclusion

The philosophical works written by the scientists of Khorezm in the 10th-12th centuries have been studied by scientists all over the world in three areas:

1) scientific research, 2) publication of the text of sources of this period in full or in part, 3) translation and publication of scientific sources in different languages of the world in the X-XII centuries in Khorezm.

In determining the ancient roots of the development of philosophical sciences in Khorezm, the main place is occupied by the materials of the archaeological and ethnographic expeditions that have been conducting research in the country for many years.

1. Muhammad ibn Musa al-Khwarizmi developed a system of counting. The positional system of zero and counting that he created spread to Europe. Decimal fractions were later discovered in the works of Ghiyasiddin Jamshid al-Qoshi, who worked at the Mirzo Ulugbek Observatory in Samarkand.

2. A comparison of geographical coordinates in the works of Abu Rayhon Beruni and al-Khwarizmi on the basis of continuity shows that Abu Rayhon Beruni did not include many cities in Western Europe (except Spain) in his tables, but at the expense of cities in Iran, Iraq, the Caucasus, Khorasan, Central Asia and India.

4. Some subjects, such as algebra and trigonometry, were separated from astronomy. Scientists from Khorezm observed the movement of the moon and conducted scientific research.

5. The geographical coordinates of settlements and cities in Central Asia, Khorasan, India and Western Europe were determined.

6. Abu Nasr ibn Iraq was the first to apply and prove the sine theorem to a spherical triangle. He found the latitude of the city corresponding to these conditions by taking the degrees of two given heights as equal. Furthermore, if the angle formed by the intersection of the horizon and the ecliptic at a given height is known, then the width of the city is also known.

7. This table shows the achievements of Khorezm scholars in mathematics and astronomy at the Al-Mamun Academy in Baghdad and the Khorezm Mamun Academy:

In Beit al-Hikmah.	At the Khorezm Mamun Academy
1. The decimal calculation system developed by Muhammad ibn Musa al-Khwarizmi, its structure and widespread use.	1. The theory of the earth's rotation around the sun was created.
2. He established a classification of linear and quadratic equations, a clear definition of the rules for their solution and application that people encounter in economic, trade, construction and legal activities.	2. The radius of the Earth was first measured by Abu Rayhon Beruni. In addition, al-Khububi revised linear and quadratic equations based on the six canonical equations. This differs from Muhammad ibn Musa al-Khwarizmi.
3. Habash al-Khasib made an important step in the development of trigonometry, replacing the Greek vatars with the sine and introducing the tangent and cotangent functions.	3. A major contribution was made to the development of trigonometry. Abu Nasr ibn Iraq proved it using the theorem of sines for a spherical triangle.
4. State astronomical observatories were built and astronomical observations were carried out in them.	4. During the time of Mamun ibn Mamun, a rich library was built and scientific research was carried out in it.
5. The famous «Map of Mamun» was created, containing information about continents, seas, settlements, climate, deserts, mountains, rivers, their tributaries, cities, etc. This map also contains information about the	5. A sector was defined for the first time in the field of geometry. Thoughts on the theory of parallels were presented. It was based on the existence of a geometry other than Euclidean. For example, the geometry

celestial spheres and planets.

6. According to the order of Al-Mamun, the accuracy of the results of measuring the length of the Earth's meridian in the Sinjar desert did not change for about 700 years.

of N. I. Lobachevsky.

6. During the Anusteghini-Khorezmshah period, attention to science increased. Mahmud al-Chaghmini's astronomy reached its peak during the Anushtegini dynasty. Scientific research in the field of astronomy during the Anushteghini-Khorezmshah period was taught from a textbook at the Mirzo Ulugbek Observatory in most countries of the East and West.

8. One of the important problems solved by Abu Rayhon Beruni in his «Geodesy» is the measurement of the Earth's radius. It is calculated with great accuracy using the formula R = in modern conditions. The proof is given in the monograph. Knowing the height of the mountain, the great scientist first determined the radius of the Earth in exact dimensions as 12851370 gas = 3212.8 miles = 6340 km.

9. The rule for finding the difference in longitude of two cities by their latitude and the distance between them can be written in the form of this formula.

$$\sin\frac{\theta_b - \theta_a}{2} = \frac{1}{2}\sqrt{\frac{\sin^2(\frac{\rho}{2R}) - \sin^2\frac{\varphi_b - \varphi_a}{2}}{\cos\varphi_a \cdot \cos\varphi_b}}$$

. In this case $\theta_b \neq 0$, $\theta_a \neq 1$, $\rho \neq 2$, $R \neq 0$, $\varphi_a \neq 1$, $\varphi_b \neq 1$.

This is why he introduced the concept of «shai saleh», which has an important mathematical meaning and by which he means any small value.

10. The rule for finding the points in the sky where the crescent is visible, that is, the rule for finding their spherical coordinates, was given by Abu Rayhon Beruni.

His rule:

$$\sinh_2 = \cos\varphi' \cdot \cos\lambda \cdot \sin\beta - \sin\varphi' \cdot \sin\lambda$$

$$\sin A_2 = \frac{\sin\varphi' \cdot \cos\lambda \cdot \sin\beta + \cos\varphi' \cdot \sin\lambda}{\cosh_2}$$

The formula occurs predominantly in the present tense, in which $h_2 \neq 1$, $\varphi' \neq 1$, $\lambda \neq 1$, $A_2 \neq 1$, $\beta \neq 0$.

11. The treatise «Kitab at-tafhim» (1029-1034) describes the basics of mathematics, astronomy and astrology. Proofs of a number of theorems in geometry and trigonometry are given in the «Treatise on the Determination of the Arcs of a Circle by Means of Broken Lines drawn within it» (1027). The work «Kanuni Masudi» (1037) is dedicated to astronomy and is a collection of knowledge in this field at that time. It also contains valuable information on the history of mathematics, trigonometry, proofs of spherical trigonometric equations and the expansion of the concept of number. In The Book of Indian Love, he justifies the rule of three, common in the Middle Ages, in terms of structural proportions. He applies it to any number of quantities and gives generalised rules. Two sections of the book «Explanations» have survived, describing the basic concepts of geometry and arithmetic. In his work «Al-asarul-baqiya» («Monuments Left by Ancient Peoples»), the great scientist reflected the achievements of many scientists who had gone before him in the fields of astronomy, mathematics, geography and other sciences. Abu Rayhon Beruni led to the solution of cubic equations: trisection of an angle, doubling of a cube and finding the side of a regular octagon. He tried to find a method of quadratic interpolation and proved the theorem of spherical sines.

12. The manuscript of Abu Ali ibn Sina's work «Usul 'ilm al-Khandasa» («Fundamentals of Geometry»), included in the third part of «Kitab al-Shifa» (№ 2720 from the Library of Ayo Sofia, Istanbul), was translated into Uzbek by the author. In it, the great scientist first presented definitions of geometry, and then postulates and propositions (axioms) that did not require proof. The first three obligatory propositions are constructive in nature. Ibn Sina teaches a student to work with geometric figures using a compass (circle) and a ruler.

13. Abu Rayhon Beruni's work «Kanuni Masudi» comprehensively covers the star catalogue and issues of functional mathematics. The work also presents his

thoughts in the field of mathematics and spherical astronomy, i.e, The origin of the shape of the universe, the location of the heavenly bodies, spherical astronomy (a system of triangles drawn inside a circle); Watters, the value of the number (= 3, 14174628) using a table of quantities for radius, cotangent («flat shadow»), tangent («reflected shadow»), the theorem of sines; The structure of the astrolabe, spherical coordinates, the maximum deviation of the ecliptic, the rise of the twelve signs, the determination of the coordinates of places on the earth, the determination of the azimuths of cities and the directions of Mecca (qibla) are of great importance today.

In addition, the structure and functions of the astrolabe, which was included in the treatises of the great scientist in the field of mathematical astronomy, were analysed.

Abu Rayhon Beruni recognised as true astronomy only that astronomy which explains the movement of the heavenly bodies on the basis of geometry. In his book Qanuni Masudi, he also described in detail previous attempts to measure the dimensions of the Earth, and focused beautifully on a new method: We have heard about the measurements of the earth», he writes, «only the words of Romanian and Indian specialists reached us, in each of which the number of units was different. The Indians measured the circumference of the earth at a distance that included one mile to our eight miles. In each of the five Siddihont, the circumference of the earth is described differently. The Romans measured it by size and called it «stadion». Galen says that Eratosthenes made his measurements in the cities of Aswan and Alexandria, which are on the same meridian. As always, Galen's book of proofs in Ptolemy's Introduction to the Art of Spherics and Geography uses different units of measurement. Such disagreements prompted Mamun ibn al-Rashid to refocus [the problem] with the help of the leaders of this science in the Sinjar desert in the land of Mosul.

Abu Rayhon Beruni obsujdal cosmogony, form of the universe and chronology and «Kanuni Masudi». Razumno zaklyuchit, chto ego astronomy was based on the geocentric system of Ptolemy. Po ego mneniyu, znachenie imeet ob'yasnenie dvizheniy Solntsa, Luny, ix zatmeniy, astronomy zvezd, planets, astrology.

Etot uchyonyy-encyclopedist podnyal mathematicheskie metody i privala na bolee vysokiy uroven vplot do vremen Ulugbeka. Eta ego work is a beautiful picture of mathematics and astronomy, and the progress of several centuries.

14. The great scientists of Central Asia, Abu Raikhan Beruni and Abu Ali ibn Sina, also studied number theory. Ibn Sina cited natural numbers and their properties in the accountancy part of his Kitab al-Shifa. He checks that operations on them are performed by 9, i.e. he first compares the numbers modulo nine.

15. Among the scientists of the Mamun Academy, the philosophical sciences are given a lot of attention along with the specific sciences. During the writing of the monograph, when we compared the comments of the Khorezm scholars Abu Abdullah al-Khorezmi, i.e. Katib Khorezmi and Ibn Sina on the «Fundamentals» of Euclid with the scientific works of foreign scholars, we witnessed that the Khorezm scholars were excellent in the field of exact sciences.

16. The scientific heritage of the Khorezm scientists in the activities of the astronomical school in Samarkand, commentary on «Kanuni Masudi» by Abu Rayhon Beruni, «Sharh al-mulahhas fi-l-haya» by Gazizada Rumi, Mahmud Chaga. mini «Brief Astronomy», Hussein al-Kubrawi's Astronomy from Arabic to Persian «Nuzhat al-mullok fi hayati-l-aflok» («The King's Review of the Structure of the Universe») and Mir Syed Sharif Jurjani's commentary on Chagmini's book. The main guide was the treatise 'Mulahas fi-l-haya'.

17. The scientific heritage of the Khorezm scientists is of great importance not only for Eastern science, but also for the development of world science, influencing the scientific heritage of Western scientists.

LIST OF REFERENCES USED

I. Regulatory documents and official literature:

1.1. Decree of the President of the Republic of Uzbekistan. «On re-externalisation of Khorezm Mamun Academy». № PF-1880. 11.11.1997// https://lex.uz/docs/198975.

1.2. Resolution of the Cabinet of Ministers of the Republic of Uzbekistan. «On the occasion of the 1000th anniversary of the Khorezm Mamun Academy». № 532. 9.11.2006/ https://lex.uz/docs/2280324.

1.3. Mirziyoyev Sh.M. We will build our great future together with our brave and noble people. - Tashkent: Uzbekistan, 2017. - 488 p.

1.4. Karimov I.A. The light of knowledge never fades. His speech on the occasion of the 1000th anniversary of the Khorezm Mamun Academy // «People's Word», 3 November 2006.

1.5. Karimov I.A. High spirituality is an invincible power. - Tashkent: Spirituality, 2008. - 174 p.

II. Books, Monographys and brochures:

2.1. Abu Ali ibn Sina. Medical laws. Book I / Editor-in-chief: T.Z.Zokhidov. Responsible editors: Askarov A.A., Ternovsky V.N., Karimov U.I. - Tashkent: Science, 1954. - 458 p.

2.2. Abu Ali ibn Sina. Medical laws. Book II / chief editor: T.Z. Zokhidov. Responsible editors: Askarov A.A., V.K.Dzhumaev, U.I.Karimov. - Tashkent: Science, 1966. - 843 p.

2.3. Abu Ali ibn Sina. Medical laws. Book III / chief editor: T.Z. Zokhidov. Responsible editors: Askarov A.A., V.K.Dzhumaev, U.I.Karimov. - Tashkent: National heritage named after. Abdulla Kadyri, 1992. - 315 p.

2.4. Abu Ali ibn Sina. Medical laws. Book IV / Responsible editors: A.A.Askarov, V.K.Dzhumaev, U.I.Karimov. - Tashkent: Science, 1960. - 802 p.

2.5. Abu Ali ibn Sina. Medical laws. Book V / Responsible editor: A.A.Askarov, V.K.Dzhumaev, U.I.Karimov - Tashkent: Science, 1961. - 348 p.

2.6. Abu Ali ibn Sina. Danish name - «Book of Knowledge». - Dushanbe: Tajgosizdat, 1967. - 180 p.

2.7. Abu Ali ibn Sina. Mathematical chapters of the «Book of Knowledge» («Donishnoma») / Trans. and com. edited by S.U. Umarov and B.A. Rosenfeld. - Dushanbe: Irfon, 1967. - 180 p.

2.8. Abu Ali ibn Sina. Book of Healing. - Tashkent: Science, 1967. - 752 p.

2.9. Abu Ali ibn Sina. Selected philosophical works. - Moscow: Science, 1980. - 552 p.

2.10. Abu Ali ibn Sina. Book of Salvation. - Tashkent: Sharq, 1986. - 322 p.

2.11. Abu Rayhon Beruni. Selected Works. 2-vol. India / Translation from Arabic by A.Rasulov, Y.Khakimjonov, G.Dzhalolov; responsible editors G.Jalolov, A.Irisov; Start a word. and the author of the comments is A.Irisov. - Tashkent: Science, 1965. - 539 p.

2.12. Abu Rayhon Beruni. Selected works. 1-vol. Monuments left by ancient peoples / Responsible editors I.Abdullaev, O.Faizullaev; Translation. A.Rasulov. - Tashkent: Science, 1968. - 486 p.

2.13. Abu Rayhon Beruni. Selected works. 5-t. Book 1. Lo Masudi. Articles 1-5 / Translation. A.Rasulov; Responsible editor: Akhmedov A.A.; The notes were compiled by A.Akhmedov and A.Rasulov. - Tashkent: Science, 1973. - 591 p.

2.14. Abu Rayhon Beruni. Selected Works. T. VI, «The Book of Understanding of the Beginnings of the Science of the Stars» [«Tafkhim»] / Introductory article, translation and notes by B.A. Rosenfeld and A. Akhmedov with the participation of M.M. Rozhanskaya, A.A. Abdurakhmanov and N.D. Sergei howl . - Tashkent, 1975. - 333 p.

2.15. Abu Rayhon Beruni. Selected works. 5-t. Book 2. Canon of Masudi. Articles 6-11 / Translation. A. Rasulov; the author of the preface and indicators is Akhmedov A.; the notes were compiled by A. Akhmedov and B. Rosenfeld. - Tashkent: Science, 1976. - 680 p.

2.16. Abu Rayhon Beruni. Selected works. 3-t. Address delimitation for determining distances (between) residential buildings. [Geodesy] / Introduction, translation. and the author of the comments A.Akhmedov. - Tashkent: Science, 1982. - 344 p.

2.17. Beruniy Abu Rayhon. Book of Understanding. - Moscow, 1973. - 328 p.

2.18. Beruniy Abu Rayhon. Monuments of Past Generations (Osor ul-Baqiya) // Selected Works. Volume I. - Tashkent: NMIU «Uzbekistan», 2022.

2.19. Beruni Abu Rayhon. India // Selected works. Volume II. - Tashkent: NMIU «Uzbekistan», 2022.

2.20. Beruni Abu Rayhon. Determination of address boundaries for determining distances (between) residential buildings (geodesy) // Selected works. Volume III. - Tashkent: NMIU «Uzbekistan», 2022.

2.21. Beruni Abu Rayhon. Kanoni Masudi // Selected Works IV. Articles 1-5. - Tashkent: NMIU «Uzbekistan», 2022.

2.22. Beruni Abu Rayhon. Kanoni Masudi // Selected works. -Tashkent, 6-11 articles. - Tashkent: NMIU «Uzbekistan», 2022.

2.23. Beruni Abu Rayhon. A book explaining the basics of the art of astrology (astrology). «Tafhim» // Selected works. Volume VI. - Tashkent: NMIU «Uzbekistan», 2022.

2.24. Beruni Abu Rayhon. Mathematical and astronomical treatises // Selected works volume VII. - Tashkent: NMIU «Uzbekistan», 2022.

2.25. Beruni Abu Rayhon. Saidana // Selected works volume IX. - Tashkent: NMIU «Uzbekistan», 2022.

2.26. Abu Nasr al-Farabi. Commentaries on the introductions of the first and fifth books of Euclid/Translated by M.F.Bockstein. Mathematical treatises. - Alma-Ata, 1972. - 324 p.

2.27. Abu Sa'id Gardizi. Zain al-akhbar. Decoration of news. Section on the history of Khorasan / Trans. from pers. A.K.Arendsa. input, comment and decree L.M. Epifanova. - Tashkent: Science, 1991. - 176 p.

2.28. Abu-l-Fazl Bayhaki. History of Mas'ud. - Moscow: Science, 1969. - 359 p.

2.29. Arabic anonymous from the 11th century. - Moscow: Eastern literature, 1960. - 221 p.

2.30. Al-Kashi Jamshid Giyaseddin. Arithmetic key. Treatise on the Circle/Trans. B.A.Rosenfeld, ed. V.S.Segal and A.P. Yushkevich. Com. A.P.Yushkevich and B.A. Rosenfeld. – Moscow, 1956. - 568 p.

2.31. Aristotle. Works: in 4 volumes. T.1- Moscow: Thought. 1976. - 682 p.

2.32. Aristotle. Essays. in 4 volumes. T.2 - Moscow: Thought. 1978. - 587 p.

2.33. Arrian. Alexander's campaign. - Moscow-Leningrad: Publishing House of the USSR Academy of Sciences. 1962. – 257 p.

2.34. Akhmedov A. Tafkhim. – Tashkent, 2005. – 390 p.

2.35. Beruni and Ibn Sina. Correspondence / Per. Yu.N.Zavadovsky. - Tashkent: Science, 1973. - 36 p.

2.36. Bulgakov P.G. Beruni and his "Geodesy" // Abu Reyhan Biruni. Favorite works: T.3. Determination of the boundaries of places to clarify the distances between populated areas [«Geodesy»] // Iss. translation and notes by P.G.Bulgakov. - Tashkent: Science, 1966. - 344 p.

2.37. Bunetov Z. State of Anushteghini-Khorezmshahs (1097-1231). – Tashkent, 1998. – 312 p.

2.38. Euclid. Beginnings / Per. from Greek D.D.Mordukhai-Boltovsky. In 3 volumes - Moscow-Leningrad: Gostekhizdat, 1948. Vol.1. - 488 p.

2.39. Euclid. Beginnings / Per. from Greek D.D.Mordukhai-Boltovsky. - Moscow-Leningrad: Gostekhizdat, 1950. T.2. - 332 p.

2.40. Muhammad ibn Musa al-Khwarizmi. Selected works. Mathematics, astronomy, geography / Responsible editors: S.Kh.Sirodzhiddinov, U.I.Karimov, M.M. Khairullayev, A. Akhmedov. – Tashkent: Science, 1983. – 470 p.

2.41. Nasir ad-Din at-Tusi. Treatise on the complete quadrilateral. / Ed. G.D. Mamedbeyli and B.A.Rosenfeld. - Baku: Publishing House of the Academy of Sciences of the AzSSR, 1952. - 255 p.

2.42. Nizami Aruzi Samarkandi. A collection of rarities or four conversations. - Moscow: 1963. - 173 p.

2.43. Nizamul Mulk. Politician or Siyar ul-Muluk. - Tashkent: Adolat, 1997. - 255 p.

2.44. Farabi Abu Nasr. City of virtuous people. - Tashkent: People's Heritage Publishing House named after Abdulla Kadyri, 1993. - 320 p.

2.45. Khayyam Omar. Treatises. - Moscow: Eastern literature, 1961. - 338 p.

2.46. Chizhevsky A.L., Shishina Yu.G. In the rhythm of the Sun. – Moscow, 1969. - 112 p.

2.47. Abu Raikhan Beruni // Uzbek Soviet Encyclopedia. Volume 1. - Tashkent: UzFE, 1971. - 632 p.

2.48. Abdullaev I. Poetry in Arabic in Central Asia and Khorasan of the 10th century. - beginning of the 11th century. - Tashkent, 1984. - 294 p.

2.49. Abdukhalimov B. "Bayt al-hikma" and the scientific activity of Central Asian scientists in Baghdad (exact and natural sciences in the 9th-11th centuries). – Tashkent: Tashkent Islamic University, – 2004. – 236 p.

2.50. Abrorova M. From the history of mathematics in Bukhara // Mathematics in the Middle Ages East. - Tashkent: Science, 1978. - pp. 97-112.

2.51. Avloni A. Turki Gulistan or ethics. – Tashkent: Publishing House Youth House, 2018. – 97 p.

2.52. Akromkhodzhaev O.M. Beruniy is one of the first researchers. – Tashkent, 1976. – 78 p.

2.53. Al-Farabi. About achieving happiness. Socio-ethnic treatises. - Alma-Ata: Science, 1973. - 350 p.

2.54. Artamonov M.I. History of the Khazars - Leningrad: Publishing house. State Hermitage, 1962. - 523 p.

2.55. Atagarriev M.N. Application of stereographic projection to determining the azimuth of the qibla: al-Biruni, al-Chagmini and at-Turkmoni // Historical and mathematical studies. Vol. XXIX. - Moscow: Science, 1980. - P.44-47.

2.56. Akhadova M. From the history of mathematics in Bukhara // Mathematics in the Middle Ages East. - Tashkent: Science, 1978. - P.97-112.

2.57. Akhadova M.V. Treatise by Abu Ali ibn Sina "The Measure of Reason" // From the history of exact sciences in the medieval Near and Middle East. - Tashkent: Science, 1972. - P.42-57.

2.58. Akhmedov A. Issues of substantiation of geometry in the medieval Near and Middle East. - Tashkent: Science, 1972. - 372 p.

2.59. Akhmedov A., Rosenfeld B.A. "Cartography" is one of the first works of Beruni that have come down to us // Mathematics in the Middle Ages East. - Tashkent: Science, 1978. - P.127-153.

2.60. Akhmedov A. About the comments of Abd al-Ali Husayn Birjandi to Ulugbek's "Zij" // From the history of science of the era of Ulugbek. - Tashkent: Science, 1979. - P.69-109.

2.61. Akhmedov A. Al-Khorezmi - astronomer and geographer // Earth and Universe. - № 6. - Moscow: 1983. - P. 28-32.

2.62. Akhmedov A. Khorezmi and geographical science // Muhammad ibn Musa al-Khorezmi. Selected works. - Tashkent: Science, 1983. - B. 225-291.

2.63. Akhmedov A., Rosendfeld B.A., Sergeeva N.D. Astronomical and geographical works of al-Khorezmi // Muhammad ibn Musal-Khorezmi. To the 1200th anniversary of his birth. - Moscow: Science, 1983. - P. 141-191.

2.64. Akhmedov A. Issues of substantiation of geometry in the medieval Near and Middle East. - Tashkent: Science, 1972. - 372 p.

2.65. Akhmedov A. "Book on extracting the edge of a cube" by al-Hasan ibn al-Haytham // Mathematics and astronomy in the works of scientists of the medieval East. - Tashkent: Science, 1977. - P.113-117.

2.66. Akhmedov A. About the comments of Abd al-Ali Husayn Birjandi to Ulugbek's "Zij" // From the history of science of the era of Ulugbek. -Tashkent: Science, 1979. - P.69-109.

2.67. Akhmedov A. Al-Khorezmi - astronomer and geographer // Earth and Universe. № 6. - Moscow, 1983. - P.28-32.

2.68.2.68. Akhmedov A.A., Bulgakov P.G. Central Asian-Indian relations in the field of exact sciences // From the history of cultural relations between the peoples of Central Asia and India. - Tashkent: Science, 1986. - P.24-33.

2.69. Akhadova M. Famous mathematicians of Central Asia. – Tashkent: Science, 1964. – 40 p.

2.70. Akhadova M. Abu Raikhan Beruni and his works in mathematics. – Tashkent: Science, 1976. – 32 p.

2.71. Akhadova M. Famous scientists of Central Asia and their works on mathematics (VIII-XV centuries). – Tashkent: Teacher, 1983. – 216 p.

2.72. Bagirova S.G. The essay "Tatimma Sivan al-Hikma al-Bayhaki" as an example of a medieval encyclopedic reference book. - Tashkent: Science, 1987. - 138 p.

2.73. Bartold V.V. History of the cultural life of Turkestan. Works in 9 volumes. II.Part 1. - Moscow: IVL, 1963.

2.74. Bartold V.V. About Christianity in Turkestan in the pre-Mongol period (About the Semirechensk inscriptions) // Works: in 9 volumes - Moscow: Science, 1964. T. 2. Part 2. - pp. 265-302.

2.75. Bartold V.V. On the issue of the confluence of the Amu Darya into the Caspian Sea. Works in 9 volumes. T.III. – Moscow, 1965. - 264 p.

2.76. Bartold V. Culture of Islam // Works in 9 volumes - T. IV. - Moscow: 1966. - 112 p.

2.77. Bakhadirov R.M. From the history of the classification of sciences in the medieval Muslim East. - Tashkent: Science, 2000. - 126 p.

2.78. Bakhadirov R. From the history of Abu Abdullah al-Khorezmi and the classification of sciences. - Tashkent: Uzbekistan, 1995. - 144 p.

2.79. Belenitsky A.M. About "Mineralogy" and Biruni // Beruni.-Moscow-Leningrad, 1950. - P. 88-105.

2.80. Questions and answers from Ibn Sina with Beruni // Translation by A.Rasulov. - Tashkent: Science, 1950. - 35 p.

2.81. Bertels E. E. Sufism and Sufi literature. - Moscow: Science, 1995. - 524 p.

2.82. Boboev H., Gafurov Z. Development of political and spiritual-educational teaching in Uzbekistan. – Tashkent: Generation of the New Century, 2001. – 240 p.

2.83. Bolshakov O. Essays on the history of Arab culture. – Moscow, 1982. - 440 p.

2.84. Bulgakov P.G. Beruni and his "Geodesy" // Abu Reyhan Biruni. Favorite Works. T.3. Determining the boundaries of places to clarify the distances between populated areas [«Geodesy»] / Translation and notes by P.G.Bulgakov. - Tashkent: Science, 1966. - 344 p.

2.85. Bulgakov P.G. Life and works of Beruni. - Tashkent: Science, 1972. - 428 p.

2.86. Bulgakov P.G. "Geodesy" of Biruni as a historical and astronomical monument // Historical and astronomical studies. Issue XI. – Moscow, 1972. - P.181-190.

2.87. Bulgakov P.G. Biruni's early treatise on the Fakhri sextant//Historical and astronomical studies. Issue XI. – Moscow, 1972. - P.211-220.

2.88. Bulgakov P.G. About two fragments from the "Canon of Mas'ud" by Beruni//Beruni. Collection of articles for the 1000th anniversary of his birth. - Tashkent: Science, 1973. - P.60-72.

2.89. Bulgakov P.G. Ibn Sina's contribution to practical astronomy//Abu Ali ibn Sina. To the 1000th anniversary of his birth. - Tashkent: Science, 1980. - P. 149-157.

2.90. Bulgakov P.G., Akhmedov A.A. Astronomy in Central Asia in the 1st – 10th centuries // Research on the history, history of science and culture of the peoples of Central Asia. - Tashkent: Science, 1993. - P. 7-28.

2.91. Bulgakov P.G. Rumi Kazi-zade. Commentary on "Compendium of Astronomy" by Chagmini. Preface, translation from Arabic and notes by corresponding member of the Ruz Academy of Sciences P.G. Bulgakov. - Tashkent: Science, 1993. - 236 p.

2.92. Boriyev O., Vakhobova B. Written sources about al-Fergani. – Tashkent, 1998. – 61 p.

2.93. Boriyev O., Toshev N. Jalaluddin Manguberdi. – Tashkent: Science, 1999. – 76 p.

2.94. Boriyev O. Khorezmshahs-Timurs (continuity of scientific traditions). – Tashkent: Science, 1999. – 48 p.

2.95. Weinberg B.I. Coins of Ancient Khorezm. - Moscow: Science, 1977. - 194 p.

2.96. Vashchenko-Zakharchenko M.E. History of mathematics. In 3 volumes. T.1. - Kiev, 1883. - 487 p.

2.97. Vakhabova B.A. Manuscripts of Ibn Sina's works in the collection of the Institute of Oriental Studies of the Academy of Sciences of the Uzbek SSR. - Tashkent: Science, 1982. - 70 p.

2.98. Vakhabov S. Two mathematical models of al-Biruni // Historical and mathematical studies. Vol. XXV. - Moscow: Science, 1980. - P.328-335.

2.99. Vakhabov S.A. Projective transformations in al-Biruni's treatise on astrolabes // Historical and mathematical studies. Vol. XXXII - XXXIII. - Moscow: Science, 1990. - P.339-344.

2.100. Ventzel M.K. A brief outline of the history of practical astronomy in Russia and the USSR (development of methods for determining time and latitude) // Historical and astronomical studies. Issue 11. – Moscow, 1956. - P.7-140.

2.101. Vildanova A.B. Manuscripts of works by Central Asian mathematicians and astronomers in the collection of the Institute of Oriental Studies of the Academy of Sciences of the UzSSR // Materials on the history and history of science and culture of the peoples of Central Asia. - Tashkent: Fan. 1991. - P.302-321.

2.102. Volin S. On the history of ancient Khorezm // Bulletin of ancient history. - Moscow, 1941. № 1. - P. 23-35.

2.103. Vorobyeva M.G., Rozhanskaya M.M. About some astronomical functions of Koi-krylgan-kala // Koi-krylgan-kala - a cultural monument of Ancient Khorezm of the 4th century. BC. - IV century AD Tr. Khorezm. expeditions. - Moscow: Science, 1967. - P. 251-264.

2.104. Vorobyeva M.G., Rozhanskaya M.M., Veselovsky I.N. Ancient Khorezmian monument of the 4th century BC. Koi-wing-kala from the point of view of the history of astronomy // Historical and astronomical studies. Vol. Kh. - Moscow: Science, 1969. - P. 15-34.

2.105. Voronovsky D.G. Astronomers of Central Asia from Muhammedal-Kharezmi to Ulugbek and his school (XIV-XVI centuries) // From the history of the era of Ulugbek. – Tashkent, 1965. - P.155; pp. 114-118.

2.106. Gafurov B.G. History of the Tajik people. - Moscow: Gospolitizdat, 1955. - 501 p.

2.107. Gafurov B.G. Tajiks. - Moscow: Science, 1972. - 476 p.

2.108. Gafurov B.G., Tsibukidis D.I. Alexander the Great and the East. - Moscow: Science, 1980. - 303 p.

2.109. Gilbert D. Foundations of geometry. - Moscow-Leningrad: Gostekhizdat, 1948. - 492 p.

2.110. Grigoryan A.T., Rozhanskaya M.M. Mechanics and astronomy in the Middle Ages East. - Moscow: Science, 1980. - 200 p.

2.111. Gumilev L.N. Ancient Turks. - Moscow: Science, 1967. - 504 p.

2.112. Gulyamov Ya.G. History of irrigation of Khorezm from ancient times to the present day. - Tashkent: Publishing House of the Academy of Sciences of the UzSSR, 1957. - 315 p.

2.113. Jalalov G.D. Some remarkable statements of astronomers of the Samarkand Observatory // Historical and astronomical studies. Issue III. - Moscow, 1957.

2.114. Jalalov G.D. Indian astronomy in Beruni's book "India" // Historical and astronomical studies. Issue XUIII. – Moscow, 1962. - P.195-220.

2.115. Jalalova Z.G. Disciple of al-Biruni about the movement of the Sun // Historical and astronomical studies. Vol. XII. – Moscow, 1975. - P.227-236.

2.116. Dovatur A.I., Kallistov D.P., Shishova I.A. The peoples of our country in the history of Herodotus. - Moscow: Science, 1982. - 495 p.

2.117. Ancient and medieval culture of southeastern Ustyurt / Responsible editor. member of the correspondent AN RUz. S.Kamalov. -Tashkent: Science, 1978. - 328 p.

2.118. Eremeyeva A.I., Tsitsin F.A. History of astronomy. - Moscow State University, 1976. - 352 p.

2.119. Zavadovsky Yu.N. Materials for the biography of Abu Ali ibn Sina. - Taj.SSR: Izv.AN. Taj.SSR, dept. total science Vol. 2. 1958. - pp. 58-59.

2.120. Star catalog of al-Biruni with the appendix of the catalogs of Khayyam and al-Tusi / Translation by S.A. Krasnova, M.M. Rozhanskaya. Ed. B.A.Rosenfeld. /Historical and astronomical research. Vol. VIII. – Moscow, 1962. - P.83-194.

2.121. Zikrillayev F. Beruni's works in the field of physics. - Tashkent, 1973.- 496 p.

2.122. Ibadov J.H. About mathematical manuscripts from the SADUM library // Collection: Mathematics in the Middle Ages East. - Tashkent: Science, 1978. - P.154-160.

2.123. Ibadov J.H. About the mathematical treatise from Khiva // Mathematics and astronomy in the works of Ibn Sina, his contemporaries and followers. - Tashkent: Science, 1981. - P.143-154.

2.124. Ibadov J.H. Mathematical treatises of al-Khububi and al-Sijavandi // From the history of medieval eastern mathematics and astronomy. - Tashkent: Science, 1983. - P. 72-81.

2.125. Ibadov J.H. Study of four manuscripts with mathematical content // Publishing house of the Academy of Sciences of the Republic of Uzbekistan. Series of physical and mathematical sciences. 1983. № 1. - pp. 69-70.

2.126. Ibadov J.H. The creativity of al-Khorezmi in the assessment of Eastern scientists-encyclopedists of the 10th-16th centuries // Great scientist of the Middle Ages al-Khorezmi. Tashkent: Science, 1985. - pp. 265-268.

2.127. Ibadov J.H. Encyclopedias of scientists of Central Asia of the 9th-18th centuries as sources on the history of exact sciences. - Tashkent: Merius, 2010. - 174 p.

2.128. Ibn Sina. Medical advice. - Tashkent: Labor, 1991. - 192 p.

2.129. Ibn Si№ Treatise on the division of existing things. - Tashkent: Shark, 1983. - P. 128.

2.130. From the history of exact sciences in the medieval Near and Middle East. - Tashkent: Science, 1972. - 248 p.

2.131. Ibodov Zh.Kh. Philosophical views of encyclopedists of the Renaissance in Central Asia and discoveries in the field of exact sciences. – Tashkent: Mevrius, 2009. – 160 p.

2.132. Ibodov J.Kh., Matviyevskaya G.P. The place of Ahmad al-Fargani in the history of mathematics and astronomy. - Tashkent: Istiklal, 1998. - 89 p.

2.133. Irisov A. Abu Ali ibn Sina. - Tashkent: Science, 1980. - 207 p.

2.134. Irisov A. The wisdom of Abu Raikhan Beruni. - Tashkent: Young Guard, 1973. - P.40-43.

2.135. Ismailov F.Yu. Continuity in social development. - Tashkent: Uzbekistan, 1986.

2.136. History of Khorezm: From ancient times to the present day / Ed. I.M.Muminova. - Tashkent: Science, 1976. - 326 p.

2.137. Kagan V.F. Foundations of geometry. - Moscow-Leningrad: Gostekhizdat, 1956. - 344 p.

2.138. Karimov U.I. Abu Rayhon Beruni (life and work). - Tashkent: Science, 1973. P. 74.

2.139. Karimov I., Valieva S., Tulenova K. Social philosophy (methodological manual). – Tashkent, 2008. – 120 p.

2.140. Krachkovsky I. Arabic geographical literature // I.Krachkovsky. Favorite Soch-i. T. IV. Moscow-Leningrad, 1957. - 954 p.

2.141. Koi-Krylgan-kala is a cultural monument of ancient Khorezm of the 4th century. BC. - IV century AD (Ed. S.P.Tolstov, B.I.Weinberg). – Moscow, 1967. - 348 p.

2.142. Conrad N.I.West and East. - Moscow: Science, 1966. - 519 p.

2.143. Konrad N.I. About the Renaissance. - Moscow: Science, 1966. - 496 p.

2.144. Konrad N.I. Selected works: History. - Moscow: Science, 1974. - 472 p.

2.145. Culture of the Middle East. Urban planning and architecture. -Tashkent: Science, 1989. - 180 p.

2.146. Lemmlein G.G. Mineralogical information. - Moscow: Publishing House of the USSR Academy of Sciences, 1950. - 470 p.

2.147. Masson V.M. Country of a thousand cities. - Moscow: Science, 1966. - 148 p.

2.148. Stars of spirituality. - Tashkent: People's Heritage Publishing House named after Abdulla Kadiri, 2000.

2.149. Matvieskaya G.P. On the history of mathematics in Central Asia in the 9th-15th centuries. - Tashkent: Publishing House of the Academy of Sciences of the UzSSR, 1962. - 125 p.

2.150. Matviyevskaya G.P. Abu Rayhon Beruni and natural sciences. - Tashkent: Science, 1963. - 48 p.

2.151. Matviyevskaya G.P. The doctrine of number in the medieval Near and Middle East. - Tashkent: Science, 1967. - 341 p.

2.152. Matviyevskaya G.P. Development of the doctrine of number in Europe until the 17th century. – Tashkent: Science, 1971. - 322 p.

2.153. Matviyevskaya G.P. Abu Rayhon Beruni and his mathematical works. - Tashkent: Science, 1973. – 96 p.

2.154. Matviyevskaya G.P. Tllashev. Mathematics and astronomy in the works of scientists of the medieval East. - Tashkent: Fan. 1977. - 230 p.

2.155. Materials on the history of progressive social and philosophical thought in Uzbekistan. 2nd ed. / Ed. I.M.Muminova and M.M.Khairullayeva. - Tashkent, Science, 1976. - 278 p.

2.156. Masharipova G.K. The influence of the natural science, socio-philosophical and spiritual heritage of scientists of the Khorezm Mamun Academy on the development of social thinking. – Tashkent: Navruz, 2019. – 264 p.

2.157. Masharipova G.K., Togaeva G. Textbook for the specialty Design from the modern concept of natural science. - Tashkent: Media lawyer. - 308 p.

2.158. Stars of spirituality (famous figures, scientists, writers of Central Asia). - Tashkent: Meros, 1999. - 370 p.

2.159. Mechanics in the Middle Ages East. - Moscow: Science, 1976. - 217 p.

2.160. Mursalimova G., Rakhimov A. Course of general disaster. – Tashkent: Teacher, 1976. – 223 p.

2.161. Nosirkhodjaeva G. Conceptual and methodological aspects of the historical and scientific, including the historical and philosophical heritage of Beruni. Problems of historical and philosophical thought in the works of Beruni. - Tashkent: Uzbekiston milliy encyclopedia, 2001. - 31 p.

2.162. Otamuratov S. Globalization and nation. – Tashkent: New Generation, 2008. – 456 p.

2.163. Rozhanskaya M.M., Rosenfeld B.A., Sokolovskaya Z.K. Abu-r-Raikhan Beruni. - Moscow: Science, 1973. - 188 p.

2.164. Rozhanskaya M.M. Mechanics in the Middle Ages East. – Moscow, 1976. - 328 p.

2.165. Rosenfeld B.A. History of non-Euclidean geometry. - Moscow: Science, 1976. -324 p.

2.166. Rosenfeld B.A., Yushkevich A.P. The theory of parallel lines in the medieval East in the 9th-14th centuries. - Moscow: Science, 1983. - 125 p.

2.167. Rosenfeld B.A., Matviyevskaya G.P. Mathematicians and astronomers of the Muslim Middle Ages and their works (VIII-XVII centuries). - Moscow: Science, 1983. - 533 p.

2.168. Sal'e M. Muhammed al-Khorezmi is a great Uzbek scientist. - Tashkent: Publishing House of the Academy of Sciences of the UzSSR, 1954. - 74 p.

2.169. Sadullayev A. The theory of shadows of Abu Raykhon Beruni (gnomonics). – Urgench, 2005. – 55 p.

2.170. Siddikov H. Works of scientists of Central Asia, the Middle East and geometry. – Tashkent: Science, 1981. – 200 p.

2.171. Siddikov H. Chagmini and his predecessors. – Tashkent: Science, 1976. – 180 p.

2.172. Collection of oriental manuscripts of the Academy of Sciences of the Uzbek SSR. T. VIII. - Tashkent: Science, 1967. - 304 p.

2.173. Collection of oriental manuscripts of the Academy of Sciences of the Republic of Uzbekistan. Exact and natural sciences/Compiled by A.B. Vildanova. - Tashkent: Science, 1998. - 314 p.

2.174. Collection of oriental manuscripts of the Academy of Sciences of the Republic of Uzbekistan. Medicine / Compiled by: Kh Khikmatullayev, S.U.Karimova. - Tashkent: Science, 2000. - 302 p.

2.175. Stavisky B.Ya. Between Pomir and the Caspian: (Central Asia in ancient times). - Moscow: Science, 1966. - 327 p.

2.176. Sulaymanova F.K. East and West: (Ancient and medieval cultural connections). - Tashkent: Uzbekistan, 1997. - 415 p.

2.177. Sura 4. Ayats // Koran / Transl. and com. I.Yu.Krachkovsky. - Moscow: Publishing House of the USSR Academy of Sciences, 1963.

2.178. Tolstov S.P. In the footsteps of the ancient Khorezmian civilization. - Moscow-Leningrad: Publishing House of the USSR Academy of Sciences, 1948. - 328 p.

2.179. Tolstov S.P. Ancient Khorezm: Experience of historical and archaeological research. - Moscow: Moscow State University Publishing House, 1948. - 352 p.

2.180. Tolstov S.P. In search of ancient Khorezm culture. – Tashkent, 1964. – 440 p.

2.181. Tolstov S.P. . Ancient culture of Uzbekistan. - Tashkent, 1944. - 528 p.

2.182. Rules of Timur (translation from Persian by Alikhon Soguni and Khabibulla Karamatov). – Tashkent: Publishing house named after Gafur Gulam, 1991. – 144 p.

2.183. Tolstov S.P. Along the ancient deltas of Oxus and Jaxartes. - Moscow: Publishing House of the USSR Academy of Sciences, 1972.

2.184. Toshlonov T. National and religious traditions. - Tashkent: Uzbekistan, 1986. - 23 p.

2.185. Tulenov Zh. Philosophy of values. - Tashkent: Uzbekistan, 1998. - 335 p.

2.186. Tulenov Zh., Gafurov Z. Independence and national restoration. - Tashkent: Uzbekistan, 1996. - 254 p.

2.187. Tulenova G. Wonderful young generation - support for independence. – Tashkent: Science and Technology, 2004. – 128 p.

2.188. Tukhliev N., Olmasov A. Dictionary of businessmen. – Tashkent: Editorial office "Komuslar Bosh", 1993. – 112 p.

2.189. Toychiev B. Scientific and philosophical correspondence between Beruni and Ibn Sina. – Tashkent, "Iod-print", 2020. – 158 p.

2.190. Tolanov Zh. Philosophy of values. - Tashkent: Uzbekistan, 1998. - 236 p.

2.191. Toraev H. Talented young people are the masters of our future. – Tashkent: Shark, 2001. – 144 p.

2.192. Umarov G.Ya. Beruni, Copernicus and modern science. - Tashkent, 1973. - 120 p.

2.193. Faizullaev A. Scientific creativity of Muhammad al-Khorezmi. – Tashkent: Science, 1983. - 32 p.

2.194. Encyclopedic Dictionary of Philosophy. – Tashkent: Shark, 2004. – 495 p.

2.195. Philosophy (textbook). Under the general editorship of E. Yu.Yusupov. - Tashkent: Shark, 1999. - 496 p.

2.196. Umar Khayyam. Treatises. - Moscow: Publishing house Vost. literature. - 1962.

2.197. Khairullayev M.M. Culture of the early Renaissance in Central Asia. – Tashkent: Science, 1994. – 78 p.

2.198. Gulomov Ya.G. Ancient history of irrigation of Khorezm. - Tashkent: Science, 1957. 313 p.

2.199. Khamidov H. Forty-five stories of Alloma. – Tashkent: Science, 1995. – 177 p.

2.200. Khikmatullayev H. Treatise of Abu Ali ibn Sina "Heart Medicines". – Tashkent: Science, 1966. – 181 p.

2.201. Usmanov T. Beruni's place in the history of physics. - Tashkent: Science, 1977. - P. 179-197.

2.202. Sharipov A.D. Great thinker Beruni. - Tashkent: Science, 1972. - 174 p.

2.203. Shermukhamedova N.A. Philosophy. Volume 1. – Tashkent: Uzbekistan, 2012. – 1215 p.

2.204. Khairullayev M.M. Farabi's worldview and its significance in the history of philosophy. - Tashkent: Science, 1967. - P. 112-127.

2.205. Khairullayev M.M. Farabi and teaching. - Tashkent: Uzbekistan, 1967. - 148 p.

2.206. Khairullayev M.M. Farabi is the greatest thinker of the Middle Ages. – Tashkent: Science, 1973. - 138 p.

2.207. Khairullayev M. Philosophical heritage of the peoples of Central Asia and the struggle of ideas. - Fergana, 1988. - 198 p.

2.208. Khairullayev M.M., Bakhadirov R.M. Abu Abdullah al-Khwarizmi. - Moscow: Science, 1988. - 144 p.

2.209. Khairullayev M.M. Culture of the early Renaissance in Central Asia. – Tashkent: Science, 1994. – 80 p.

2.210. Ergashev I. Philosophy of development. – Tashkent: Academy, 2000. – 112 p.

2.211. Yushkevich A.K. History of mathematics in the Middle Ages. – Moscow, 1961. - 448 p.

2.212. From history and interethnic relations in Uzbekistan/Editor in charge: prof. Murtazaeva. – Tashkent: University, 1998. – 104 p.

2.213. From the history of superstitions of the peoples of Central Asia. – Tashkent, 1990. – 110 p.

2.214. 2.214. Brief political dictionary. Developers: L.A. Opikov and N.V. Shishlin. - Tashkent: Uzbekistan, 1983. - 423 p.

2.215. Brief political dictionary. Completed and revised second edition. - Tashkent: Uzbekistan, 1975. - 311 p.

2.216. Kasimov B. National awakening: courage, enlightenment, sacrifice. - Tashkent: Spirituality, 2002. - 400 p.

2.217. Kochkarov V. National identity and socio-political processes. – Tashkent: Academy, 2007. – 155 p.

2.218. Avicenne. Le ivre de science, t.1. Paris, 1955; T.II. (Physique – mathematiques), trad. par. M. Achenaet H.Masse. - Paris,1958. - 276 p.

2.219. Ahmad I. Al-Biruni's astronomical works, Cairo Universiti Press, Bulletin No 48. – Cairo, 1959.- 432 p.

2.220. Barani S.H. Muslim Researches in Geodesy // «Al-Biruni – Commemoration Volume». - Calcutta, Iran Society, 1951. -52 p.

2.221. Boncompagni B. Trattaty d'Arifmetica publicati de Baldassare Boncompagni I. Algoritmi de numero indorum. II. Ioanni Hispalensis Liber algoritmi de praticaarismetrice. - Roma, 1857. - 23 p.

2.222. Brockelmann. C. Geschichte der arabischen Litteratur. 1-2. - Leiden, 1898-1902; 2. Ausl. 1-2. Leiden, 1943-1944. - 324 p.

2.223. Suter H. Die Mathematiker und Astronomen der Araber und ihre Werke. - Leipzig, 1900. - 167 p.

2.224. Khayyam Omar. Discussion of difficulties of Euclidd. Erani. - Teheran. 1936. - 345 p.

2.225. Khayyam Omar. Explanation Of the diffeculties in Euclids postulates. By A.I.Sabra. – Alexandria, 1961. – 278 p.

2.226. BrowneA.A.A. Literature History of Persia from Earliest Times until Firdawsi. Vol. 1. - Cambridge, 1902. - 224 p.

2.227. Enestrom G., Kleine Bemerkunden zur 2. Auflage von Cantors «Vorlesungen». Bibl. math., F. 3. Bd. I. 1900. - P. 499-500; Bd. VII. 1907. - P.284.

2.228. Encyclopedia of the History of Arabic Science⸺Ed. B.Rushdi. - London, 1996. - 304 p.

2.229. Islam ansiclopedisi, cilt 5/1. 257-268.- Istanbul, 1950. - 229 p.

2.230. Carra de Vaux, Les penseurs de L'Islam. – Paris, 1921. V. II. 216. - 309 p.

2.231. Neugebauer O. Theearly history of theastrologe. Isis. Vol., II, 1949. - 534 p.

2.232. Chasles M. Apersu historique sur l'origineet le developpement des methodes en geometrie. – Paris, 1837. - p. 211-223.

2.233. Gartz J. De interpretibus et explanatoribus Euclidis arabicus. – Halee, 1823. - P. 504.

2.234. Gandz S., The origin of the term Algebra, Amer. math. monthly, vol, 33, 1926. - 223 p.

2.235. Gandz S. Mishnat ha middot, the first Hebrew geometry of about 150 c. E, and the Geometry of Muhammad ibn Musaak-Khowarizmi, thearabic Geometry (p. 820), representatio thearabic version of the Mishnat ha-middot. – Berlin, 1932.

2.236. Gandz S. The sources of Al-Khowarizmi's Algebra.- Osiris. Vol. I. 1936. – 435 p.

2.237. Wustenfeld von F. Die Geschichtschteiber der Araber und ihre Werke. - Gottingen, 1882. - 278 p.

III. Articles in scientific journals and conference proceedings:

3.1. Abdullaev I. New information about As-Saalibi // Oriental Studies. - Tashkent. 2005. - № 1. - P.28-37.

3.2. Abdurimov K. Origins of the Khorezm Mamun Academy: calculation, observation technology and culture of Central Asia, their invariants // Khorezm Mamun Academy and its place in the development of world science. Proceedings of the international scientific conference. - Tashkent-Khiva: Science, 2006. - P.25-27.

3.3. Abdukhalimov B.A. Khorezm Mamun Academy and its influence on the development of medieval science // Khorezm Mamun Academy and its place in the development of world science. Proceedings of the international scientific conference. Tashkent-Khiva: Science, 2006. - P. 163-165.

3.4. Abdukhalimov B. About Haji Khalifa Abu Rayhon Beruni./Oriental Studies. - Tashkent, 1994. - № 4. - P.82-89.

3.5. List of Abu Raikhan Beruni's own works / translation by A. Rasulov // To the 1000th anniversary of the birth of Abu Raikhan Beruni. - Tashkent: Science, 1973. - P.230-243.

3.6. Abdullaev A.A. Academy of Khorezmshah Mamun in Khorezm // Medical Journal of Uzbekistan. - Tashkent, 1971. - № 8. - P. 57-59.

3.7. The collection is dedicated to the 1000th anniversary of the birth of Abu Rayhon Beruni. – Tashkent: Science, 1973. – 260 p.

3.8. Azizov S.Kh. "Kaptarkhana" in Khorezm - the address of the time service // Khorezm Mamun Academy and its place in the development of world science. Proceedings of the international scientific conference. - Tashkent-Khiva: Science. 2006. – pp. 23-25.

3.9. Alimzhanov H. Study of the activities of Abu Raikhan Beruni // Public education. - Tashkent, 1994. № 1-2. - P. 69.

3.10. Akhmedov A. Ibn Sina and questions of substantiation of geometry // Abu Ali ibn Sina. To the 1000th anniversary of his birth. - Tashkent: Science, 1980. - P.183-189.

3.11. Akhmedov A.A., Rosenfeld B.A., Sergeeva N.D. Astronomical and geographical works of al-Khorezmi // Muhammad ibn Musaal-Khorezmi. To the 1200th anniversary of his birth. - Moscow: Science, 1983. - P.141-191.

3.12. Akhmedov A. The theory of the movement of planets in "Zij" by al-Khorezmi // Social sciences of Uzbekistan. - Tashkent, 1983. - № 7. - P.59-64.

3.13. Akhmedov A., Rosenfeld B. A. Unknown treatises of al-Khwarizmi. // Social sciences of Uzbekistan. - Tashkent, 1984. - № 2. - P. 4.

3.14. Akhmedov A. Muhammad al-Khorezmi – historian // Social Sciences of Uzbekistan. - Tashkent, 1985. № 11 - P.51-55.

3.15. Based on the works of Akhmedov A. Al-Khorezmi // Science and life. - Tashkent, 1986. - 12 issues. - P. 8-9.

3.16. Akhmedov A. Some questions of mathematics and spherical disaster in the "Kanoni Masudi" by Abu Rayhon Beruni // Collection dedicated to the 1000th anniversary of the birth of Abu Rayhon Beruni. - Tashkent: Science, 1973. - P.111-122; 260.

3.17. Akhmedov A. Mathematicians and astronomers-contemporaries of Abu Ali ibn Sina // Collection of articles dedicated to the 1000th anniversary of the birth of Abu Ali ibn Sina. – Tashkent: Science, 1980. – 99 p.

3.18. Akhmedov A. Muhammad al-Khorezmi - historian // Social Sciences of Uzbekistan. - Tashkent, 1985. - № 11. - P. 51-55.

3.19. Akhmedov A. Ulugbek and his "Zij" // Oriental Studies. - Tashkent, 1994. - № 5. - B.10-17.

3.20. Akhmedov A. On the preparation of a reliable basis for clarifying Abu Rayhon Beruni's concept of the passage of light // Oriental Studies. - Tashkent, 1994. - № 12. - P.58-63.

3.21. Akhmedov A. A. Bulgakov P. G. Central Asian-Indian relations in the field of exact sciences. - On Sat. From the history of cultural relations between the peoples of Central Asia and India. -Tashkent: Science, 1986. - 24-33 p.

3.22. Boltaev M. Ibn Sina is an outstanding philosopher of the Medieval East. - Moscow: Knowledge, 1983. – 47 p.

3.23. Boltaev M. Questions of epistemology and logic in the works of Ibn Sina and his school. - Dushanbe: Irfon Publishing House, 1965. - 98 p.

3.24. Boltaev M. Abu Ali Ibn Sina is a great thinker, scientific encyclopedist. - Kazan: Master Line, 1999. – 400 p.

3.25. 3.25. Boltaev M. Philosophical and social teachings of Abu Ali ibn Sina. – Bukhara, 2001. – 30 p.

3.26. Boltaev M. Abu Ali ibn Sina. – Moscow: Sampo, 2002. – 396 p.

3.27. Boltaev M. Great Thinker of the East. – Bukhara, 2006. – 196 p.

3.28. Bulgakov P.G. Sextant in "Geodesy" by Biruni // Social sciences in Uzbekistan. - Tashkent, 1963. № 6. - P. 43-46.

3.29. Bulgakov P.G. Globe Biruni // Social sciences in Uzbekistan. - Tashkent, 1965. № 1. - P. 24-27.

3.30. Bulgakov P.G., Akhmedov A. Biruni and al-Kindi on the theory of parallel // Society. science in Uzbekistan. - Tashkent, 1977. - № 8. - P. 30-36.

3.31. Bulgakov P.G. Determining the dimensions of the medieval Muslim East // Oriental Studies. - Tashkent: Science. - 1991. - № 2. - P. 18-24.

3.32. Bulgakov P.G. Activities of Central Asian scientists in Baghdad // Oriental Studies. - Tashkent, 1994. - № 1. - P. 19-28.

3.33. Boriyev O. Continuity of the scientific heritage of Ahmed al-Fargani and Abu Raikhan Beruni // Oriental Studies. - Tashkent, 1994. - № 12. - P. 63-71.

3.34. Boriyev O. Geographical knowledge in the Khorezm Mamun Academy and its role in the revival of the Timurids // Khorezm Mamun Academy and its role in the development of world science. Proceedings of the international scientific conference. - Tashkent-Khiva: Science, 2006. - P. 27–32.

3.35. Jamol ad-Dabbah. Book of measurements of figures of Banu Musa // "Historical and mathematical studies". Vol. XII. - Moscow: Publishing House of the USSR Academy of Sciences, 1965. - P. 389-426.

3.36. Jalolov G'. The work of Abu Ali ibn Sina entitled "Al-Hisab" // Collection of articles dedicated to the 1000th anniversary of the birth of Abu Ali ibn Sina. - Tashkent: Science, - 1980. - P. 122-134.

3.37. Ibadov J.H. Physics and mathematics chapters of the encyclopedia "Collection of Sciences" ("Jami ul-ulum") Fakhr ad-Dinaar-Razi. Dep. AT VINITI. - Moscow: 1987. № 1066. - 14 p.

3.38. Ibadov J.Kh., Bulgakov P.G. To the history of mathematics of Khorezm at the end of the 10th century. // Social sciences in Uzbekistan, 1988. № 5. - pp. 62-65.

3.39. Ibadov J.H., Matviyevskaya G.P. Exact sciences in the encyclopedia "The Wisdom of the Source ("Hikma al-ain") al-Qazwini" // Izv. AN UzSSR. Ser. Physics and mathematics, 1989. - pp. 29-31.

3.40. Ibadov J.H., Matviyevskaya G.P. Physical and mathematical sciences in the encyclopedia "Keys of Sciences" by Abu Abdallahaal-Khorezmi // Izv. AN UzSSR. Ser. Fiz.-mat.nauk, 1990. № 3. - P. 34-39.

3.41. Ibadov J.H. Classification of physical and mathematical sciences in the medieval encyclopedias of Abu Abdullahaal-Khorezmi, Fakhr ad-Dinaar-Razi, Qutb ad-Dinaash-Shirazi and Bahaad-Dinaal-Amili // Abstracts of the XXXIV Scientific

Conference ideas of postgraduate students and young specialists in the history of natural sciences and technology of Institute of Electrical Engineering and Technology RAS. - Moscow: Literature, 1992. - P. 35-36.

3.42. Ibadov J.H. "Book of research on algebra" by Hassan ibn Harisaal-Khububi al-Khwarizmi // Theses of scientific and theoretical studies. and tech. conferences of professionals, lecturers Tashkent State Technical University named after A. Beruni. – Tashkent: Science, 1992. - P. 123-125.

3.43. Ibadov J.H. Comparative analysis of the physical and mathematical chapters of the universal encyclopedias "Keys of Sciences" by Abu Abdallah al-Khwarizmi (X-XI centuries) and "Collection of Sciences" by Fakhr ad-Din ar-Razi. - Tashkent State Technical University named after. A. Beruni, 1992. - pp. 135-136.

3.44. 3.44. Ibodov J.H. On the mathematical treatise of al-Khububi al-Khorezmi // TashKhTI, 1994. - pp. 81-85.

3.45. Ibadov J.H. "Book of Research" by al-Khububi as a source on the history of mathematics of the East // International Conf. from Ulugbek to the twentieth century. – Tashkent: Science, 2003. - P. 84-90.

3.46. Ibadov J.H. Predecessors of the scientific school of Ulugbekaal-Khububi al-Khorezmi // Abstracts of the international conference dedicated. 600th anniversary of Mirza Ulugbek. - Tashkent-Samarkand, 1994. - pp. 118-119, 139-140.

3.47. Ibodov Zh.Kh. Matviyevskaya G.P. Ulugbek's student – Ali Kushchi – Tashkent: Science, 1994. – 36 p.

3.48. Ibodov J.H. Physics and mathematics chapters of "Keys of Sciences" (Mafotih al-ulum) Abu Abdallahaal-Khorezmi. -Tashkent: TUIT, 2005. - 56 p.

3.49. Ibodov Zh.Kh. Studying the rich scientific heritage of our country // Problems of improving the quality of personnel training for the field of communications and information. Scientific conference TATU. Volume 1. - Tashkent: Science, 2012. - P. 105-107.

3.50. Ibn al-Haytham. Treatises on burning mirrors (preface by B.A. Rosenfeld, translation by I.O. Mohammed and N.V. Orlova, notes by N.V. Orlova and

B.A.Rosenfeld). - Historical and astronomical research. Vol. XV. - Moscow: Publishing House of the USSR Academy of Sciences, 1980. - P.305-338.

3.51. The historical legacy of the learned thinkers of the Middle Ages, its role and significance for modern civilization // Proceedings of the international conference on May 15-16, 2014. - Samarkand-Tashkent: Uzbekistan, 2014.

3.52. Karimov U.I. On the question of Ibn Sina's views on chemistry // Materials of the scientific session of the Academy of Sciences of the Uzbek SSR. dedicated to the 1000th anniversary of Ibn Sina. - Tashkent: Science, 1953. - P. 13-38.

3.53. Karimov U.I. Classification of sciences according to Ibn Sina // Materials of the First All-Union Scientific Conference of Orientalists in Tashkent on June 4-11. 1957. - Tashkent: Science, 1958. - P. 986-990.

3.54. Karimov U.I. Essay on the life and work of Abu Raihan Biruni // Social sciences in Uzbekistan. - Tashkent. 1961. - № 7. - P. 65-66.

3.55.3.55. Karimov U. About the medical heritage of Ibn Sina // On the 1000th anniversary of the birth of Ibn Sina. - Tashkent: Science, 1980. - P. 122-149.

3.56. About Al-Khorezmi al-Kasi and his work "Ain al-Sana" // Oriental Studies. - 2004 - № 8. - P.58 - 62.

3.57. Karimova S.U. Scientific activity of Abu Ali ibn Sina at the Khorezm Mamun Academy // Khorezm Mamun Academy and its role in the development of world science. Proceedings of the international scientific conference. - Tashkent-Khiva: Science, 2006. - P. 168-170.

3.58. Karimov B.R. The contribution of Khorezmi, Ferghani, Farabi, Beruni, Ibn Sina to world science as the basis of the scientific achievements of Ulugbek and his school // Mirzo Ulugbek merosi va gozirgi zamon. - Tashkent: Uzbekistan Milliy Universiteti, 2014. - P.52-61.

3.59. Kasymova E.G. Beruni's treatise on spherical trigonometry // Beruni. Collection of articles for the 1000th anniversary of his birth. - Tashkent: Science, 1973. -P.81-85.

3.60. Comments by Abu Nasraal-Farabi on the difficulties in the introductions to the first and fifth books of Euclid // Problems of Oriental Studies. - 1959. - № 4. - P. 93-104.

3.61. Livshits V.A. Khorezm calendar and the era of Ancient Khorezm // History, culture, languages of the peoples of the East. - Moscow: Science, 1970. - P. 5-16.

3.62. Livshits V.A. Khorezm calendar and era of Ancient Khorezm // Palestine collection. Vol. 21 (84): Middle East and Iran. - Leningrad: Science, 1970. - P. 161-169.

3.63. Lunin B.V. Bibliographic index of Soviet literature about Abu Rayhon Beruni and editions of the texts of his works (1918-1972) // Collection of articles for the 1000th anniversary of Beruni's birth. - Tashkent: Science, 1973. - P.186-202.

3.64. Lunin B.V. The life and works of Ibn Sina in Russian science // Abu Ali ibn Sina. To the 1000th anniversary of his birth. - Tashkent: Science, 1980. - P. 212-243.

3.65. Matviyevskaya G.P. From the early history of studying the mathematical and astronomical heritage of Beruni // Collection of articles for the 1000th anniversary of the birth of Beruni. - Tashkent: Science, 1973. - pp. 173-186.

3.66. Matviyevskaya G.P., Tllashev H. On the scientific heritage of the astronomer of the 10th-11th centuries. Abu Nasr ibn Iraq // Historical and astronomical studies. Vol. XIII.- Moscow: 1977. - P.219-234.

3.67. Matviyevskaya G.P. Arabic medieval encyclopedias as sources on the history of mathematics and astronomy of the Near and Middle East // Mathematics in the Middle East. - Tashkent: Science, 1978. - P.88-96.

3.68. Matviyevskaya G.P. From the history of studying the physical and mathematical heritage of Ibn Sina // Mathematics and astronomy in the works of Ibn Sina, his contemporaries and followers. - Tashkent: Science, 1981. - 149 p.

3.69. Matviyevskaya G.P. Abd ar-Rahman al-Sufi and his role in the history of astronomy // Historical and astronomical studies. Vol. XV1. - Moscow: Publishing House of the USSR Academy of Sciences, 1983. - P.93-138.

3.70. Matviyevskaya G.P., Rosenfeld B.A. Mathematicians and astronomers of the Muslim Middle Ages and their works (VIII-XVII centuries). Book 1, 2, 3. - Moscow: Publishing House of the USSR Academy of Sciences, 1983.

3.71. Matviyevskaya G., Tllashev H. Mathematical and astronomical manuscripts of scientists of Central Asia of the X-XIII centuries. - Tashkent: Science, 1981. – 148 p.

3.72. Matviyevskaya G.P. Mathematics and astronomy in the works of Ibn Sina, his contemporaries and followers. - Tashkent: Science, 1981. – 155 p.

3.73. Matviyevskaya G.P. Essays on the history of trigonometry. – Tashkent: Science, 1990. - 148 p.

3.74. Medova M.I. Abu-l-Hasan Ali ibn Ahmad an-Nasawi. Enough about Indian arithmetic // Historical and mathematical studies. Vol. XV. - Moscow: Fizmatgiz, 1963. - P. 423.

3.75. Masharipova G.K. Kazi-Zade Rumi "Chagmini Compendium of Astronomy" // Social Sciences in Uzbekistan. - Tashkent, 1994. - № 7. - pp. 62-63.

3.76. Masharipova G.K. "Fundamentals of Geometry" by Abu Ali ibn Sina // Oriental Studies. - Tashkent, 1994. № 5. - P.41-49.

3.77. Masharipova G.K. Postulates and axioms in mathematics of Abu Ali ibn Sina // Khorezm Mamun Academy and its role in the development of world science. Proceedings of the international scientific conference. - Tashkent-Khiva: Science, 2006. - P. 76-78.

3.78. Masharipova G.K. Beruni on measurements of the size of the Earth // Russia. - Moscow: Modern Hanamite Studies, 2011. - № 4. - P.29-31.

3.79. Masharipova G.K. Philosophical views of the thinkers of the Khorezm Mamun Academy // Social Thought, 2012. № 4. - P. 37-43.

3.80. Masharipova G.K. Scientific discoveries of the great scientist from Khorezm Abu Nasra ibn Iraq // New University. – Russia, 2014. – № 6. – P. 93-95.

3.81. Masharipova G.K. Philosophical views of the teachings of the Khorezm Mamun Academy // Science. – Russia, 2014. – pp. 20-23.

3.82. Masharipova G.K. Khorezm Mamun Academy - a treasury of knowledge // Science. – Russia, 2015. – pp. 25-28.

3.83. Masharipova G.K. The role of science in the formation and development of a democratic society // Fen-science. – Russia, 2015. – pp. 29-30.

3.84. Masharipova G.K. Ancestor's heritage and spiritual education. Spiritual promoter support. Republican Center for Spiritual Encouragement. – Tashkent: Ma'naviyat, 2015. – 100 p.

3.85. Masharipova G.K. Reflection of moral ideas in the heritage of scientists of the Khorezm Mamun Academy // Methods and means of spiritual and moral education. Materials of the republican scientific and practical seminar. – Tashkent, 2015. – P. 167-169.

3.86. Masharipova G.K. The contribution of Abu Ali ibn Sina to the development of mathematics // The significance of the scientific and cultural heritage of Ibn Sina and its place in the development of science. IX Readings of Ibn Sina. Collection of articles of the international scientific and practical conference. – Bukhara, 2017. – pp. 166-169.

3.87. Masharipova G.K. Coverage of socio-political and moral issues in the works of Abu Raikhan Beruni // Light of civilization. 2019. - № 1. - P. 63-67.

3.88. Masharipova G.K. Problems of religious tolerance and the formation of a culture of information consumption among young people // Islam Ziyasi. - 2019. - № 3. - 58–65 pp.

3.89. Masharipova G.K. The role of the hadiths of Imam Bukhari in the education of youth // Lessons of Imam Bukhari. – Samarkand, 2019. № 3. – 40-41 p.

3.90. Masharipova G.K. Study of the scientific heritage of Mahmud al-Chagmini in the countries of East and West // Bulletin of the National University of Uzbekistan. – Tashkent, 2019. – № 1. – P. 76-78.

3.91. 3.91. Masharipova G.K. The origin of society and its purpose (Based on the work of Abu Rayhon Biruni) // Scientist of the 21st century. - Russia, 2019. - № 3. - pp. 23-26.

3.92.3.92. Masharipova G.K. Social relations in the scientific heritage of Abu Raikhan Beruni // Heritage. – Tashkent, 2019, № 2. – P. 28-35.

3.93. Masharipova G.K. Natural scientific and philosophical views of Abu Ali ibn Sina // Scientist of the XXI century. – Russia, 2019. – № 9. – P. 47-50.

3.94. Masharipova G.K. The influence of the scientific, philosophical and spiritual heritage of Abu Ali ibn Sina on the life of society. – Tashkent: Navruz, 2020. – 144 p.

3.95. Masharipova G.K. The role of the education system in the development of the intellectual potential of youth // Current issues of national development and increasing the social and political activity of youth. Materials of the Republican Scientific and Theoretical Conference. – SAMDAKI, 2020. – pp. 116-118.

3.96. Masharipova G.K. Innovative technologies - improving the quality of education based on modularity and technology of the educational process and the effectiveness of its implementation // Prospects for the development of legal, economic, socio-philosophical, educational directions of innovative ideas in Uzbekistan in the context of globalization. Materials of an online scientific and practical conference on a republican scale. - TSPU. 2020. - P.472-475.

3.97. Masharipova G.K. Religious views of Abu Raikhan Beruni // Man, his faith, society, the Universe: problems of development and modernity. Materials of the Republican Scientific and Theoretical Conference. – Bukhara, 2020. – P. 243-246.

3.98. Masharipova G.K., Israilov B., Diyorova G. Bulletin of the Khorezm Mamun Academy: There is no salvation except knowledge // The need to fight "enlightenment against ignorance." – Khiva, 2020, № 4/2. - pp. 54-58.

3.99. Masharipova G.K. The role of national and universal values in the spiritual heritage of Eastern scientists in the education of youth // Current problems of innovative cooperation in improving the quality of higher education. Proceedings of the international conference. – Navoi, 2020. – pp. 250-252.

3.100. Muhammadiev Kh.M. Planimetric part of "Kitob al-Shifo" // Scientific notes of the Leninabad State Pedagogical Institute. Vol. XV. - Dushanbe, 1962. - P.5-8.

3.101. Muhammad ibn Musaal-Khorazmi. Mathematical treatises / Executive editor S. Sirazhiddinov. - Tashkent: Science, 1983. - 483 p.

3.102. Muhammad al-Khwarizmi. Mathematical treatises / Translation by Yu.Kh.Kopelevich and B.A. Rosenfeld, comments by B.A. Rosenfeld. - Tashkent, 1964. - P. 9-24.

3.103. Neugebauer O. Exact sciences in antiquity / Transl. E.V. Gokhman: ed. and from before A.P. Yushkevich. - Moscow: Science, 1968. - 224 p.

3.104. Nosirov A. List of works of Abu Raikhan Beruni // In the collection "Abu Raikhan Beruni - the great scientist of the Middle Ages." - Tashkent: Science, 1950. - B. 108-125 p.

3.105. K. Norkhodjaev Abu Raikhan Beruni and the science of geodesy // Collection dedicated to the 1000th anniversary of the birth of Abu Raikhan Beruni. - Tashkent: Science, 1973. - B. 145-159.

3.106. Pigulevskaya N.V. Byzantium and Iran at the turn of the 6th and 7th centuries. - Moscow-Leningrad: Science, 1946. - 412 p.

3.107. Raik E.A. Essays on the history of mathematics in ancient times. - Saransk, 1967. - 352 p.

3.108. Rakhimov S. Abu Ali ibn Sina on education and upbringing. -Tashkent: Teacher, 1967. - 77 p.

3.109. Rozhanskaya M.M. Mechanics. - Moscow: Science, 1967. - P. 238.

3.110. 3.110. Rozhanskaya M.M. Ibn Sina as a mechanic // Abu Ali ibn Sina. To the 1000th anniversary of his birth. - Tashkent: Science, 1980. - P. 163-183.

3.111. Rosenfeld B.A. About the mathematical works of Nasireddin Tusi // Historical and mathematical studies. – Moscow, 1951. - Issue. IV. - pp. 489-512.

3.112. Rosenfeld B.A. An attempt at quadratic interpolation by Abu r-Rayhon al-Biruni // Historical and mathematical studies. - Moscow, 1959. - Issue. XII. - pp. 421-430.

3.113. Rosenfeld B.A., Krasnova S.A., Rozhanskaya M.M. About the mathematical works of Abu-r-Raikhanal-Biruni // From the history of science and technology in the countries of the East. – Moscow, 1963. - Issue. III. - P. 71-92.

3.114. Rosenfeld B.A. Arabic and Persian physical and mathematical manuscripts in libraries of the Soviet Union // Physical and mathematical sciences in the countries of the East. - Moscow: Science, 1966. - P. 256-289.

3.115. Rosenfeld B.A., Dobrovolsky I.G., Sergeeva N.D. On the astronomical treatises of al-Fargani // Historical and astronomical studies. – Moscow, 1972. - Issue XI. - P.191-210.

3.116. Rosenfeld B.A., Abdurakhmanov A. Beruni's treatises on astrolabes // Beruni. Collection of articles for the 1000th anniversary of his birth. - Tashkent: Science, 1973. - P.85-90.

3.117. Rosenfeld B.A., Sergeeva N.D. On the astronomical treatises of al-Khorezmi // Historical and astronomical studies. - Moscow, 1977. - Issue. XIII. - P.201-218.

3.118. Rosenfeld B.A. [Some questions of mathematics of variables in Biruni's treatise on shadows] // Historical and mathematical studies. Vol. XXIII. - Moscow: Science, 1978. - P.226-231.

3.119. Rosenfeld B.A. About the zodical light among the Arabs // Historical and astronomical studies. Issue XV. – Moscow, 1980. - P.290-292.

3.120. Rosenfeld B.A. About Ibn Sina's works on mathematics and astronomy // Abu Ali ibn Sina. To the 1000th anniversary of his birth. - Tashkent: Science, 1980. - P. 342-349.

3.121. Rosenfeld B., Matviyevskaya G. Mathematicians and astronomers of the Muslim Middle Ages and their works (VIII-XVII centuries). Book 1. - Moscow: Publishing House of the USSR Academy of Sciences, 1982.

3.122. Rosenfeld B.A., Akhmedov A. Unknown treatises of al-Khwarizmi. // ONU. 1984. - № 2. - P. 4-6.

3.123. Sadykov H.U. Beruni and his works on astronomy and mathematical geography. - Moscow: Publishing House of the USSR Academy of Sciences, 1953. – 30 p.

3.124. Semenov A.A. Biruni - an outstanding scientist of the Middle Ages // Biruni - a great scientist of the Middle Ages. – Tashkent: Science, 1950. - P. 38-39.

3.125. Siddykov H. Mahmud ibn Muhammad ibn Omar al-Chagmini al-Khorezmi - a great scientist of the Middle Ages // Bulletin of the Karakalpak branch of the Academy of Sciences of the Republic of Uzbekistan. – Karakalpakstan, 1965. - № 4. - P.49-52.

3.126. Siddykov H. Early lists of treatises of al-Chagmini and Ali Kushchi // Bulletin of the Karakalpak branch of the Academy of Sciences of the UzSSR. - Karakalpakstan, 1967, № 3-4. -WITH. 157-158.

3.127. Siddykov Kh.S. About the scientific creativity of the Khorezm astronomer and mathematician of the 12th–13th centuries. Mahmuda al-Chaghmini // From the history of exact sciences in the medieval Near and Middle East. Ed. S.Kh.Sirozhiddinova. - Tashkent, 1972. - P. 200-206.

3.128. Sirazhdinov S.Kh., Matviyevskaya G.P. On the study of the history of mathematics in Central Asia // Historical and mathematical studies. Issue XXI. - Moscow: Science, 1976. - P.51-60.

3.129. Sirazhdinov S.Kh., Akhmedov A. From the biography of Ibn Sina // Mathematics and astronomy in the works of Ibn Sina, his contemporaries and followers. - Tashkent: Science, 1981.- P. 3-15.

3.130. Tagi-Zade A.K. Quadrants of the Middle Ages // Historical and astronomical studies. Vol. XIII. - Moscow, 1977. - P.183-200.

3.131. Targ S.M. The force of inertia // Physical encyclopedia: [in 5 volumes] Ch. editor A.M. Prokhorov. – Moscow, 1994. - P. 494-495.

3.132. Tllashev Kh., Ramazanova S.A. Treatises of Abu Nasr ibn Iraq on the astrolabe // Mathematics and astronomy in the works of scientists of the Middle Ages East. - Tashkent: Science, 1977. - P.89-97.

3.133. Tolstov S.P. New Year's holiday «Kalendas» among Khorezm Christians at the beginning of the 11th century (In connection with the history of Khorezm-Khazar relations) // From historical and ethnographic comments to al-Biruni. - Soviet ethnography. - Moscow: Publishing House of the USSR Academy of Sciences, 1946. - № 2. - P. 99-102.

3.134. Tolstov S.P. Works of the Khorezm expedition of the USSR Academy of Sciences on the excavation of a monument of the 4th-3rd centuries. BC. Koi-Krylgan-kala. Bulletin of Ancient History. - Moscow, 1953. - № 1. - P.160-174.

3.135. Tolstov S.P. Biruni and problems of ancient and medieval history of Khorezm // Materials of the First All-Union. scientific con. orientalists in Tashkent June 4-11, 1957 - Tashkent, 1958. - pp. 125-130.

3.136. Tolstov S.P. Abu Raygon Beruniy va uning zamoni // Abu Raygon Beruniy – ÿurta asrning buyuk olimi týplamida. - Toshkent: Science, 1960. - 16 b.

3.137. Proceedings of the Khorezm archaeological and ethnographic expedition, 1958. T.2. – Tashkent, Fan. - P.7-258.

3.138. Tuychiev B.T. Problems of formation of political culture and democratization of modern society. - Tashkent, 1991. - P.228.

3.139. Usmanov A. Ibn Sina and his merits in the history of the development of mathematical sciences // Mathematics and astronomy in the works of scientists of the medieval East. - Tashkent: Science, 1977. - P. 55-58; 142.

3.140. Fry R.N. Heritage of Iran. - Moscow: Science, 1977. - P. 64-65.

3.141. Khayyam Umar. Treatises. - Moscow: Publishing house Vost.lit. - 1962. - P. 113-127; 271-281.

3.142. Khairetdinova N.G. Trigonometry in the works of al-Farabi and Ibn Sina // Questions of the history of natural science and technology. Vol. 3(28). – Moscow, 1969.

3.143. Kholidov A.B, Erman B.T. Preface to Beruni's "India" // India. T. II. – Moscow, 1963. - P.47.

3.144. Khorezm Mamun Academy and its role in the development of world science. Proceedings of the international scientific conference. - Tashkent-Khiva: Science, 2006. - P.215.

3.145. Sharipov M., Mukhsimova H.V. The settlement of secular sciences in Central Asia // Philosophy of Secularism. - Tashkent: Tashkent State Economic Institute, 2007.

3.146. For information about Abul Abbas from Iran. Western India, Volume II. -

Tashkent: Science, 1965. - P.477.

3.147. Yusupova D. Letter from Giyasiddin Koshi from Samarkand to his father Koshan // In memory of Amir Temur and contemporaries of Ulugbek. - Tashkent: Science. - P.266-298.

3.148. Yusupova D. Letter from Ghiyas ad-Din Kashi to his father from Samarkand to Kashan // From the history of science of the era of Ulugbek. - Tashkent, Science, 1979. - P. 37-64.

3.149. Yushkevich A.P. On the mathematics of the peoples of Central Asia in the 1st-15th centuries // Historical and mathematical studies. Issue 1V. - Moscow: Science, 1951. - P.455-489.

3.150. National Encyclopedia of Uzbekistan. Volume 4. - Tashkent - 2002. - 703 p.

3.151. Kariev O. Issues of marriage in "Hindistan" by Abu Raikhan Beruni and "Khidaya" Marginani // Oriental Studies. - Tashkent, 1994. - № 5. - B.49-54.

3.152. Khabibullaev A. Works of Abu Rayhon Beruni in Oxford // Oriental Studies. - Tashkent, 1994. - № 8. - B.89-95.

3.153. Hazratkulov J. Rashid Vatvot - writer // Oriental Studies. - Tashkent, 1994. - № 8. - B.189-196.

3.154. Khaitov Sh. Introduction to the history of compromise and philosophy in Uzbekistan. -Tashkent: Institute of Philosophy and Law, 2010. - 431 p.

3.155. Hasanov H. Geographers and tourists of Central Asia. - Tashkent, 1964.

3.156. Hasaniy M. Abu Raikhan Beruni and Ibn Sina: poetry and medicine // Oriental Studies. - Tashkent, 1994. - № 12. - B.71-76.

3.157. Herman Vambery. History of Bukhara or Movarunnykhra. – Tashkent: Literature and Art, 1990. – 96 p.

3.158. Abu Ali ibn Sina. Kunuz al-Marifa. Manuscript of the Academy of Sciences of the Republic of Uzbekistan, Institute of Oriental Studies named after Abu Rayhon Beruni, № 2385/XXII, Persian.

أبو على بن سينا. كنوز المعرفة. أبو ريحان البيرو ى اميده گى شرقشناس ليك إستيتوتى قولیازمه سى،

۲۳۸۵/۲۲

3.155. Abu Ali ibn Si№ Ganj al-maruf. Manuscript of the Academy of Sciences of the Republic of Uzbekistan, Institute of Oriental Studies named after Abu Rayhon Beruni, №3374/V, in Persian.

أبو على بن سينا. گنج المعروف. أبو ريحان البيرو ى اميده گى شرقشناس ليك إستيتوتى قوليازمه سى،
٥/٣٣٧٤

3.156. Abu Ali ibn Sina. Tahriri Uqlidis. Microfilm of the manuscript from the library of Ayo Sofia № 2720.

أبو على بن سينا. تحرير أقليدوس. أيا صافية كتبخا ه سى قوليازمه سى، ٢٧٢٠

3.157. Abu Ali ibn Sina. Usul ilm al-Khandasa was published in Cairo in 1976.

أبو على بن سينا. أصول علم الهندسة. قاهرة، ١٩٧٦.

3.158. Manuscript of Abu Ali al-Hasan ibn Harit al-Khububi "Kitab al-istiksa' wa-t-tajnis fi 'ilm al-hisab".

أبو على الحسن بن الحارث الحبوبى. كتاب الإستقصاء و التجنيس فى علم الحساب. قوليازمه

3.159. Abu Nasr Farabi. Risola fi mo yasuh wa mo lo yasuh min ahkom an-nujum. Manuscript of the Academy of Sciences of the Republic of Uzbekistan, Institute of Oriental Studies named after Abu Rayhon Beruni, №2385/III.

أبو صر الفارابى. رسالة فى ما يصوح و ما ا يصوح من أحكام النجوم. أبو ريحان البيرو ى اميده گى شرقشناس ليك إستيتوتى قوليازمه سى، ٣٢/٢٣٨٥

3.160. Abu Rayhon Beruni. At-tafhim li avail sina'at-tanjim. Manuscript of the Academy of Sciences of the Republic of Uzbekistan, Institute of Oriental Studies named after Abu Rayhon Beruni, №3423.

ابو ريحان البيرو ى. التفهيم لأوائل صناعة التنجيم. أبو ريحان البيرو ى اميده گى شرقشناس ليك إستيتوتى قوليازمه سى، ٣٤٢٣

3.161. Abu Rayhon Beruni. Tamhid al-mustaqar li tahqiq meaning al-mamar. Hyderabad, 1367/1948. - Б.1–107.

أبو ريحان البيرو ى. تمهيد المستقر لتحقيق معنى الممر. حيدرآباد، ١٣٦٧. ب. 107 - 1

3.162. Al-Baihaqi Zahir ad-Din. Tatimmat Siwan al-Hikma. Lahore, 1354.

البيهقى ظهير الدين. تتمة سوان الحكمة. لاهور، ١٣٥٤.

3.163. Jabra mokobale, naveshte-e Muhammad ibne Musa Khorezmi, translation-e Hossein Khedivjam (Persian) - Tehran. 1348.

جبر و مقابلة. ويشته محمد بن موسى خوارزمى. ترجمهء حسين خديوجمع. طهران، ۱۳۴۸

3.164. Zaki Salih. Osori Bakiya, Volume 1. Istanbul Printing Science. 1329. Manuscript of the Academy of Sciences of the Republic of Uzbekistan, Institute of Oriental Studies named after Abu Rayhon Beruni, from source № 18464.

زكى صالح. آثار باقيه. ۱ جلد. استا بول مطبعه سى، ۱۳۲۹. أبو ريحان البيرو ى اميده گى شرقشناس ليك إستيتوتى منبعه سى، ۱۸۴۶۴.

3.165. Ibn al-Athir. Al-kamil fi-t-tarikh. T. 1-9. - Cairo. 1348.

إبن الاثير. الكامل فى التأريخ. ۱-۹ جلد. قاهرة، ۱۳۴۸.

3.166. Ibn Abi Usaybia. Uyun al-anbo fi tabakot al-atibbo. - Kohira. 1882. II zhuz, 4 p.

ابن أبى أسيبعه. عيون الأ باء فى طبقات الأتباء. ۲ جلد. قاهره، ۱۸۸۲.

3.167. Ibn al-Fuwati. Talkhis majma al-adab fi mujam al-alqab. - Volume 4. Section 1-4. Damascus, 1962-1968. № 1234.

إبن الفواتى. تلخيص مجمع الآداب فى معجم الألقاب. ۴ جلد. دمشق، ۱۹۶۲-۱۹۶۸

3.168. Ibn al-Fuwati. Talkhis majma' al-adab fi mujam al-alqab. 5th volume. - Lahore, 1932. № 7651.

إبن الفواتى. تلخيص مجمع الآداب فى معجم الألقاب. ۵ جلد. لاهور، ۱۹۳۲.

3.169. Ibn al-Qifti. Kitab akhbar al-ulama bi-akhbar al-hukama. Cairo, 1326/1908, 177-178-б.

إبن القفطى. كتاب أخبار العلماء بأخبار الحكماء. قاهره، ۱۳۲۶.

3.170. «Kitab Tahrir Usul li-Uklidis min ta'lifi Nasir ad-Din al-Tusi.» A copy written in Arabic is kept in the manuscript collection of the St. Petersburg Branch of the Russian Academy of Sciences under number 49/672. The work was published in Rome in 1594.

كتاب تحرير أصول لأقليدوس من تأليف صير الدين الطوسى. راسيه فن لار أكديميه سى سنكت-پتيربورگ بوليمى قوليازمه سى، ۴۹/۶۷۲

3.171. Mahmud ibn Muhammad ibn Umar al-Chaghmini. Al-mulahas fi-l-haya. Manuscript of the Academy of Sciences of the Republic of Uzbekistan, Institute of Oriental Studies named after Abu Rayhon Beruni, 10417; 7761/III; 8796/II; 11599/III.

محمود بن محمد بن عمر الچغمینی. الملخص فی الهیئة. أبو ریحان البیرونی امیده گی شرقشناس لیك إستیتوتی قولیازمه لاری، ۱۰۴۱۷، ۳/۷۷۶۱، ۱۱/۸۷۹۶، ۳/۱۱۵۹۹.

3.172. Mahmud ibn Muhammad ibn Umar al-Chaghmini. Ash-Sharkh «Al-mulahhas fi-l-haya». Manuscript of the Academy of Sciences of the Republic of Uzbekistan, Institute of Oriental Studies named after Abu Rayhon Beruni, №2655.

محمود بن محمد بن عمر الچغمینی. شرح ملخص فی الهیئة. أبو ریحان البیرونی امیده گی شرقشناس لیك إستیتوتی قولیازمه سی، ۲۶۵۵

3.173. Mahmud ibn Muhammad ibn Umar al-Shagmini. Commentary «Al-mulahhas fi-l-haya». Manuscript of the Academy of Sciences of the Republic of Uzbekistan, Institute of Oriental Studies named after Abu Rayhon Beruni, № 8217, № 3935.

محمود بن محمد بن عمر الچغمینی. شرح ملخص فی الهیئة. أبو ریحان البیرونی امیده گی شرقشناس لیك إستیتوتی قولیازمه لاری، ۸۲۱۷، ۳۹۳۵

3.174. Muhammad ibn Umar Fakhriddin ar-Razi. Manuscript of «Jome al-ulum».

محمد بن عمر فخر الدین الرازی. جامع العلوم. أبو ریحان البیرونی امیده گی شرقشناس لیك إستیتوتی قولیازمه سی،

3.175. Muhammad Tahir ibn Abu-l-Qasim, Ajaib at-Tabakat, Manuscript Fund of the Russian Federation Academy of Sciences. Institute of Oriental Studies, №. 9042, p. 175a.

محمد طاهر بن أبی القاسم. عجایب الطبقات. أبو ریحان البیرونی امیده گی شرقشناس لیك إستیتوتی قولیازمه سی، ۹۰۴۲.

3.176. Nasir ad-Din al-Tusi. Majmu'a al-Raso'il was published in Hyderabad (India) in 1358/1939.

صیر الدین الطوسی. مجموعة الرسائل. هندستان، حیدرآباد، ۱۳۵۸

3.177. Nasir ad-Din al-Tusi. «Tahrir Uqlidis fi 'ilm al-handasa». Tehran, 1881.

صیر الدین الطوسی. تحریر اقلیدوس فی علم الهندسة. طهران، ۱۸۸۱

3.178. Risola ila Abu Rayhon Muhammad ibn Ahmad al-Beruni. Manuscript of the Academy of Sciences of the Republic of Uzbekistan, Institute of Oriental Studies named after Abu Rayhon Beruni, 2385/14, in Arabic.

رسالة إلى أبى ريحان محمد بن أحمد البيرونى. أبو ريحان البيرونى اميده گى شرقشناس ليك إستيتوتى قوليازمه سى، ۱۴/۲۳۸۵

3.179. "Fehrist kutub al-Sheikh ar-rais." Manuscript from the Institute of Oriental Studies of the Russian Academy of Sciences, № 2385/X1

فهرست كتب الشيخ الرئيس. أبو ريحان البيرونى اميده گى شرقشناس ليك إستيتوتى قوليازمه سى، ۱۱/۲۳۸۵

3.180. Sharifzhan Makhdum Sadri Zia, Tazkiray Shuara Mutakaddimiin and Salatin, Foundation of the Academy of Sciences of the Republic of Uzbekistan, Institute of Oriental Studies named after Abu Rayhon Beruni, № 2193/X, p. 272a.

شريفجان مخدوم صدر ضيا. تذكره شعراء متقدمين و سلاطين. أبو ريحان البيرونى اميده گى شرقشناس ليك إستيتوتى قوليازمه سى، ۱۰/۲۱۹۳

3.181. Hajjaj ibn Yusuf ibn Matar (late 8th - early 9th century). «Kitab Uklidis fi-l-Usul.» - Manuscript of the Manuscript Fund of the Russian Academy of Sciences in St. Petersburg №. C 2145.

حجاج بن يوسف بن مطر. كتاب أقليدس فى الأصول. راسيه فن لار أكديميه سى سنكت-پتيربورگ بوليمى قوليازمه سى، ۲۱۴۵

3.182. Hussein ibn al-Hasan al-Khwarizmi al-Kubrawi. Nuzhat al-mallok fi hayat al-aflok. Manuscript of the Academy of Sciences of the Republic of Uzbekistan, Institute of Oriental Studies named after Abu Rayhon Beruni, №1207/III.

حسين بن الحسن الخوارزمى الكبروى. زهة الملاك فى هيئة الأفلاك. أبو ريحان البيرونى اميده گى شرقشناس ليك إستيتوتى قوليازمه سى، ۳/۱۲۰۷

3.183. Abul-Rayhan al-Biruni, The Book of instruction in theelements of astrology. Ed. And transl. By R.Wright. – London, 1934. - P. 99-102.

3.184. Adu-r-Rayhon al-Biruni/Al-Qanun'l Masudi (Canon Masudicus). - Hayderabad-Dn. - Osmania Press, 1954-1956, vol. III. - pp.1014-1126.

3.185. Avicenna. Le livre de science. vol. 11, Physique-mathematiques trad. par V.Achenaet Henri Masse. – Paris, 1958. - P. 91-239.

3.186. Ahmedov A.A., Al-Dabbagh J., Rozenfeld B.A. Itanbul Manuscripts of Al-Khwarizmu's Treatisas. – Erdem, Ankara, 1987. R. 3. N 7. - P. 163-186.

3.187. Ahmedov A.A., Al-Dabbagh J., Rozenfeld B.A. Harezmi'nun Eserlerinin Istanbul Yazmalari Geviren: Melek Dosay. - Erdem, Ankara, 1987. - P. 187-210.

3.188. Barani S.H. Al-Biruni and his Magnum Opus Al-Qanunu'l-Mas'udi, Al-Biruni, Al-Qanunu'l-Mas'udi китобида, Hyderabad, V. III, 1956. - P. 203-221.

3.189. Bosmans H., Le fragment du commentaire d'Adrien Romain zur L'algebre de Muhammed ben Musael-Chowarezmi, Ann. De la Soc. Seiry de Bruxelles, 30; 2, 1906. - P. 34.

3.190. Karpinski L.C. Robert of Chester's Translation of al-Khowarizmi, Bibl. Math.. F. 3. Bd. XI. 1911. - P. 125-131.

3.191. Karpinski L.C. Bobert of Chester's Latin Translation of theAlgebraof al-Khowarizmi, N.-Y., 1915. - P. 123-134.

3.192. MarreA. Le Messahat de Mohammad ben Moussa, extrait de son Algebre.- Nouvelles Ann. De Math. T. 5. 1846. - P. 86-98.

3.193. Al-Khayyami Omar. Discussion of difficulties in Euclid. Transl. by A.R.Amir-Moez. - Scripta math. 1959. - Vol. 24. № 4. - P. 275-303.

3.194. Rosen T. Thealgebra of Muhammed ben Musa. - London, 1831. - P. 234-278.

3.195. Brockelmann C. Geschichte der Arabischen Literatur. Bd. I. - Weimar, 1898. - PP.215-216; 452-458.

3.196. Brockelmann C. Geschicte der Arabishen Literatur, 1. - Berlin, 1902. - p.452- 458.

3.197. Brockelmann C. Geschichte der Arabischen Litteratur, Erster Supplementband. – Leiden, 1937. - P. 381-382.

3.198. Ed.Sachau zur Geschichte und Chronologie von Khwarizm, SBWAW. Ph HCL. B. 73. 1873. - P. 225-229.

3.199. Ensyslopedia of the History of Arabic Science // Ed. B.Rushdi. -London, 1996.

3.200. Jensen C. Abu Nasr Mansur's approach to spherical astronomy as developed in his treatise «The Table of Minutes» Centaurus, 1971. Vol.16. No 1. - P. 1-19.

3.201. Johannes Thomann. Abu Mansur b. Iraq's criticism of the Shi'a calendarical methods // Khorezm Ma'mun Academi fnd its role in the development of world scince. - Tashkent-Khiva: Science, 2006. - P.111-112.

3.202. Brockelmann C. Geschichte der arabischen Litteratur. Weimar-Berlin-Leiden, Bd 1, 1943-1944. -P. 857.

3.203. Gandz S. The Origin and Development of the Quadratic Equation in Babylonian, Greek and Early Arabic Algebra.-Osiris, 1937. Vol. III. - P. 405-557.

3.204. Gandz S. TheAlgebra of Inheritons. A. Reabilitation of al-Khowarizmi-Osiris, 1938. Vol. V. – P. 229-302.

3.205. Ibadov J.H. The new data in the History of mathematics in the Islamic Mesieval East/ Abctract the international congress for theadvancement of scienceand technology in the Islamic world. - Tehran, Iran, 1993. - P. 102-109.

3.206. Ibadov J.H. Mathematical maniuscripts by al-Hububi, as-Sijawandi und al-Amili in the library of the Muslim Religions Board for Central Asiaand Kazakhstan // Studies in History Medicineand Science. New Selhi. - India, 1994. - P. 81-88.

3.207. Ibadov J.H. Al-Hubibi al-Khorezmi and his «Researh Book». - International conference. - Tashkent, 2005. - P. 140-145.

3.208. Ibadov J.H. On discoveries in exact sceences by the scienfists of Mirzo Ulughbek Acasemy of sdences/International conference - T.: Promotion on DSVA. - Tashkent, 2007. - P. 225-228.

3.209. Kazim M.A. Al-Biruni and Trigonometry // «Al-Biruni - Commemoration Volume». - Calcutta, 1951

3.210. Karpinski L.C. Winter J.G. Contributions to the History of Science. Ann Arbor, 1930. - P. 66-125.

3.211. Kennedi E.S. Biruni's graphical determination of the local Meridian. Scripta Mathematica, XXIV, 195.

3.212. Kennedy E.S. and Mustafa Mawaldi. Abu al-Wafaand the Heron Theorems, Journal for the History of arabic science. - 1970. Vol. 3. № 2. - P.119-128.

3.213. Kennedy E.S. Parallax theory in islamic astronomy. JSIS, u. 47 (1156). - P. 33-53.

3.214. The Cambridge History of Arabic Literature, Relision, Learning and Science in theAbbacid Period. - Cambridge, 1990.

3.215. Klamroth M. Veber den Arabischen Euklid. Zeitschr. d. Deutsch Morgenland. Ges.. Bd. 35. 1881. - P. 270-326.

3.216. Krause M. Die Spharik von Abu Nasr Mansur b. 'Ali b. Iraq , mit Untersuchungen zur Geschichte des Textes bei den islamischen Mathematiker. - Berlin, 1936. - P.10.

3.217. Kramers G.H. Al-Biruni's Determination of Geographical Longitude by measuring of the distances // «Al-Biruni - Commemoration Volume». - Calcutta, 1951.

3.218. Kremer A.V. The Orient under the Caliphs (Translated from von Kremer's Culturgeschihte des Orients) by Khuda Buksh. - Calcutta, 1920. - P. 291-302.

3.219. Lambert J.H. The oriocder Parallel-Linien - Leipziger Magazin der reine und angewandte Mathematik. 1786, № 2. S. 137-164 - P. 325-358.

3.220. LegendreA.M. Elements de geometrie 1^{eme}et. P. 3^{eme}et. ed. - Paris, 1823. - P. 299-303.

3.221. Le Strange G. Baghdad during theAbbasid Caliphate from Contemporary Arabiv and Persian Sonrses by G. Le Strane/ 2 nd ed. - London, 1920.

3.222. Libri G., Histoire des sciences mathematiques en Italie, vol. 1. – Paris, 1839. - P. 253-297.

3.223. Lexicon Bibliographicum et Eucyclopaedicum a Mustafa ben Abdallah… Haji Khalfa celebrato compositum.Editit G. Fluegel. - London, 1835-1858.

3.224. Markwart I. Wehrot und Arang. Unterchungen zur mithischen und geschichtlicheh I.Wehrot und arang. - Oxford, 1951. - P. 22-28.

3.225. Masharipova G. K. The scientific heritage of the scholars of Khorazm Mamun Academy who made great inventions of the MiddleAge. Europaische Fachhochschule. European applied sciences # 9. 2014. - P. 13-14

3.226. Masharipova G. K. Philosophical views of Abu Reikhan Biruni. International Journal of Advanced Research in Management and Social Sciences // India, 2019. – P. 126-138.

3.227. Masharipova G.K., Z. Kattahodzhayeva.Development of scientific creativity in theera of renaissance. Iinternational conference bridge to science: research work april, 15, 2019 - San Francisco, California, USA conference proceedings. - P. 6-10.

3.228. Masharipova G. K. The natural-scientifig heritage of the Khwarezm Ma'mun Academy and its socio-philosophical views. – International Journal of Philosocial Rehabilitation. Vol 24, Issue 09, 2020. - PP. 3683-3694.

3.229. Masharipova G. K.Khorezm Ma'mun academy - at the crossroads of world civilization. International Journal on Integrated Education. Volume 3, Issue XI, November 2020. - PP. 64-65.

3.230. Montucla J.E. Histoire des mathematiques, t.1, - Paris, 1758; 1802.- 680 p.

3.231. Nallino K. Zu Giagmini's Astronomie, Zeitschr. Der Deutsch. Morgenland. Gesselschaft, Bd. 48. - 1894. -P.120.

3.232. Haji Khalfa. Lexicon bibliograph. et encycl. a Haji Khalfa, ed. G.Flugel. – Lipsiae, 1835-1958. - P. 544.

3.233. Henning W.B. The Choresmian Documents. - P. 158-168.

3.234. Henning W.B. Zoroastr: Politician or Witch-Doktor. – Oxford, 1951. - P. 225-238.

3.235. Rasailu Abu Nasr 'Arraq. Osmania Oriental Publication Bureau, Hyderabad - Deccan, 1943-1947.

3.236. Rodet L. L'algebre d'Alkarizmi et les methodes indiens et grecques. Journ. as. ser. 7. T. 11. 1878. - P. 5-100.

3.237. Rudloff G., Hochheim A. DieAstronomie des Mahmud ibn Muhammed ibn 'Omar al-Cagmini // Zeitschrift der Deutschen Morgenlandischen Geselschaft, Bd.47, 1893. -P.213-275.

3.238. Ruska I. Zur altesten arabishen Algebra und Rechenkunst. Sitzungsberichte der Heidelberger Akad. d. Wissenschaften. 1917. - P. 227-323.

3.239. Ruska J. Zur altesten arabischen Algebra. Ruska J. Zue Geschichte der arabischen Algebra und Rechenkunst der Islam. Bd. 9. 1919. - P. 116-117.

3.240. Sayili A. Abdulhamid ibn Turk'un «Katisik Denklemlerde Mantiki Zaruretler» adli yazisi ve zamanin cebri (Logical nacassities in mixed equations by 'Abd al-Hamid ibn Turk and thealgebra of his time), Text in turkish, english and arabic, Turk Tarih Kurumu Jayinlardan. – Ankara, 1962. VII. Seri. 41. - P. 95.

3.241. Sayili A. The observatory in Islam. -Ankara, 1960. - 343 p.

3.242. Saccheri G. Euclides ab omni naevo vindicanus red. and transl. G.B.Halsted Chicago.- London, 1920. - P. 212-234.

3.243. Sarton G. Introduction to thehistori of science, vol. I-III. – Baltimore, 1927-1948. - vol.I. - P.707.

3.244. Sarton G. Adrian von Romen's commentary on Al-Khowarizmi (1598). Isis. vol. 21. 1934. - P. 18-23.

3.245. Sezgin F. Geaschichte des arabischen Schrifltums. Bd. V. - Leiden, 1974. - P. 45-52.

3.246. Sezgin F., GAS, Bd V. – Leiden, 1974. Bd. VI. 1978.

3.247. Simon M. Zu Hwarizmi's hisab algabr wal muqabala, Archiv Scripta. math. und phys. Reihe 13. Bd. 28. 1919. – P. 28-39.

3.248. Sourdel D. Et Sourdel J. La Civilisation de l'Islam classique. - Paris, 1968. - 453 p.

3.249. Suter H. Rezinsion Rushka, Zur altesten arabishen Algebra, Archiv s. math. u phus. Bd.28, 1919. - 232 p.

3.250. Suter H. DieMathematiker und Astronomen der Araber und ihre Werke, Leipzig, 1900. - P. 20-38, 72.

3.251. Steinschneider M. Diearabischen Bearbeiter des Almagest. Bibl. math. F. 2. b. 6.1892.- P. 29-34.

3.252. Steinsneider M. Euklid bei Arabern. Eine bibliographische Studie. «Zeitschr. fur Math. u. Phys». Bd 31. 1886. - P. 81-110.

3.253. Steinschneider M. Diearabischen Ubersetzungen aus dem Griechischen. Zweiter Abschnitt. Mathematik Zeitschr. d. Deutsch. Morgenland. Ges. Bd. 50. 1896. - P. 161-219; P. 337-417.

3.254. Le Strange G. Baghdad during theAbbasid Caliphate from Contemporary Arabic and Persian. - London, 1924. - 345p.

3.255. The Kitab al-Ansab of Abd al-Karim ibn Muhammad al-Sam'ani repreduced in Facsimile.- Leyden-London, 1912. - 98 p.

3.256. The Cambridge History of Arabic Literature, Religion, Learning and Science in theAbbasid Period. -Cambridge, 1990. - 299 p.

3.257. Farooq M. Al-Qanun-al-Masudi. –Aligarh, 1929. – 576 p.

3.258. Schoy C.. Die trigonometrischen Lehren des persischen Astronomen Abul-Rayhon Muh. ibn Ahmad al-Biruni, dargestellt nach al-Qanun al-Mas'udi, Hannover, 1927. - P. 2-73.

3.259. Wallis J. De postulato quinto et definitione quinta lib. 6 Euclidis; disceptatio geometrica. - Opera mathematica. – Oxoniae, 1693. T. 2. - P. 665-678.

3.260. Wiedemann E. Zur Geschichte der Astrologie. «Das Weltail». - Bd. 22. - 1922. 121-126.

3.261. Wiedemann E. Uber ein von Avicenna hergestelltes Beobachtungsinstrument. «Zeitschr., fur Instrumentenkunde». Bd. 45. 1925. - 269-275.

3.262. Wiedemann E. Einleitung zu dem astronomischen Teil des Kitab al Schifa (Werk der Genesung) von Ibn Sina , «Sitzungsber, d. phys.-med. Soz. In Erlangen» - Bd. 58-59, 1926-1927, 225-227.

IV. Dissertation and dissertation abstracts:

4.1. Abdulla-zade Kh.F. History of astronomy in medieval Khorasan and Maverannahr (1X - 15th centuries): Author. dis... . doc. ist. science - Dushanbe, 1990. - 43 b.

4.2. Abdukhalimov B.A. "Kashf az-zunun" as a source on the history of the exact sciences of Maverannahr and Khorasan: Author. dis... cand. ist. science - Tashkent, 1994. - 23 b.

4.3. Abdukhalimov B.A. "Bayt al-hikmah" and the scientific activity of Central Asian scientists in Baghdad (IX–XI centuries). Natural sciences. – History of the East of the Academy of Sciences of the Republic of Uzbekistan named after. Abu Rayhon Biruni: Author. for a degree in thesis.dis.historical sciences. - Tashkent: 2001. - 47 p.

4.4. Ahadova M. Physico-mathematical works of Ibn Sina in the Tajik language: Author's abstract. dis... Ph.D. physics and mathematics - Tashkent, 1965. - 11 p.

4.5. Akhmedov A. Scientific heritage of Khorezmi and its place in the history of science and culture: Abstract of thesis... doctor of history. - Tashkent, 1985. - 34 p.

4.6. Ibadov Zh.Kh. Arabic and Persian encyclopedias of the 10th–18th centuries. as sources on the history of exact sciences: Author's abstract. dis . . . Doctor of History - Tashkent, 1994. - 42 p.

4.7. Imamkhodjaeva A. Ibn Sina and Aristotle: development of logical ideas. Diss. for the job application PhD student - Tashkent, 1990. – 139 b.

4.8. Isakdzhanov R. Epistemological principles in the theological teaching of Ibn Sina. Doctor of Philosophy (PhD) diss. – Tashkent, 2020. – 138 p.

4.9. Karimova S.U. The role of scientists from Maverannahr and Khorasan in the development of chemistry and pharmacology in the Middle Ages (According to written sources of the 9th–11th centuries): Author. dis... .doc. ist. science – Tashkent, 2001. - 57 p.

4.10. Kocharev V.G. From the history of the organization and development of public education in Turkestan. - Dissertation...candidate of historical sciences. - Tashkent, 1967. - 304 s.

4.11. Kulieva G.Z. Basic concepts of mathematics among Nasiriddin Tusi's predecessors: Abstract. dis.cand. physics and mathematics science – Baku, 1962. - 11 p.

4.12. Mazhidova O.U. Abu Ali ibn Sino falsafasida khaqikatga erishishning mantiqiy concept: Diss. halyard fan. byyicha fan doctor (PhD). – Tashkent, 2021. – 135 b.

4.13. Matviyevskaya G.P. The doctrine of number in the Middle Ages: Author. dis . . . doc. physics and mathematics - T., 1968. - 28 p.

4.14. Masharipova G.K. "Usul 'ilm al-Khandasa" by Abu Ali ibn Sina as a mathematical source in the history of science: History of science... dis. – Tashkent, 1995. – 138 p.

4.15. Muhammadiev Kh. Mathematical chapters of the "Book of Healing" by Ibn Sina: Author. dis.candidate of historical sciences. - Dushanbe. 1967. - 22 p.

4.16. Romanova B.R. Pedagogical thoughts of Khorezm poets-educators of the late XIX - early XX centuries: Author. dis... .can.ped.science. - Tashkent, 1978. - 17 p.

4.17. Tagi-Zade A.K. Mathematical methods used in the construction of astronomical instruments in the Middle East: Author. Dis... .cand. physics and mathematics - Moscow: 1974. - 23 p.

4.18. Sharipova M.S. Mathematical chapters of the "Book of Healing" by Ibn Sina: Abstract of thesis. - Dushanbe, 1967. - 11 p.

www.ingramcontent.com/pod-product-compliance
Lightning Source LLC
LaVergne TN
LVHW080352070526
838199LV00058B/3799